W9-AYG-165

1695

ISRAEL AT FORTY

Land of PROMISE

Land of STRIFE

Wesley G. Pippert

WORD BOOKS
PUBLISHER
WACO, TEXAS

A DIVISION OF
WORD, INCORPORATED

LAND OF PROMISE, LAND OF STRIFE

Copyright © 1988 by Wesley G. Pippert. All rights reserved. No portion of this book may be reproduced in any form, except for brief quotations in reviews, without written permission from the publisher.

All quotations from the Bible in this volume are from the Revised Standard Version, unless otherwise indicated. Copyright 1946, 1952, 1971 by the Division of Christian Education of the National Council of the Churches of Christ in the U.S.A. Used by permission. Those quotations indicated PHILLIPS are from *Four Prophets: Amos, Hosea, First Isaiah, Micah* by J. B. Phillips, © 1963, 1969 by The Macmillan Company. Used by permission.

The map of UN Palestinian Refugee Camps (p. 180) is published by the Public Information Division of the United Nations Relief and Works Agency, 1987. The map of the Middle East (on endpapers) is published by the U. S. Central Intelligence Agency

Permission to reprint three maps from *Israel, the Embattled Ally*, by Nadav Safran © 1978, 1981 by the President and Fellows of Harvard College, is gratefully acknowledged.

Library of Congress Cataloging-in-Publication Data

Pippert, Wesley G., 1934–
   Land of promise, land of strife.

   Includes index.
   1. Israel. 2. Jewish-Arab relations. I. Title.
DS102.95.P57   1988   956.94   88–88
ISBN 0–8499–0640–7

Printed in the United States of America

8 9 8 0 1 2 3 9 AGF 9 8 7 6 5 4 3 2 1

To

Elizabeth Marie

Israel's Greatest Gift to Me

Contents

Illustrations

Introduction

Israel is a land of religion, romance, and hard realities. Two peoples are striving for a homeland—one partly on the basis of a promise made four thousand years ago, the other on the basis of their constant residency for more than one thousand years.

I came home to America from a three-year assignment in the Middle East with love and affection for both the Jew and the Arab. And I understand more fully the attachment and affection each feels toward that beautiful but oft-bruised land.

There are lots of heroes in Israel and the Arab territories—Sam Nissan, the Hadassah surgeon; Shlomo Drori, who lives near the Dead Sea, and his counterpart Mendel Nun, who lives near the Sea of Galilee; Jonathan Kuttab, the young human-rights lawyer; all the courteous Arab shopkeepers. I wish the leaders of the Israelis and the Palestinians were half as skillful and dedicated to justice and peace as these men and women are in their various duties.

Two key themes in this book are:

—Despite the pain each side has suffered, neither Israeli nor the Palestinian leaders work very hard for justice and peace. Both sides must share the fault.

—But the real villain in the Middle East is the West, particularly the British and the French for deceitfully withholding Arab independence after World War I, and now, the Soviet Union and the United States for turning the region into an arsenal of death.

This book is not intended to be a history text. Yet, I occasionally have gone back to review the historical record to put modern events into context. I did this particularly in discussing the role of the West and the long story of the Jews and Arabs.

I firmly believe the fundamental enmity in the Middle East is religious in nature. This is why I have sought to interpret Israel and the Arab so frequently in terms of religion and the Bible.

Modern Israel is forty years old. It was reborn to be, as its founding fathers declared, quoting the prophet Isaiah, "a light to the nations" (Isa. 49:6).

In the Bible, the number forty has significance. It rained forty days and forty nights during Noah's flood. The Israelites wandered in the wilderness forty years. In the earliest days of the nation of ancient Israel, during the cycles of the Judges, we read, Israel "rested" forty years during the administrations of Othniel, Deborah, and Gideon. But after the rule of Abdon, Israel was oppressed for forty years. Always, during these cycles, periods of rest were followed by times of oppression, or vice versa. Several kings also reigned forty years.

So with modern Israel's first forty years, it has been involved in at least a war a decade with its Arab neighbors and it remains in a formal state of war with almost all of them. Hardly a person in Israel has not been scarred by those battles. The quest for peace has been long and largely unfulfilled.

In the view of Israeli President Chaim Herzog, Israel's main problem is internal, not external. The band of hardy Jews and their brethren have transformed Israel into one of the world's strongest nations. Now, Israel is no longer perceived as David, but as Goliath. In being so transformed, however, Israel has become increasingly harsh toward the Palestinian—the stranger and alien in its midst for whom the Bible repeatedly orders it to care. The quest for justice has been often perverted. Further, the ultra-Orthodox are growing bolder and more aggressive in trying to impose their Pharisee-like rules and demands on the rest of the nation. The light is flickering.

The Arabs must answer to the same universal and inalienable laws of justice and peace as the Jews. Have their leaders' methods of the "armed struggle" and acts of violence served their cause? Is it really true that the Israelis are the cause of all the Palestinians' problems?

Is the biblical formula applicable today? If so, has Israel been through forty years of rest—or oppression? And, therefore, will Israel's next forty years be ones of oppression—or rest? Israel faces profound choices. Must its need for security compel it to be oppressive? How does it reconcile the ancient Promise of the Land with the biblical mandate to be just and to care for the widow, the orphan, and the alien?

In this book, Part I looks at modern Israel and the occupied Arab territories. Part II examines the people of the conflict, their backgrounds, and their beliefs. Part III looks at peace, more as a hope than a probability.

The most vivid way the problems of the Middle East come home to me is as the father of a daughter born in Jerusalem. Will she ever be able to travel in the Arab world? And, if she returns to the land of her birth as an 18-year-old, would the Israelis nab her at Ben-Gurion Airport and draft her into the army? I am equally told yes and no to these questions.

This book has been shaped by almost every part of my life. As United Press International manager for Israel and as senior Middle East correspondent for three years, unless otherwise noted, I observed firsthand almost all of the people and events described in this book. Ohad Gozani, Gerald Nadler, James Dorsey, Patricia Behre, Joel Greenberg, James Hershberg, Raya Rotem, and Jocelyn Noveck were my colleagues in that most trying and exciting time. Years earlier, I studied the Old Testament under J. Barton Payne, and participated in the final season of the archeological excavation at Dothan in what is now the West Bank. And afterward, while a Fellow at Harvard's Institute of Politics, I studied the Middle East under Nadav Safran. I have discussed many of the ideas here presented with my students in Politics of the Middle East classes at Gordon College. Moshe Gershovich, an Israeli doctoral student at Harvard, read and critiqued the manuscript as did Marvin Wilson, chairman of the Bible department at Gordon, and Robert Cooley, president of Gordon-Conwell Theological Seminary and my colleague on the 1964 excavation at Dothan. Frank Cross, archeologist at Harvard, read the Dead Sea Scrolls section of chapter 9, and Marvin Kalb, director of Harvard's Center for Press, Politics, and Public Policy, and former NBC chief diplomatic correspondent, read chapters 2 and 5. But mostly, it has been the love and appreciation of the Bible that has whetted and sustained my interest in Israel and the Middle East. This I owe to my parents, and my chief regret is that they are not here so that I might share the following with them. My wife Becky gave great meaning and cheer in Jerusalem, not only to me but to many others.

I want to thank the professional and gracious people at Word Books, my publisher—especially Ernie Owen, Dr. Jim Nelson Black, publicist Nancy Guthrie, and my highly competent and conscientious editor, Carey Moore. They turned my early dream of merely telling my children about my life in the Middle East into a much broader reality.

Wes Pippert
Cambridge, Mass.
1987

PART I
MODERN ISRAEL AT FORTY

1

Streams in the Desert

"I will restore the fortunes of my people Israel, and they shall rebuild the ruined cities and inhabit them; they shall plant vineyards and drink their wine, and they shall make gardens and eat their fruit. I will plant them upon their land, and they shall never again be plucked up out of the land which I have given them," says the Lord your God.

—Amos 9:14–15

At any hour, the view is filled with romance and mystery. In the silence of the night, one can see the headlights of a lone truck or car making its way along the narrow blacktop encircling the walled Old City. By day, Jerusalem's stone buildings and shrines are bathed in rose hues, the colors varying at the whim of the slant of the sun's rays.

We lived in the integrated neighborhood of Abu Tor on the top floor of what was a luxury apartment, by Jerusalem standards. From our balcony, looking north across the Valley of Hinnom, so close that it seemed you could hit it with a stone, was Mount Zion, the traditional but unlikely site of David's Tomb. Out of our view behind Mount Zion rose the black dome of the Church of the Holy Sepulchre, the traditional and likely site of Christ's crucifixion and resurrection. Just to the right stood the golden Dome of the Rock, on the site where the patriarch Abraham prepared to sacrifice his son Isaac, where Solomon built the temple, and, according to Moslem tradition, where the prophet Mohammed began his nighttime celestial journey. Farther to the right one could see the south end of the well-worn Mount of Olives, now bearing the sleek Intercontinental Hotel. In the Kidron Valley "V" between the Old City and the Mount of Olives, a clump of ancient olive trees could be seen. That would be the Garden of Gethsemane, where Jesus prayed on the night before he was crucified (Matt. 26:36 and Mark 14:32). Beyond this to the north atop Mount Scopus was the modernistic campus of the Hebrew University.

The poignancy of the disappointments and dreams permeating this scene touched me most at two different times. One was in the nighttime hours, when I would wander out on our balcony, if unable to sleep. The view always proved a balm for whatever weariness I felt. The other occasion was when our child Elizabeth, herself a daughter of Jerusalem, would toddle out on the balcony, step up on the foot ledge, and gaze long moments through the railing. Her thoughts and wonder at all she saw are known only to herself and God. I promised her some day to try and tell her the meaning of what she was seeing.

From that balcony, I always enjoyed the three towers soaring above the Mount of Olives—the tower of Hebrew University to the far north, that of the Russian Church and Monastery to the south, and in the middle, the tower of Augusta Victoria Hospital. They signified the three approaches, I thought—education, medicine, and theology.

Our next-door neighbors were the Samuelses, a devout and saintly French-speaking couple whose apartment remained dark and silent in devotion every Shabbat,[1] from sunset Friday to sunset Saturday. The ground-floor apartment belonged to Betty Solomon, the widow of a rabbi in Kansas City. In the other part of the building were the Shalits and Rick Hurst. Lilli Shalit, pioneer of the Israeli airline industry, served as company secretary of Palestine Airways Ltd. when it was founded in 1937 with two five-passenger, twin-engine *Scion Junior* planes—long before the days of the El Al airline. Opposite them lived Hurst, a Pentecostal Christian with artistic flare who designed and established one of Jerusalem's most attractive coffeehouses just inside the Old City's Jaffa Gate.

---

1. This is the modern Hebrew spelling of Sabbath.

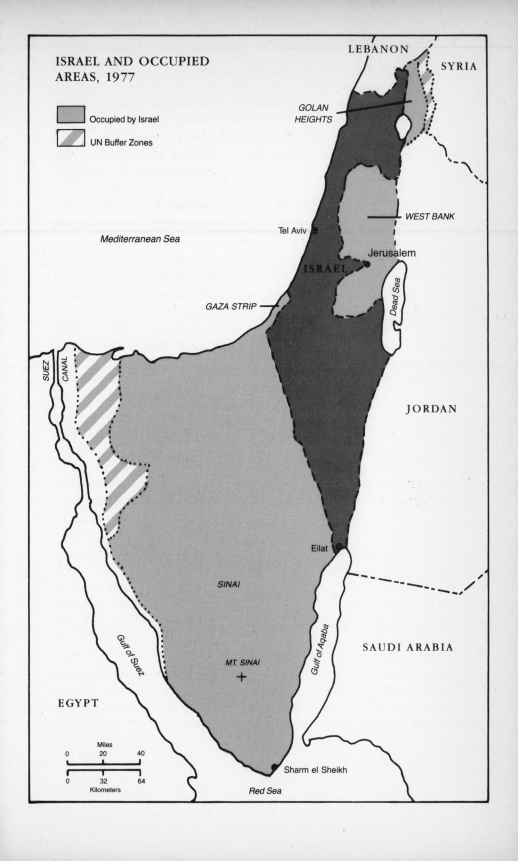

ISRAEL AND OCCUPIED
AREAS, 1977

Occupied by Israel

UN Buffer Zones

LEBANON

SYRIA

GOLAN
HEIGHTS

WEST BANK

Mediterranean Sea

Tel Aviv

Jerusalem

ISRAEL

Dead Sea

GAZA STRIP

JORDAN

SUEZ

CANAL

Eilat

SINAI

Gulf of Suez

Gulf of Aqaba

SAUDI ARABIA

MT. SINAI

EGYPT

Miles

0   20   40

0   32   64

Kilometers

Sharm el Sheikh

Red Sea

These were kin. They all shared a love of Israel, and the conviction they had come home to the Land of Promise.

Several times a week I jogged around the circumference of Abu Tor. Just past the bend in the road, only a few meters from our apartment, scores of Arab children played in the streets in the daytime, occasionally offering up in careful English a "Hello. How are you?" It bothered me that they were bashfully speaking my language to me, and I, an American, was unable to address them in their tongue. Their mothers, wearing full-length robes and head-dress, tended them.

Every day, Arab boys brought a camel along our street and persuaded tourists, who had come to enjoy the view from Abu Tor, to pay a few coins for a ride. The boys would give tourists a ride and use the tourists' cameras to snap a picture. It was quite clear the tourists were more interested in a photo to take home than in the ride itself.

Chickens scampered about always. On the roof of one building where Arab families lived—about the size of our apartment building, but lacking our conveniences—a dog on a chain barked so loudly that the sound bounced off the rocky hillside of Silwan across the Kidron Valley.

That section of Abu Tor seemed light years away from our affluent neighbors. Indeed, for the two decades between the 1948 Israeli War of Independence and the 1967 Six-Day War, when Israel reunited Jerusalem, the dividing line between Israel and Jordan lay only a few feet to the east of our apartment building. It cut Abu Tor in half. I hardly ever saw Jews in the Arab half of Abu Tor and rarely did I see Arabs in the Jewish half.

From our apartment, the distance to two tiny grocery stores in Abu Tor was almost identical. One was in the Jewish section, and the other was in the Arab section. At either store, we bought milk in plastic bags and our eggs were put in a paper sack. The Jewish store was known as the *makollet*. When we went to the Arab grocery and said, *Ma-salaami; Keef halik*, the proprietor immediately lit up and became warm. Abu Tor was a peaceful neighborhood. It symbolized both the separation and the closeness that mark Israel today.

Importance: The Land of the Bible

As President Chaim Herzog points out, Israel has the third largest concentration of foreign correspondents of any country in the world. News agencies from the United States, Britain, West Germany, France, Italy, and Spain all maintain bureaus in Israel. There are as many British reporters in Israel as there are Americans. Events that otherwise would not be considered news would make the front page in the United States, because they happened in Israel. Why? Why this insatiable interest in Israel?

The Middle East is strategically important because of its location between the West and the East, between the Mediterranean Sea and the Indian Ocean. Russia always has cast a covetous eye toward the Middle East because it is the route to all-season ports on the Persian Gulf. Part of the global confrontation between the United States and the Soviet Union is being played out in microcosm in the Middle East by their surrogates, Israel and Syria.

Israel lies at the hub of the vast Middle East and, over the centuries, many nations have used the Holy Land as a crossroads and a battlefield. Twenty times in three thousand years the Valley of Megiddo, a narrow cut through the Hill Country on the historic main route between Egypt and Mesopotamia, has been overrun and conquered. And the Battle of Armageddon (literally, mountain of Megiddo) will be fought there on its plains, the Bible says (Rev. 16:16).

Israel is the only democracy in the Middle East. The Middle East came forcibly to American consciousness in 1973 when the Arab oil embargo sent gasoline prices rocketing. Yet, the geopolitical reasons fall short of offering an adequate explanation for Israel's constant newsworthiness.

Israel is the Land of the Bible, and any news about that land touches the hearts and minds of Jews, Moslems, and Christian faithful everywhere. To the Jews, even those who have never visited there, Israel is the Promised Land, the location of the most sacred site in Judaism, the Temple Mount. Termed the Wailing Wall—or Western Wall, as the Jews call it—it is the last remaining part of the foundation of the Second Temple, which the Romans destroyed in A.D. 70.

To the Christian, Israel is highly important too, for there Jesus was born, there he ministered and died and rose again, and to Israel he is expected to return at his second coming. In Islam, Jerusalem is the third most holy city. Here lies the answer to our question: The real reason why day after day, week after week, month after month, Israel and the Middle East are Page One stories in the Western press is that the Land of Israel was the cradle of Judeo-Christian belief.

Jerusalem's mayor, Teddy Kollek, recognized this when he sought to explain why his city became great. "It enjoys none of the physical features which favored the advancement and prosperity of other important cities," he said. "It stands at the head of no great river. It overlooks no great harbor. It commands no great highway and no crossroads. It is not close to abundant sources of water. . . . It possesses no mineral riches. It was off the main trade routes. It held no strategic key to the conquest of vast areas prized by ancient warring empires."[2] The importance of Jerusalem, he said, sprang from the Hebrew prophets and kings who propounded the concept of good and evil, brotherly love, and the rule of law. Kollek quoted the prophet Isaiah, who said, "Out of Zion shall go forth the law, and the word of the Lord from Jerusalem" (2:3b).

For all this, there remains a mystery. There is an indefinable something that seems to capture those who visit Israel, even antagonists. There is a passion that grasps the person who visits or lives in Israel. It is impossible to be indifferent; one either loves or hates Israel.

"We don't possess the land," says Dr. Samuel Nissan, chief of surgery at Hadassah-Mount Scopus Hospital and a *sabra* (native-born Israeli). "The land possesses us."

---

2. Teddy Kollek and Moshe Pearlman, *Jerusalem: Sacred City of Mankind, a History of Forty Centuries* (Jerusalem: Steimatzky, 1972), 12.

Geography: The Hub of the Middle East

Israel has a population of about 4.2 million, of which 81 percent are Jews and almost all of the others are Palestinians. Of the Jews, approximately 57 percent are *sabras*. The Israeli-occupied West Bank has a population of 813,000 Palestinians and 65,000 Jewish settlers, and the Gaza Strip has a population of about 525,000 Palestinians and 2,700 Jewish settlers, making Gaza one of the most densely populated areas in the world.[3]

Israel is an awkward-shaped land about the size of Massachusetts. The Mediterranean forms the western boundary. There Israeli gunboats patrol the sea all the way from Gaza to Beirut. Arab countries form the other boundaries—Lebanon to the north, Syria and Jordan to the east, and Egypt to the south.

Along the Mediterranean lies a lush plain of farms and citrus groves. Running north and south in the middle of the country are the well-worn and rounded mountains, two thousand to three thousand feet in height, called the "Hill Country." This high land drops off sharply in the east to perhaps Israel's best-known physical features, two lakes that are both hundreds of feet below sea level. In the north is the Sea of Galilee. The purplish aura always suspended above it seems to suggest the constant presence of Jesus, who once walked the shores (and on the lake itself!). And in the south is the Dead Sea, with tiny iceberg-like cakes of salt floating on it. The two seas are connected by a muddy stream flowing straight south—its importance all out of proportion to its tiny size—the Jordan River.

In Israel's south is the triangular-shaped Negev, or desert, and its capital, Beersheba. Centuries ago, the camel caravans of the Nabateans carried gold, frankincense, and myrrh over the ancient paths in the Negev between the Red Sea and the Mediterranean. They started their journey into the Negev by passing through the narrow channel in the mountains at rose-red Petra,

---

3. From 1987 report of the West Bank Data Base Project by Meron Benvenisti, published by *The Jerusalem Post*, pp. 1, 52.

which the prophet Obadiah may have had in mind when he spoke of "the clefts of the rock" (v. 20).

In the north is the Galilee where, for much of the year, the whole countryside is ablaze with yellow wild mustard, red poppy, and white parsley. There also is the Galilee's most famous city, Nazareth, Jesus' hometown. Today it has a communist mayor. Nazareth is not a particularly attractive city, and the single, winding main street through the city can become impossibly clogged with traffic. One person remarked, only half joking, "Now I know why Jesus left Nazareth after he was grown, and why Nathanael asked, 'Can anything good come out of Nazareth?'" (John 1:46). When Joseph and the pregnant Mary departed Nazareth on their trip to Bethlehem, they had a choice of routes to take. They could go straight south through the rugged hill country. Or, they could swing west along the Mediterranean and then scoot east along the route of the present Tel Aviv-Jerusalem four-lane highway. Or, they could have headed east and then southward through the Jordan Valley to within a few miles of Bethlehem. Although tradition has it that Joseph and Mary traveled through the Samaritan hill country, I think they chose the Jordan Valley route as most foreign correspondents do nowadays when traveling between Jerusalem and the Galilee. Because of dangers from the Arabs, modern Israelis generally take the coastal route.

The occupied West Bank, a Delaware-sized area in the hill country shaped like a backward B, is located just where its name suggests—on the west bank of the Jordan. The West Bank was 100 percent Arab at the time of the 1967 War. Since then, Jewish settlers have planted about one hundred twenty settlements throughout the occupied territories. The belt buckle of that backward B is Jerusalem, a city over which Mayor Teddy Kollek says there have been fifteen major battles, beginning with David. In fact, the concentration of Arab population was a circular bulge on the west side of the Jordan. But Israeli troops pushed their way in to capture the western half of the Holy City in 1948, squeezing the bulge into a B. It later became known as the West Bank.

Jerusalem and Tel Aviv are classic twin cities. Each with approximately a half million in population, they are Israel's

Number 1 and Number 2 cities. The likeness ends there. Jerusalem has an ancient past, dating back to Canaanite days. Lance Lambert, a charismatic Christian and staunch supporter of Israel, speaking at the Feast of Tabernacles celebration in Jerusalem in October 1984, quoted the Psalms: "For the Lord has chosen Zion . . . here I will dwell, for I have desired it" (132:13–14). Zion, the name of one of the mountains forming Jerusalem, has come to be a poetic name for the city.

The status of Jerusalem is the single issue in the Arab-Jewish dispute. Neither side will compromise on this—never. Neither will Arab or Jew ever relinquish its claim to Jerusalem. Even the United States is officially ambiguous toward Jerusalem. On U.S. passports, the place of birth is usually identified by the name of the country. But on my daughter Elizabeth's U.S. passport, the place of birth reads: "Jerusalem."

Who can say for sure, but Jerusalem appears to be lovelier today than at any time in its five thousand-year history. It is once again the capital city of the Jewish state—for the first time in two thousand years. Kollek, probably the world's best-known mayor, has been a genius in soliciting the wealth of ideas and funds that have gone to make Jerusalem a well-run and aesthetically beautiful city. The tiny shanties that lined the wall of the Old City before the 1967 War, for instance, have been cleared away, and now grass and flowers accent the ancient walls, illumined by floodlights. Increasingly, black-clothed ultra-Orthodox Jews have filled the neighborhood of Mea Shearim in the heart of the Jewish sector and are spilling beyond its borders. At noonday on Friday, the city's residents may be thinking of anything but this city's beauty, for then Jerusalem is clogged with its worst traffic jams of the week. An hour later, the streets are quiet in anticipation of Shabbat, but in Tel Aviv it's raucous until much later.

Tel Aviv, to the west, was built by some of the first Jews to return to the Promised Land in the early 1900s. It is a largely unattractive city of commerce, coffeehouses, and fun whose main claim to beauty is the spectacular Mediterranean beach and a new promenade. Tel Aviv's claim to biblical history is the now-annexed Jaffa, on the city's south side. At Jaffa, Jonah defied God's orders to go to Nineveh, and wound up inside a big fish; and there Peter received

27

the vision for the Gentiles (Acts 10). On Friday afternoon in Tel Aviv, the sidewalk cafes on Dizengoff Street are jammed.

One can drive from Jerusalem to anywhere in Israel and return the same day. From Jerusalem, via the four-lane superhighway, Tel Aviv and an evening of fun is less than an hour away. It is three hours by auto from Jerusalem to Metullah (220 kilometers, or 136 miles), the northernmost town in Israel, within view of Mount Hermon. Foreign correspondents have come to know Metullah well for it is one of the two checkpoints for entry into Lebanon. It is a four-hour drive (200 miles) from Jerusalem to Eilat, King Solomon's port (1 Kings 9:26) on the Gulf of Aqaba, touted as one of the best winter vacation spots in the world. Foreign correspondents have come to know Eilat well, too, for its snorkeling and its beaches, where one might see three topless generations—grandmother, daughter, and child—all at once.

The People: A Zest for Life

Israelis are a boisterous lot. They are verbal, assertive, argumentative, nosey; they themselves joke, "Two Jews, three opinions." Although a growing number of public officials have doffed the short-sleeved, open-neck shirt in favor of a suit and tie, no one has ever accused the Israelis of being best dressed. The majority, it seems, chain-smoke, but rarely do they drink anything other than a single glass of wine. Many have high blood pressure.

Their public behavior can be infuriating. They are wild drivers—but not *that* bad. According to the International Road Federation, Israel in 1981 had four deaths per 100 million kilometers driven, twice that of the United States but much less, for instance, than Chile (nine deaths per 100 million km.), South Africa (eighteen), or Togo (an unbelievable ninety-one deaths). Any attempt at persuading intransigent Israeli officials or clerks to change their minds likely will be met with an elaborate shrug, or something worse. On the other hand, No never means No in the Middle East. No merely means you are at the starting point of negotiations.

In the always-long queues at the Post Office or the bank, when your time at the window comes, you can expect to see the two Israelis directly behind you step up and stand next to you, one on each side, unashamedly looking over your shoulder to see to whom you are writing and how much you are depositing. This practice got to the point that, according to *The Jerusalem Post*, the Education Ministry called jumping the queue a sin and asked teachers to instruct their pupils to observe the rules of lines just as they observe the Shabbat and other religious institutions.

The long queues at the Post Office are worth the wait. Since Israel is very socialistic, one can mail a letter, send a cable, buy telephone tokens, and pay parking fines and telephone, water, and electricity bills—all in one stop.

An Israeli asked my wife once, "How much do you pay for your apartment?" "What does your husband do?" "Can he afford to pay that rent?"—all without apology. In line at the bank, my wife noticed a man looking over her shoulder at her balance sheet. She said to him with bemusement, "What do you think?" He replied, "Doesn't look good to me."

Yet, there is a caring quality to the Israelis' candor that more than redeems the discourtesy and inquisitiveness. You know where you stand with an Israeli. And the warmth and hospitality shown you after you get to know an Israeli must equal that of any people in the world.

We may think they are being rude, but Israelis see their public behavior as being straightforward. Israeli clerks don't smile much, and you would never hear them mouthing the inane remark, "Have a nice day." Yet, clerks at Mahane Yehuda, the huge open market in Jerusalem, or Super Sol, Israel's supermarket, once they get to know a customer, will almost leap over a counter to tell him or her about some especially good strawberries freshly arrived.

We often were invited to the home of ordinary Israelis, who had nothing to gain except mutual friendship. We ate numerous Shabbat dinners—the traditional Friday night meal that combines food and worship—as well as the annual Pesach (Passover) meal, at which the head of the home reads the story of the first Passover (Exodus 11–12) and all recite: "Next year in Jerusalem!" Shortly after we arrived in Israel, I was sent on assignment to Beirut. An electronics man whom my wife had called to repair our stereo looked at her countenance and asked, "What's wrong?" When she explained that I was in Beirut, he refused to give her a bill on that trip, saying, "You have enough on your mind now." And the next day, his wife called to invite her to their home for Shabbat dinner, but she couldn't accept—an Israeli neighbor couple, also concerned about her being alone, already had invited her.

When our nanny fell while carrying Elizabeth (they were frightened but not hurt), several cars stopped to help. A taxi driver took my wife and them across town and refused to accept a fare. "The baby is OK, thank God," he said. "Children are our most precious treasure—the only resource we have."

The Jews are a people who have been despised for four thousand years. They have known the persecution of the Crusaders, the Russian pogroms, the Nazi Holocaust, and now, nearly forty years of war with their nearest neighbors. These have not left the people unscathed. One of the most abrasive women I have ever met was in Tel Aviv. Intimidating one and all, she was likely to call anyone who disagreed with her a Nazi. I had compassion on her when I noticed blue numbers tattooed on her arm—Auschwitz!

The Israelis have a reverence for life. This reverence unquestionably grows out of the Torah as well as the great loss of life they have suffered in their wars, and it also is the result of their own desire to repopulate the land. This has nurtured two things—the delight they show toward all children, and their medical research. Dr. Joseph Schenker, of Hadassah Hospital, world-renowned for his fertility research, says it all is quite consistent with the biblical mandate, "Be fertile and multiply the earth and master it" (Gen. 1:28, his translation). Parents take their children everywhere—to the restaurants, to parties, to the movies. If the children fuss, "no problem, no problem." My wife found that on long, tiring, transoceanic flights, flight attendants on El Al were eager, even overjoyed, to help with the baby. They were much less so on American flights.

"A man, Arab or Jew, who does not have children, is often regarded as impotent," says Schenker, who has delivered several of Israel's thirteen test-tube babies. "It affects his prestige, his status in society. A barren woman regards herself as a failure, a disappointment to her family."

The loss of a single Israeli soldier is the subject for national mourning. Cabinet ministers frequently attend the funeral of a fallen soldier. Time and again, Israel has arranged for lopsided prisoner swaps in order to get back a few of their own. In May 1985, Israel almost emptied its prisons, releasing 1,150 Arabs (including the surviving perpetrators of the worst terrorist attacks committed against Israel) in exchange for three Israeli soldiers who had been captured in the Lebanon War.

This same reverence extends to all of life. Since 1948, Israelis have planted 185 million trees. In fact, one of the ways to memorialize a person who has died is through the planting of a tree. Every kibbutz and every Jewish settlement in occupied Arab territories has lush lawns and flower gardens. Flower stands are scattered throughout Jerusalem, and roses sold for the equivalent of fifty cents each while we lived there. It is easy and inexpensive to have cut flowers in one's home all of the time, and we did.

Israel, paradoxically, is one of the most religious and most secular countries. Through the influence of religious political parties, the country almost literally comes to a halt every Shabbat. The national transportation systems—Egged and Dan buses and El Al Airlines—do not operate, the newspapers do not publish, and Israeli stores are not open. The more resourceful—and irreverent—Jewish residents of Jerusalem simply drive across town to the Arab sector, where all shops are open and doing a thriving business—Saturday not being a Moslem holiday.

Politics: Rough and Tumble and Proportionate Representation

This same exuberance extends to politics. "Ladies and gentlemen," Foreign Minister Shimon Peres told an American audience, "whatever you may think about Israel, it is a fiercely democratic country—never short of argument, never in need of parties, never out of debate, never forgetting to do it with full strength and devotion, on every particular issue."

In 1986, then-Foreign Minister Yitzhak Shamir was nearly involved in a brawl at the Herut convention. Sessions of the Knesset, Israel's parliament, are often nasty, with none of the politeness and deference that mark the United States Congress or the British Parliament. Israelis are remarkably informed about politics; and even if they aren't, they argue as if they are. Israel Radio broadcasts hourly newscasts. Many Israelis carry radios and would not think of missing the hourly 'cast. Egged, the Israeli bus line, pipes the newscasts over its vehicles' public-address systems.

Israel's first generation of leaders—David Ben-Gurion, Menachem Begin, Golda Meir, Moshe Dayan—is gone. A new generation has taken their place. Men like Yitzhak Shamir, Shimon Peres, and Yitzhak Rabin are more colorless than charismatic, more technocrats and long-time party functionaries than visionaries.

Shamir, a short, swarthy, reticent man, had been a member of Mossad, Israel's equivalent of the CIA. His aides said that Shamir, tough in his public policies, was generous and friendly when dealing with subordinates. By contrast, his predecessor, Moshe Dayan, would ride for three hours without saying a word to his driver. Peres, a man of equal calm and determination, often simply wore down opposition. He would keep Cabinet in session all night—as he did in getting passage of his economic austerity program on July 1, 1985, and in pursuing a closer relationship with Egypt in January 1986.

Israel's system of government rewards the party faithful who have worked their way up. In the national coalition that ruled after the 1984 elections ended in a dead heat, there were three present or past prime ministers and one former president in the Cabinet. This is almost half of all the prime ministers modern Israel has had. In 1986, Peres was prime minister and Rabin defense minister; a decade earlier, Rabin was prime minister and Peres the defense minister.

The good side of what essentially amounts to a de facto oligarchy is that it assures that Israel's leaders always are people of experience and seniority. Abba Eban, for instance, has been ambassador to the United Nations, ambassador to the United States, foreign minister, and now chairman of the Knesset Foreign Affairs and Defense Committee. In the United States, only two recent presidents could boast anything like the leadership experience that is so common in Israel. These were Lyndon B. Johnson and Gerald R. Ford, who rose to congressional leadership posts; both of them ascended to the White House only because the elected president died or was disqualified.

But Israel's system of government makes it very difficult for fresh faces with new ideas to emerge. George McGovern, Jimmy Carter, or even Ronald Reagan probably would not have made it to the top in Israel; they hadn't spent enough time working their way up in the party.

One sure way into public life in Israel has been through the military; this is not surprising given its frequent wars (although only Dwight Eisenhower was able to capitalize on this background in the United States in recent years). Yitzhak Rabin was chief of staff in the 1967 War, and several other generals have served in the Cabinet. Ironically, Israel's most famous soldier, Moshe Dayan, was defense minister and foreign minister but never prime minister.

So, the makeup of the next generation of leaders is not firm.

One of the most prominent is David Levy, a Sephardic Jew who was born in Morocco and came to Israel as a construction worker in Beit Shean. He now is deputy prime minister and has a huge following in the Likud bloc. Levy doesn't speak English—the thought of an Israeli prime minister who doesn't speak English is somewhat mind-boggling. His mother believes in him, however. In an interview in an Israeli newspaper, she said he was born circumcised, which she took to have messianic implications.

Israel has pure proportional representation, or, democracy in its truest form. In Israel's system, the various parties nominate slates of candidates for the Knesset at their conventions, ranking them 1-2-3-4 etc. The party leaders and senior members are given high ratings, assuring them of a seat in the Knesset no matter how well or how poorly the party does. In the election, the citizens vote for the party of their choice, not for individual candidates. The votes are tabulated and totalled, and then each party is assigned a percentage of seats in the 120-member Knesset according to the party's share of votes in the election.

No party has yet received even a bare majority of 61 seats. For instance, in 1984, Labor got 44 and the Likud 41; and in 1981, the Likud received 48 and Labor 47. After the 1984 election, in which the centrist Labor Party and the rightist Likud bloc reached a standoff, a compromise was worked out so that *both* parties would rule—Labor's Peres would be prime minister for the first twenty-five months, then the Likud's Shamir would serve twenty-five months. It was as if, in the close 1976 election in the U.S., Carter and Ford decided they would split the next term, each serving two years. Joked Peres: "We did it because we didn't have a choice. The only person to console me was our former chief rabbi who said there was precedent for it in the Bible. When I asked him where, he said in Paradise, because when Adam discovered there was no other lady but Eve and Eve discovered there was no other gentleman but Adam, they decided to make a national unity government, and it lasted until the snake, or quite a while. So we are used to this sort of Paradise, of equal forces."[4]

This has meant that Labor and the Likud must woo the smaller, often religious-oriented parties. In exchange for their support, Labor or the Likud is forced to grant concessions to the small parties. This has the effect of giving the smaller parties and their platforms disproportionate strength and influence.

One unusual role played by the religious parties has been that of peacemaker or mediator between the major parties. When Prime Minister Shimon Peres tried to fire Ariel Sharon, the popular but abrasive ex-general, from the Cabinet, it was Interior Minister Yitzhak Peretz, of the Sephardic Torah Guardian party, who played mediator.

The Economy: The Land and the Dead Sea

Israel was refounded by men and women who loved the Land and worked it with their hands. The stereotype of Jews as merchants and men and women of commerce may be accurate in recent centuries. But the Jews who returned to the Promised Land also returned to the soil.

Israel literally has created "streams in the desert" (Isa. 35:6). It has imposed a large-scale water system that enables it to use water from the Sea of Galilee for irrigation, and its engineers have devised a method of "drip irrigation" that avoids the evaporation of aerial irrigation by letting water ooze from irrigation pipes just below the surface. Micah's prophecy that in the latter days, they

---

4. From a public address in the forum sponsored by the Kennedy School of Government at Harvard University, September 21, 1987. See Genesis 2:18–3:24.

would "beat their swords into plowshares" (4:3b) has come true:
A factory in the old Philistine city of Ashkelon that once produced tanks now makes tractors.

Today Israel exports more food than it imports. Its main
agricultural exports are citrus fruits, valued at approximately
$500 million a year, and tomatoes, valued at about $300 million a
year. Israel imports beef from Argentina, although most of its
imports are feed grains.

Nowhere have "streams in the desert" flowed quite so dramati-
cally as in the Dead Sea region. The Dead Sea lives!—yet not at
first glance. The body of water forty miles by eleven miles is
approximately 1,300 feet below sea level. It is so mineral-laden
that to drink a cup of its "water" brings death in a half hour in the
most horrible way. Every year five or six persons die just that way.
Cakes of salt float on it like tiny icebergs, although its water feels
more oily than salty. Every tourist goes into the Dead Sea, if only
long enough to have a picture snapped while afloat reading the
paper. The temperature reaches 125° F in the daytime shade and
this becomes worse at night because the adjoining mountains
reflect heat like a furnace.

But waters from the Dead Sea, mudpacks from the shore, and
the blazing sun work miracles in treating psoriasis and other skin
disorders. Every year several hundred people, from all over the
world, fill five-star hotels along the sea for three to four weeks of
treatments. Dr. David Abels of the Ein Bokek Clinic on Psoriasis
credits the healing qualities to the mineral-rich, germ-free mud
and the unique climatic conditions—the high level of oxygen in
the air (the richest air in the world!) and the heavy atmospheric
pressure combine to filter out ultraviolet rays, leaving the infrared
rays to penetrate deep into the flesh in a therapeutic way—
without the danger of sunburn. The bromide in the Dead Sea acts
like a tranquilizer for the person bathing in it.

"We know it works," Abels says. The "certificate" Israel gives
to people who have visited the Dead Sea quotes Ezekiel 47:9,
". . . these waters shall be healed and whosoever cometh there,
shall live" (47:9).

Millennia ago, Abraham's nephew Lot was told to flee Sodom
and Gomorrah because of their sin. (The sin of Sodom, contrary

to popular speculation, was not sexual in nature, but was pride, gluttony, and the failure to care for the poor and needy. See Ezekiel 16:49, 50.) The Pentateuch says the Lord rained brimstone and fire on Sodom and Gomorrah, and when Lot's wife looked back she was turned into "a pillar of salt" (Gen. 18:16–19:28). The account says that Abraham looked at the ruins of Sodom and Gomorrah and the picture was "like the smoke of a furnace."

Traditionally Sodom has been located in what is now the six-mile Salt Mountain on the western shore of the Dead Sea's even more highly mineral-concentrated southern basin. Now, the Dead Sea Works Inc., one of Israel's main industries, is located in the area, illuminating the night air "like a furnace" as did Sodom of old. Organized in the 1930s as Palestine Potash Works, the company mines minerals from the sea, and sells bromine and potash for export. Potash is a main ingredient of fertilizer. Bromine is used in pesticides, paint, and fireproof building materials. Within the next decade, the Works proposes to convert the Dead Sea's three hundred annual cloudless days into solar energy.

"The Dead Sea is the future of Israel," says Shlomo Drori, 65, director of information for the Dead Sea Works. Some twenty families, including Drori's live in Newe Zohar, which may come closest to being on the location of biblical Sodom. Drori is an Austrian Jew who came to Palestine at seventeen and has worked for the firm for twenty-seven years. No one now alive has lived near the Dead Sea longer than he.

Drori has his own theory as to where Sodom and Gomorrah were located, pointing out that according to Genesis 13, Lot chose to settle in Sodom and Gomorrah because the cities bloomed "like the garden of the Lord." Drori takes this to mean like the Garden of Eden. Across from the Dead Sea Works on the Jordanian (eastern) side, the small Zered River flows between the mountains of Moab and Edom into the Dead Sea. In the winter, the Zered floods and erodes the mountains to form new soil. Over the years, the floods have created a fertile delta in the middle of the salt sea, resulting in the sweetest springs in the Middle East and an open-air hot house.

Drori says, "The result is the sweetest fruits and a blooming area which I compare to the Garden of Eden. This is Paradise. This also was the reason for the degeneration and perversity of the people of Sodom and Gomorrah. If you have everything you need and you don't have to work or struggle, you become degenerated."

The Kibbutzim and Diamonds

If Paradise lives on, Israel's grand social experiment—the kibbutz—is undergoing change. The kibbutzim were organized collectively, almost always on an agricultural basis. Men and women lived communally and kept beautiful dairy herds and tilled the fields. Their children were raised separately in the "children's house." Out of this regimen came a large percentage of Israel's army officers and some of its most illustrious citizens—patriarchs David Ben-Gurion and Golda Meir, among others.

Today, 120,000 men, women, and children live on Israel's 250 kibbutzim. The kibbutz now reflects more traditional family values. And far fewer "kibbutzniks" go into the standing army. Children in the kibbutz are more likely to spend the night with their parents, and their parents are more likely to work in a kibbutz factory than in the fields. "It boils down to the night. Where will the children be?" asks Raphael Lancer, a member of Nof Ginosar on the Sea of Galilee. Previously, children were "the property of the kibbutzim," he says. "They ignored the needs of the mother."

It is believed that within a short time, every third kibbutz will have an industrial project of some kind. Most of the kibbutzim still have herds of dairy cows, hundreds of chickens, and lush fruit groves. The kibbutz cares for every need of its members. There are no salaries, but the kibbutz has annual individual budgets for such things as vacations, clothing, books, gifts, cosmetics, and coffee. Twenty-five kibbutzim have guest houses, making this the largest hotel chain in Israel.

At the Orthodox Kibbutz Lavi in central Israel, the six hundred to seven hundred people eat communally. More than half of those in its guest house are religiously oriented, approximately 70 percent of them Christians who, traveling from Lavi, can make a round trip to Nazareth or the Sea of Galilee in a single day. Lavi was founded in 1949 on a barren hilltop by fifty settlers from England. The people of the kibbutz have planted trees, built a synagogue,

37

and furnished it—and now they make synagogue benches and supplies for export to the United States.

Surprisingly, perhaps, diamonds are Israel's top export by far. The gross income from diamonds was reportedly $1.5 billion in 1986, more than twice the amount received for electronic equipment, the No. 2 export. Over the years, Israel has specialized in the medium-sized or "melee" diamond of a half-carat, or perhaps slightly larger, all of which are imported. Some 55 percent of its stones, after cutting and polishing, go to the United States. During World War II, Palestine took over most of the world's diamond-cutting and polishing because the Nazis had overrun the traditional centers of Antwerp and Amsterdam. But after the war, Belgium and the Netherlands started up again, and Palestine lost business. In the early 1980s, a worldwide slump hit the diamond business, causing 80 percent of the big dealers to go under. Then Jewish entrepreneurship took over.

"It is the special nature of Jews to be independent," says Moshe Schnitzer, president of both the Israel Diamond Exchange and the World Federation of Diamond Exchanges. "The cutters in the big factories were fired . . . so they started on their own. They had the courage." They were following the model of Schnitzer himself, a history and philosophy major at Hebrew University who turned to diamond cutting as a trade, and then went into business for himself in 1946 after he was laid off. More than ten thousand Israelis work in diamond cutting and polishing factories, almost all of them small shops employing fewer than one hundred workers.

Now, a handful of oil wells dots the Negev, although all together Israel's production is only three hundred barrels a day. The first Hebrew to reach the Negev was the patriarch Abraham (Gen. 12:9). Wags have suggested that Abraham misunderstood God's directions. Had he made a sharp left turn as God intended, they say, today Israel would be awash in all that Saudi oil instead of dwelling in an oil desert. Israel's most recent producing well was drilled in the Negev near Arad, where a Canaanite king tried to stop the children of Israel's advance toward the Promised Land thirty-five hundred years earlier (Numbers 21). While petroleum is in short supply, Israel has taken steps to draw

Lifestyle in flux on Israel's kibbutzim

By WESLEY G. PIPPERT
United Press International

CHANGE IS SWEEPING the kibbutz, Israel's grand social experiment. Nowadays children stay at home overnight instead of living separately and their parents go off to work in factories.

The 120,000 men, women and children on Israel's 250 kibbutzim still keep customs and values the first kibbutzniks had at the turn of the century when they worked the land and lived communally.

But change is obvious. Some is a return to the traditional. Instead of the children living, eating and sleeping by themselves, many of them now eat the evening meal and spend the night with their parents.

"It boils down to the night. Where will the children be?" said Raphael Lancer, a member of Nof Ginosar. Previously children were considered "the property of the kibbutzim," Lancer said. "They ignored the needs of the mother."

Now many kibbutzim provide the parents with apartments large enough to let the children eat the evening meal and sleep overnight.

"The parents like children sleeping at home," Raphael said.

"It was the mothers' struggle. It never came from the children," said Yuval Peleg, a member of Kibbutz Shefayim.

Peleg has a 14-year-old son who he says decides where he will stay.

"I have never made a decision for him since he was 2," Peleg said. "He decided to stay home until he was 13. All his peers stayed at the children's home. But he had gotten his own computer and didn't want to."

The homecoming has occurred gradually. The orthodox Kibbutz Lavi in the Galilee voted in 1957 to let children live with their parents and spend only the working hours of the day in the children's houses.

"This 'revolutionary' step is one we have never regretted," a Lavi member said.

Most of Israel's kibbutzim still have herds of dairy cows, hundreds of chickens and lush fruit groves. A typical kibbutz has several hundred members and several hundred acres.

THE KIBBUTZ CARES for every need for its members. There are no salaries, but the kibbutz has annual individual budgets for such things as vacations, clothing, books, gifts, cosmetics, coffee.

Peleg's kibbutz, a "club-type" resort village on the Mediterranean nine miles north of Tel Aviv, is typical of the change in the economy of the kibbutzim.

Twenty-five kibbutzim have guest houses—the largest hotel chain in Israel—with pleasant accommodation and prices that attract not only hard-pressed Israelis but thousands of tourists.

Journalists crossing into Lebanon through the Rosh Hanikra checkpoint frequently stay overnight or eat breakfast at Kibbutz Gesher Haziv, nestled among the hills of Lebanon, the hills of Galilee and the sandy beach of the Mediterranean.

The price: $21 per person for bed and breakfast. Guests occasionally pick their own grapefruit for breakfast or an avocado to take home.

Gesher Haziv's main source of income, however, is a factory that makes high chairs, rockers and play tables.

The Kibbutz Industries Association says that within four years every third kibbutz will have an industrial project.

At orthodox Kibbutz Lavi, the 600 to 700 members eat communally. More than half the guests in its guest house are religiously oriented—and 70 percent of these are Christians who can make a roundtrip to Jesus' hometown of Nazareth or the headquarters of his ministry at Capernaum on the Sea of Galilee in a single day.

LAVI WAS FOUNDED on a barren hilltop in 1949 by 50 settlers from England. It planted trees, built a synagogue, furnished it—and now makes synagogue benches and supplies for export to the United States.

Spring-fed Kibbutz Ein Gedi, overlooking the stark Dead Sea, takes in about a dozen 15-year-olds from broken homes. The teen-agers stay by themselves with a nanny the first year, then are assimilated into the kibbutz, each family adopting one.

Ein Gedi member Mark Shamir said 99 percent of them become permanent members of the kibbutz. He said 22 of the original 24 people who founded Ein Gedi 29 years ago are still on the kibbutz—and the oldest is only 46 or 47.

upon another energy source—nuclear power. A nuclear reactor is located at Dimona in the Negev. Since it began operation in 1964 it has added greatly to speculation that Israel has an arsenal of nuclear weapons and bombs.

Israel has done something that few industrialized nations have been able to do—stopping inflation dead in its tracks. In 1984, inflation reached 451 percent, and during October that year, prices were shooting up at an annual rate of 1,260 percent. But on July 1, 1985, the hybrid government of Peres-Shamir pushed through a harsh austerity program. It voted to fire a number of civil workers (although it is now questionable if the dismissals actually took place), reduce government subsidies on basic foods and transportation that Israelis enjoy, devalue the shekel, freeze prices, and trim the national budget by about 4 percent. Israel's standard of living was lowered, but inflation was abruptly halted. The state's unemployment hovers around 6 or 7 percent, quite low for an industrialized nation; it is even lower in the occupied Arab territories.

Israel has a very socialistic economy. As we have noted, the air and bus lines, radio and television, telephone, telegraph, and electricity all are state-owned. The kibbutz and its brother movement, the moshav, an agricultural cooperative settlement, have socialistic elements. The government traditionally has heavily subsidized transportation and basic foods for poor people. "The Zionist view . . . considers the state as an instrument for solving the Jewish Problem," says Nadav Safran.[5]

Foreign correspondents have their own way of dealing with the cost of living in Israel. Most of us from the United States established "dollar accounts" in Israeli banks and made deposits in them from our American banks. Periodically, we would go to the bank, write a check for, say, three hundred dollars, and then take the dollars to an Arab money-changer. He would pay us in Israeli shekels anywhere from 5 to 15 to 25 percent more than what we could have gotten at our banks. Then, with a wad of shekels in our pocket, we paid various bills. This clearly is a concession to

---

5. Nadav Safran, *Israel: The Embattled Ally* (Cambridge, Mass.: Harvard University Press, 1981), 113.

foreigners, because Israelis may take only a limited number of dollars out of the country.

The Press

In my opinion, the press's view of Israel has changed greatly. From 1948 until the 1967 War, many foreign correspondents saw Israel romantically, in the sort of way Leon Uris portrayed Israel in *Exodus*. This is no longer true. This change may be because Israel has been perceived as the aggressor in the 1967 War that netted the West Bank, Gaza, and the Golan, and because of its bombing of the Iraqi nuclear reactor in 1981 and its invasion of Lebanon in 1982. This may be in part due to the sharp outward difference between the two peoples, the brash Israelis and the courteous Arabs. For whatever reason, most foreign correspondents I know are now more sympathetic to the Palestinian cause than to Israel. But they are highly professional journalists who do not let their feelings get in the way of their coverage of a particular story. It is debatable how much their feelings may affect the *selection* of stories they write, or how much this affects public opinion and public policy.

Choices

Despite these rivers of life flowing through modern Israel, the land faces tough choices. Will Israel be a secular or a religious nation? Will Israel be a democracy, or a state that imposes its will on others? Will Israelis be a people of justice and peace, or will they be oppressors and aggressors? Will they choose blessing or cursing, life or death? The answer is not clear, as we shall see.

2

The Problem Without

And the Lord gave them rest on every side just as he had sworn to their fathers; not one of all their enemies had withstood them, for the Lord had given all their enemies into their hands.

—Joshua 21:44

Israel has fought a war with its Arab neighbors every decade since its birth as a nation, and uncounted skirmishes between the wars. In forty years the nation has lost 12,950 soldiers in its wars, a rate of casualties that would have left 750,000 Americans dead in the same period. And Israel remains in a formal state of war with most Arab nations, Egypt being the sole exception. From 1967, the year of the Six-Day War, through 1985, 389 tourists and Israeli civilians had been killed and 2,561 wounded in terrorist activities in Israel, the West Bank, and Gaza.[1]

The toll of Israel's conflicts with the Arabs has been costly. Hardly a family in Israel has been spared. Our next-door neighbor in Jerusalem was a rabbi who had four sons. One son was killed in one war, and a second was killed in another war. The third, distraught in his grief, turned to crime and pulled a robbery in our own neighborhood. Only a fourth son has been able to lead a normal life, and pressures recently drove him back to the calm of a kibbutz.

Dr. Samuel Nissan told us of his son, a paratrooper, who witnessed the scraping of the remains of a baby off the side of the hijacked bus that was blown up on the Haifa-Tel Aviv coastal highway on March 11, 1978, in the worst guerrilla attack against

---

1. Reported in *Ha'aretz* on September 27, 1985.

Israel. The young man took part in Israel's Litani River campaign in southern Lebanon immediately after that attack. Since then, he has taken to climbing mountains in the Americas. He would work only long enough to make enough money to climb another mountain, but no summit climb could erase the memories.

When Israel invaded Lebanon in 1982, the young man was in Colorado. Seeing the news in the paper, he promptly hitchhiked to New York, flew back to Israel, and hitched a ride from Ben-Gurion Airport to his parents' place, arriving at about 10 P.M.. His parents were away for the evening, and their watchdog, not remembering him, would not let him near the house. So, he was asleep in his sleeping bag outside their fence when they returned. His parents begged him to stay for a day or two, but he refused; and the next morning at six o'clock he was reporting for duty for service in Lebanon. After serving his stretch, he flew back to America and resumed his mountain climbing.

Nissan, who had fought with the British in World War II, walked from Kibbutz Huldah to besieged Jerusalem in order to join his family and friends in the 1948 War of Independence. "All of us thought we had fought to make Israel secure," he told my wife and me. "We never dreamed our sons also would fight wars." One day, he said, while operating on a wounded soldier, he was overwhelmed to learn that the soldier was the son of a colleague. He said he then realized his generation had passed on to the next generation the mantle of war. Nissan's family has lost six of its own to wars and terrorism since 1970.

The tension, always close to the surface, has fostered the frenetic nature of the Israeli personality. Even Shimon Peres, foreign minister and former prime minister, with as calm a demeanor as imaginable, smokes so heavily that he lights up during a meal.

Modern Israel's security problems are no less acute than what Joshua and David encountered. (See my discussion in Appendix D.) In fact, it took ancient Israel four hundred years to secure its borders; it seems unrealistic or premature to think modern Israel can do so in only forty.

Israel contends that its wars have been fought either to protect its security or because its security had been threatened. The westernmost boundary of the West Bank comes to within eight miles of the Mediterranean. This means that when Jordan controlled that area, as it did from 1948 to the 1967 Six-Day War, the Arabs in a surprise attack from the West Bank border towns of Tulkarm or Qalqilyah could have reached the sea in a half hour, thus cutting Israel in two and eventually strangling it to death. When my wife and I heard flutist Jean-Pierre Rampel at the festival at the Ein Gev kibbutz on the eastern shores of the Galilee, I looked up and saw the towering Golan Heights looming so close that I thought a modern-day David with a slingshot could lob grenades from those mountains into the audience and kill hundreds. That suggests something of the risk Israelis live with each day.

Few Israelis assert that Israel conquered the West Bank, the Golan Heights, and the Gaza Strip in the 1967 War in order to reclaim land God had promised Abraham.[2] Rather, they state bluntly, it was done for purposes of security and survival. Israelis also explain that they launched the invasion of southern Lebanon in 1982 to stop the rocket attacks which had been launched across the border on the Galilee; but the reasons for that invasion are more complex, as we shall discuss later. I once was at dinner with a British diplomat and an Israeli professional, in the latter's home. The diplomat said: "The issue is land." "Absolutely not," the Israeli answered. "It's survival."

To look at the security problem from the standpoint of land area, Israel is the size of Massachusetts, the West Bank the size of Delaware—and the Arab states bordering Israel are more than half the size of the contiguous forty-eight U.S. states.

The constant threat of war has led to a militaristic society. Tiny Israel is number 15 among arms importers, and number 22 among arms exporters in the world, according to the U.S. Arms Control and Disarmament Agency, although it doesn't differ from most of its Arab neighbors in this respect.[3] Israel has developed a mentality whose immediate response often seems to be to pull the trigger

---

2. Golan and Golan Heights, and Gaza and Gaza Strip are used interchangeably in this book.

3. *World Military Expenditures and Arms Transfers*, 1986, published by the U.S. Arms Control and Disarmament Agency, p. 19.

or launch another air raid. Every provocation, big or small, seems to demand a response of force.

It appeared the Iran-Iraq War was shifting attention away from the Palestinian problem, but recent events in Gaza and the West Bank may be caused in part by a Palestinian determination to keep attention focused on them. The Arab League in 1987 voted to present a solid bloc opposition against Moslem (non-Arab) Iran. This mood of opposition was so intense that the League decided to let Arab countries reestablish relations with Egypt, broken since that nation's 1979 treaty with Israel, in order to encourage the Egyptians to join the opposition. Many countries quickly did so. As news commentator John Chancellor said, an old Arab adage, "the enemy of my enemy is my friend," might create the miracle of an Israeli-Arab bond as a result of a mutual hostility toward Iran. The focus of Arab concern moved from Israel to the Persian Gulf, and that was good news for Israel.

But the quiescence was short-lived. The Arabs revolted and the Israeli army responded harshly in late 1987 and early 1988 in the worst violence since the 1967 War. The fury exploded throughout Israel and the occupied territories, but the worst spot was the Gaza Strip. The number of Arabs killed by the army rose to nearly fifty in the first two months.

With the United States abstaining but significantly refusing to exercise its veto on behalf of Israel, the U.N. Security Council voted unanimously January 5 to urge Israel not to deport the nine Palestinian ring leaders as it had said it would.

What had happened? Some Westerners speculated that the Palestinians were determined not to let the focus of world attention shift to the Persian Gulf. Perhaps the terrible conditions in Gaza had predictably erupted into violence. Perhaps the fighting dramatized the truth that no army can subjugate a people indefinitely. *The Washington Post* reported January 10, 1988 that the Ateret Cohanim yeshiva (seminary) had been buying property in the Moslem Quarter of the Old City in Jerusalem, a provocative act. Jerusalem's mayor, Teddy Kollek, said that what inflamed Palestinians was that Defense Minister Ariel Sharon had moved into the Moslem Quarter and had promptly thrown a Hanukkah party.

The Arab revolt does not bode well for Israel. John Peterson,

45

dean of St. George's College, believes there will be no return to the status quo. Reuven Pedatzur, military correspondent for *Ha'aretz*, quoted an Israeli Defense Ministry spokesman as saying, "World military history shows that in a protracted war, quantity wins out." This means that despite Israel's show of force, the more numerous Palestinians ultimately will prevail.

Internal Security

The security problem is most acute within Israel's own boundaries. Guerrilla attacks have scarred every part of the body Israel. Here is a list, by no means complete, of some of the worst attacks, in descending order of numbers of casualties, including both victims and perpetrators:

44 killed on March 11, 1978—Thirteen Fatah commandoes from the Palestine Liberation Organization penetrated from the sea near Maagan Michael and commandeered a taxi and two buses, killing thirty-three civilians and fatally wounding eleven guerrillas.

28 killed on May 30, 1972—Three members of the Japanese Red Army attacked in the baggage-pickup area of Lod (now Ben-Gurion) Airport on behalf of the Popular Front for the Liberation of Palestine (P.F.L.P.); twenty-six civilians and two team members were killed.

28 killed on May 15, 1974—Three guerrillas held students at the Ma'alot school near the Lebanese border as hostages; twenty-four persons, mostly children, one soldier, and all three guerrillas were killed.

21 killed on April 11, 1974—A three-man squad from Lebanon infiltrated the northern town of Kiryat Shmona, and sixteen civilians, two soldiers, and all three guerrillas were killed.

18 killed on March 5, 1975—An eight-man Fatah squad broke into the Savoy Hotel in Tel Aviv; eight civilians, three soldiers, and seven guerrillas were killed.

11 killed in April 1969—A bomb exploded in the market in Jerusalem.

6 killed on May 2, 1980—Six Palestinians who had infiltrated from Jordan killed six Jewish yeshiva (seminary) students near Beit Hadassah in Hebron on the Occupied West Bank.

6 killed on April 22, 1979—A guerrilla squad attacked an apartment in Nahariya, killing three civilians, one policeman, and two of the four guerrillas.

3 killed on March 11, 1969—Guerrillas infiltrated Jiftlik and killed three soldiers.

2 killed on May 14, 1979—A bomb was planted in the Tiberias bus station, killing two children and wounding thirty-six persons.

29 wounded on March 6, 1969—A bomb was planted in the cafeteria at Hebrew University.

In every case above, all surviving perpetrators were released in the massive 1985 prisoner swap in which Israel freed 1,150 guerrillas in exchange for three Israeli soldiers taken prisoner of war in Lebanon.

One day in Gaza, an Israeli army officer told me during a discussion about the Arabs, "I appreciate the (desire) to be free. I can understand it. But in order for him to be free, I'm not ready to die. If the meaning of freedom is throwing bombs on Israeli citizens and soldiers, I have to fight this." Armed operations are waged against Israelis almost everywhere they are in the world. In the worst, terrorists killed eleven Israeli Olympic team members in Munich in September 1972.

This is not to suggest that all terrorism is perpetrated by the Arabs. As we shall see in the next chapter, there have been perhaps even more Arab casualties of Jewish terrorism than vice versa. Terrorist acts often have been initiated by Arabs; the terrorist acts by Jews often have been retaliatory in nature. The atmosphere in which terrorism has occurred often has been under control of the Israelis. Neither side is faultless; neither side bears all the guilt.

Terrorism is a harsh fact of life that lurks in the minds of everyone who lives in or visits the Middle East. Israeli Air Force planes flying over Jerusalem often broke the sound barrier, producing a deep "boom" that never failed to startle me for a moment. During my own tenure in Jerusalem, in December 1983, a bomb went off on an Israeli bus in west Jerusalem, killing six and wounding forty-one. The PLO claimed responsibility. The following April, three Arab young men walked out of a sports shop near the main intersection of King George Street and Jaffa Road in Jerusalem and started spraying bullets, wounding forty-eight, one of whom died later. While I was in Jerusalem, on numerous occasions sharp-eyed Israelis noticed a suspicious bag left under a bus seat or at a bus stop and we reporters received messages on our beepers signaling that Jerusalem police sappers were investigating. Sometimes the package was harmless, sometimes it contained explosives, and sometimes the explosives discharged.

Terrorism may be defined as random violence directed at innocent civilians. Often it has a political objective; at other times it seems senseless. It is largely a twentieth-century phenomenon that has proved to be the worst kind of war. Throughout much of western history, wars were fought between nations with recognized governments. War was tidy, as much as war can be. The warring governments knew how to get in touch with each other, negotiate, and eventually sign peace treaties. But terrorism is waged by nameless, faceless commandoes.

Terrorism has been a political weapon in the Middle East for years, so much so that many people link one with the other. It is only fair to remember, however, that terrorism is not confined to one group of people. In light of our American Revolution, Civil War, and Indian wars, we Americans may have forfeited the right to sit in judgment on others who resort to the armed struggle.

There are Arab terrorists, Jewish terrorists, American terrorists, Irish terrorists. Often Palestinian groups have resorted to terrorist tactics to further their objective of Palestinian self-determination; on the other hand, a group of Jewish settlers in the Occupied West Bank waged a three-year reign of terror against Arab residents.

Terrorism came abruptly and forcefully to the attention of most Americans in 1985 after two things happened. A TWA jetliner was held hostage in Beirut for nearly three weeks, and three months later, the *Achille Lauro* cruise ship was hijacked and an American Jewish passenger was killed. Tourists and would-be Holy Land pilgrims cancelled their trips to the Middle East in droves. There appeared to be a hiatus in terrorist attacks following the U.S. bombing of Libya in early 1986, but it was difficult to establish a

48

clear cause-and-effect. Just as an uneasy calm seemed to be prevailing, a Pan Am flight was hijacked in Pakistan, and seventeen of the four hundred persons aboard were killed. Then a Jewish synagogue was bombed in Istanbul, killing twenty-three.

There was provocation for the TWA hijack. The Israelis had taken twelve hundred prisoners of war, mostly Shiite Moslems, from the Ansar detention camp in southern Lebanon in late 1983 to prisons in Israel. This was an apparent violation of the Geneva Convention which prohibits taking POWs across a border. One of the demands of the hijackers was the release of the 766 who remained in Israeli prisons. Israel released the last of them from its Atlit prison south of Haifa two months later. TWA pilot John Testrake, an evangelical Christian, said later that although he condemned their terrorism, he saw valid reasons for the hijack— "a desperate move by oppressed people to try to break out of the injustice imposed on them." Two other former hostages, David Jacobsen and Benjamin Weir, both Christians, made similar statements; victims of terrorism often express sympathy for the perpetrators of it.

"Terrorism Is Going to Go Further"

Clinton Bailey, an expert on Shiite Moslems and a professor at Tel Aviv University, narrates a cycle of terror from the standpoint of a Shiite: "One day they put a booby-trapped car in our neighborhood. It blows out a building. It kills children. We carry them out. We cry and we scream. We denounce the inhumanity, the treason, the treachery. Next week we put a bomb in their neighborhood . . . the next week they put something in ours. . . . It's been going on that way for years."

In international terrorism, the tactics change a bit, Bailey says. "Hostages are part of it. (Terrorists) realize the West is very sensitive to loss of life." He says that in adopting terrorist tactics, the Shiites simply use the means that had been used in the 1960s and 1970s by the PLO.

For a land under an almost constant threat of terrorism, from both Arabs and Jews, Israel has been remarkably successful in preventing attacks that would take a heavy toll of lives. Rafael Eytan,

Israel's leading authority on terrorism, attributes the record to painstaking planning and lightning-fast responses. A short, balding man with an easy laugh, Eytan offered his views while sitting in the lobby of Jerusalem's King David Hotel, the target of one of the most notorious terrorist acts ever committed in the Middle East. With Menachem Begin as mastermind, the Irgun, a Jewish, preindependence terrorist organization, planted a bomb in a milk can that blew up the King David on July 22, 1946, killing ninety-one. It was one of the last deadly acts before the British gave up their mandate over Palestine the next year. Later, Eytan gained notoriety as the senior Israeli official responsible for the activities of Jonathan Pollard, the American Jew who was hired by Israel to spy on the United States. But when I spoke with him, Eytan's target was terrorists, not the United States.

"Is it possible for one man to make terrorism?" Eytan asked. "No. For terror, you need many people—smuggling, communicating, making the explosives, concealing the charges, setting the charges."

Because Israel is small, intelligence agents are able to keep track of suspicious people. Terrorists' lives intersect with many other people, and in the process they drop clues that superperceptive intelligence agents pick up. Clues are dropped not only by paid informers or the disenchanted but also unwittingly by the most competent and dedicated of terrorists. Intelligence agents pour over all kinds of data. Often, what seems like insignificant information may be the tiny piece that completes a big puzzle.

"Eight or nine times out of ten we head off an attack," Eytan said. "Even in operations where they succeed there is generally a small toll."

Nowhere is Israel's record against terrorism better illustrated than by its El Al airlines. An El Al airliner has not been hijacked successfully since 1968. The security people at El Al, often young women who look like they are high-school age, can teach the most skillful reporter about asking tough, probing questions. The departing passenger at Ben-Gurion Airport runs into a barrage of questions: Where are you going? Why? What neighborhood do you live in in Jerusalem? Where is it located? Do you know any Israelis? What are their names? Did anyone give you packages to mail or to deliver? Who packed your bags? Have you had your bags with you since you packed them? Do you know why I am asking you these questions? In their minds, they are using one question to double-check on another. They ask to examine your ticket and your passport. They may or may not go through your baggage, carefully scrutinizing every piece, no matter how embarrassing to you. Then, their supervisor must approve what they have done.

The case of the pregnant young Irish woman who carried a bomb in her suitcase as she tried to board an El Al jumbo jet in London in 1986 illustrates the efficiency of Israeli security. The woman was asked why she was flying to Israel. For Passover, she replied. So far, so good. Where are you going to stay? In Bethlehem, she said. (Passover is not observed in Bethlehem; the town is 100 percent Arab.) At what hotel? The Hilton, she said. (The nearest Hilton Hotel is in Jerusalem.) Security agents took another look at the young woman's baggage and found hidden in the lining a sophisticated plastic explosive that her Arab boyfriend had given her.

El Al, however, has been targeted more effectively in its ground operations. At Christmastime 1985, attacks at El Al counters at airports in Rome and Vienna left eighteen dead. This was also the year of the three-week hijacking of the TWA jetliner and the hijacking of the *Achille Lauro* cruise ship elsewhere in the Middle East.

The acts led Israel's U.N. Ambassador Benyamin Netanyahu to predict grimly that terrorism would increase in intensity and violence. Netanyahu spoke from a unique standpoint. His brother Jonathan was the only soldier who was killed in Israel's daring 1976 rescue of hijacked airline passengers in Entebbe, Uganda. The Jonathan Institute on International Terrorism was founded in his memory.

"Terrorism is going to go further," Netanyahu told me. "It has to. There is an inexorable internal dynamic about terrorism that will make these attacks grow and increase both in intensity and scope of violence and probably in number as well. Terrorism seeks to frighten, to stupefy, to shock. Once the West gets accustomed to a certain level of violence, there is no more shock, so you [the terrorists] have to come up with 'new and better' things, more horrifying ways of killing people. You used to hijack an airplane. That used to make tremendous headlines. Today, no. You have to hijack an airliner and kill a few hostages. In the future, they'll probably have to kill a lot more hostages—and they will."

Population

Demographic figures suggest a greater, long-term threat to Israel's internal security. There are 700,000 Arabs living in Israel, a sizeable 18 percent of the total population. In the territories that Israel has occupied since the 1967 War, the West Bank has a population of 813,000 Arabs and 65,000 Jewish settlers, and the Gaza Strip is home for 525,000 Arabs and 2,700 Jewish settlers. (See Appendix C.)

The odds are worsening from the Israeli point of view, so much so that the Jews could become a minority in their own state. Demographers Dov Friedlander and Calvin Goldscheider found that the present fertility rate for Jewish women is 2.7 births and for Arab women on the West Bank it is 7.5 births. They predict that by the year 2015, the birth rates will decline to between 2 and 2.5 births for Jewish women and 4.5 to 5.5 births for Arabs. Friedlander and Goldscheider say the Jewish population of "Greater Israel," the name they applied to modern Israel and the occupied territories, thus could range from 62 percent to less than 50 percent of the population.[4]

"The resulting Greater Israel would then be a bi-national, if not, indeed, an Arab-dominated state. If Israel chooses not to extend political rights to the incorporated populations, the extreme result would be a potentially inflammable 'colonial' relationship between a minority of Jews and the large proportion of disenfranchised Arabs living within the boundaries of Greater Israel."[5]

Not everyone agrees with the Friedlander-Goldscheider

---

4. See Dov Friedlander and Calvin Goldscheider, *Israel's Population: The Challenge of Pluralism*, vol. 39, no. 2 (Washington, D.C.: Population Reference Bureau), 1984, 32.

5. Ibid., 37.

conclusions. Michael I. Teplow points out that birth rates are influenced by a nation's level of education and income, and that the Arab birth rate has declined since the founding of Israel. Thus, he says, the percentage of Arabs in Israel plus the occupied territories has stayed at about 36 or 37 percent since 1967.[6]

We will discuss the West Bank and the Palestinians more fully in chapters 4 and 7. Outwardly, Jews and Arabs alike do not believe Israeli Arabs would pose a threat to Israel's security in the event of another Israeli-Arab conflict soon. "There would not be a revolt. There might be some demonstrations, some political protest," says Walid Fahoum, a lawyer and member of an eminent Arab family that has lived in Nazareth for five hundred years. His cousin is chairman of the Palestine National Council, the legislative body of the PLO. "We don't know. We can't predict. . . . You can't know what people are thinking if they are not speaking what is inside their minds." Fahoum's words have an ominous ring.

External Security

David has become Goliath. The promise of the land to Abraham became a full reality only in the halcyon days of King Solomon (1 Kings 4:21 and 2 Chronicles 9:26) when he ruled from Egypt to the Euphrates. Israel today is the strongest that it has been since the days of Solomon, who contributed to its grandeur not so much through war as through slave labor. Israel now is acknowledged to have one of the strongest armies in the world after the superpowers, though with only 170,000 regulars, it is quite small in comparison with the size of the Arab regular armies.

There are several reasons for Israel's strength and effectiveness in war:

1. Israel is physically compact, a sort of hub in the middle of a wheel.

2. According to Israeli intelligence officers, Israel makes highly effective use of quick and frequent troop movements, simplified by the physical compactness of the land. Troops fighting in Gaza

---

6. A letter to the editor of *The New York Times*, October 23, 1987.

on the Egyptian front would find themselves a few hours later fighting against the Syrians in the north.

3. Its "citizen-soldier" army enables the forces to be doubled or tripled within a few hours in case of a call-up of the reserves.

4. Many of the new buildings in the new settlements in Israel and the West Bank were constructed like fortresses, with narrow slits that easily can accommodate a weapon. Israelis frankly acknowledge that the new neighborhoods of Gilo, Ma'ale Adumim, and the French Hill provide an almost impenetrable ring around Jerusalem.

5. Israel used the preemptive strike, that is, to hit first and draw first blood, in every one of its wars except the 1973 Yom Kippur War. Then the Egyptians struck on the most solemn Jewish holiday, even as the Israeli Cabinet was meeting and discussing a preemptive strike.

6. According to official Western analysts, Israeli generals also give their field commanders much more freedom to make tactical decisions on the spot, often with innovative and astonishing results. This is unlike the Arab pattern of following the Soviet model of a strict centralized command.

7. According to these Western strategists, Israel's technological edge plus a critical psychological edge in "leadership" overcomes any advantage the Arab countries might gain by obtaining sophisticated equipment from the Soviets.

The Wars

The 1948 War of Independence

A small statue on Jaffa Street in West Jerusalem demonstrates the homemade rifles that Jews were forced to use in their War of Independence in 1948. The rifle is little more than a tin pipe and scrap metal.

To the world, the odds seemed stacked against the relative handful of Jews in their war against the vastness of the Arab lands and people. Chaim Herzog says, however, that the actual forces at the outset numbered about fifteen thousand Jews and thirty thousand Arabs. Neither side was especially unified. Menachem

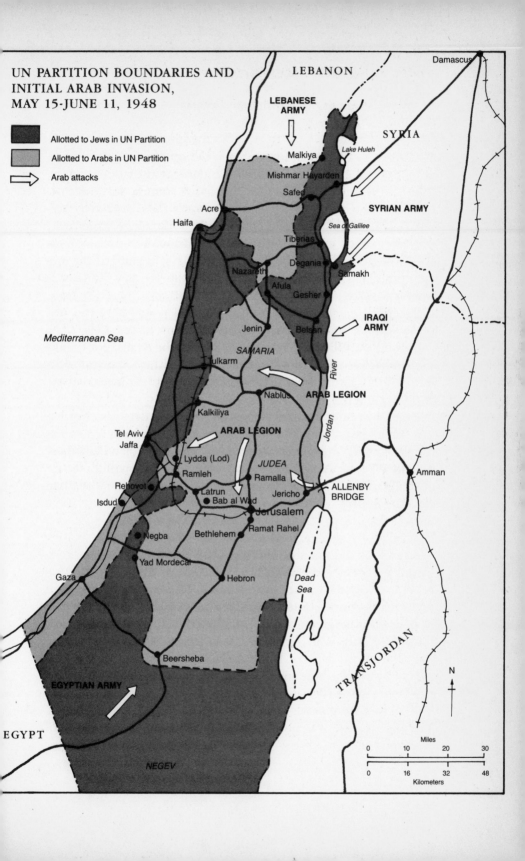

UN PARTITION BOUNDARIES AND INITIAL ARAB INVASION, MAY 15-JUNE 11, 1948

Allotted to Jews in UN Partition

Allotted to Arabs in UN Partition

Arab attacks

LEBANON

Damascus

LEBANESE ARMY

SYRIA

Malkiya

Lake Huleh

Mishmar Hayarden

Safed

SYRIAN ARMY

Acre

Haifa

Sea of Galilee

Tiberias

Degania

Nazareth

Samakh

Afula

Gesher

Jenin

Belsan

Mediterranean Sea

SAMARIA

Tulkarm

IRAQI ARMY

Nablus

ARAB LEGION

Kalkiliya

Jordan River

Tel Aviv

Jaffa

ARAB LEGION

Lydda (Lod)

JUDEA

Ramleh

Ramalla

Amman

Rehovot

Jericho

ALLENBY BRIDGE

Isdud

Latrun

Bab al Wad

Jerusalem

Negba

Ramat Rahel

Bethlehem

Yad Mordecai

Dead Sea

Gaza

Hebron

TRANSJORDAN

Beersheba

N

EGYPTIAN ARMY

EGYPT

Miles

0   10   20   30

NEGEV

0   16   32   48

Kilometers

Begin's militant Irgun continually was at odds with the Jewish regulars, or Haganah. The various Arab states were even more divided.

The key to the Israeli triumph was the agreement for a twenty-eight-day truce starting in June 1948. Jerusalem had been under siege and was near the point of starvation. During the truce, the Israelis were able to smuggle arms in with their approved shipments of food and medical supplies for Jerusalem. The Israeli army was reorganized and strengthened with material, especially from Czechoslovakia. When the war resumed, Israelis grabbed the momentum. The second truce took effect July 18, and a cease-fire went into force January 7, 1949.

Israel had much more land than the Jews would have received under British proposals in the 1930s or under the 1947 U.N. Partition Plan, all of which were rejected by the Arabs. But thanks to the effectiveness of the Arab Legion under the command of Sir John Glubb, Jordan kept control of East Jerusalem including the Old City and the Wailing Wall.

Israel now stretched from Beersheba to the Lebanese border. But three key parcels of land—an area that came to be known as the West Bank, the teeming Gaza Strip, and the Golan Heights—remained under Arab control and provided them with bases for guerrilla attacks against Israel. Indeed, there were more than eleven hundred Israeli casualties between the 1948 and 1956 wars, according to official Israeli figures. There were also 750,000 Palestinian refugees, a problem that persists to this day.

The blood did not stop flowing, even among the peacemakers. Count Bernadotte, the Swedish U.N. mediator who wanted to give Israel the Western Galilee instead of the Negev and put Jerusalem under U.N. control, was assassinated, presumably by Jews yet not named, on a Jerusalem street September 17, 1948. And Jordan's King Abdullah, who had been negotiating secretly with Israel, was assassinated in 1951, by a Palestinian. Abdullah's teenage son Hussein was at his side and succeeded him.

The prospects for peace looked bleak. The Arabs, after all, had little to gain from peace—and little to lose by going to war again. The Jewish state was now a reality and occupied large parts of Arab land.

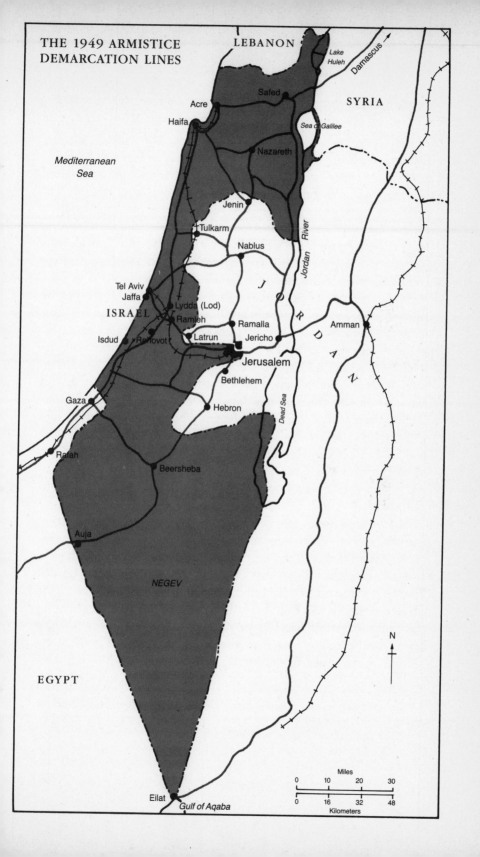

THE 1949 ARMISTICE
DEMARCATION LINES

LEBANON

Lake
Huleh

Damascus →

SYRIA

Safed

Acre

Haifa

Sea of Galilee

Mediterranean
Sea

Nazareth

Jenin

Tulkarm

Nablus

Jordan River

J

O

Tel Aviv

Jaffa

Lydda (Lod)

ISRAEL

Ramleh

Ramalla

Amman

Isdud

Rehovot

Latrun

Jericho

R

Jerusalem

Bethlehem

D

Gaza

Hebron

Dead Sea

A

Rafah

N

Beersheba

Auja

NEGEV

N

EGYPT

Eilat

Gulf of Aqaba

Miles

0   10   20   30

0   16   32   48

Kilometers

1956 Sinai Campaign

The superpowers—the United States, the Soviet Union, Britain, and France—played important roles in this war between Israel and Egypt. The Soviets, courting the Arabs, had completed an arms deal with Egypt through Czechoslovakia in late 1955 as part of its attempt to foil the U.S. "cold war" containment policy. In reaction, the United States extended, then in July withdrew, an offer to help Egypt build a new Aswan Dam. Within days, Egypt's Gamal Abdul Nasser, infuriated, nationalized the Suez Canal. Even earlier he had closed it to Israeli shipping.

Israel, meanwhile, for years had been the target of attacks by Palestinian *fedayeen,* or commandoes, with a particular religious fervor, operating under the auspices of Egypt. "We are compelled to make a supreme effort for security," Prime Minister Ben-Gurion told the Knesset on October 15.[7] Following the plan of their three-way alliance, Israel attacked on October 29, and the British and French followed the next day. Moshe Dayan, Israel's most famous soldier, was chief of staff. Ariel Sharon, a burly, George Patton-like leader who some Israelis say was their finest field officer ever, was one of ten brigade commanders. The Israelis roared across the Sinai and took the Gaza Strip in what Herzog called "a work of art."[8] "After 3,300 years, we were at Mount Sinai again," Ben-Gurion said.[9]

The United States and the Soviet Union cooperated in getting the United Nations to impose a cease-fire that took effect November 6. After the war, Israel withdrew from all but Sharm el Sheikh, which controlled access to the Gulf of Aqaba and the Israeli port of Eilat. The war effectively removed Britain and France as major players in the Middle East; from then on, the United States became the most important western nation in the region. By supplying arms, the Soviets emerged as the friend of the Arabs. Nasser's seizure of the Suez from the West overshadowed his defeat in

---

7. David Ben-Gurion, *Israel: Years of Challenge* (New York: Holt, Rinehart and Winston, 1963), 110.

8. Chaim Herzog, *The Arab-Israeli Wars* (New York: Vintage, 1982), 141.

9. Ben-Gurion, 131.

combat and he emerged as the hero of Arab nationalism. Israel's victory was decisive enough to assure it relative calm with its Arab neighbors for ten years. It used the period to develop, among other things, a nuclear capability in cooperation with France.

The 1967 Six-Day War

The Soviet friendship with the Arabs had continued into 1967, helping Egypt build the Aswan and supplying arms. For years there had been little tension, and few people believed war was imminent. But in 1966 the Israeli-Syrian border heated up; Israel shot down seven Syrian planes at one point. Nasser worked himself to a feverish pitch during a few days late in May 1967, with only mild responses from Levi Eshkol, the Israeli prime minister and defense minister. He massed troops along the border with Israel, blockaded the Gulf of Aqaba, and escalated his rhetoric by saying the existence of Israel and Palestinian rights were the issues. Moshe Dayan became Israel's defense minister.

On June 5, Israel attacked first. It destroyed almost all of Egypt's air force within three hours, and for all practical purposes, the outcome of the war had been decided. By the end of the week, Israel had captured the Sinai and Gaza Strip from Egypt, the West Bank and East Jerusalem from Jordan, and the Golan Heights from Syria, increasing its land area fourfold.

The 1967 War was a watershed. The outcome drastically affected the balance of power in the Middle East. Previously, the Arabs had little to gain from recognizing Israel's right to exist. Now, Israel held sizeable chunks of Arab land that might be useful as negotiating chips. The outcome also drastically affected world opinion toward Israel. U.S. President Lyndon B. Johnson assured Israel that the United States would not force Israel to give back conquered territory without something in return. The United States also realized that Israel's military superiority in the Middle East was now unchallenged. For the first time, Israel was seen in world opinion as an aggressor who captured the territory of other nations.

The U.N. Security Council passed Resolution 242 on November 22, 1967, which provided for "withdrawal of Israeli armed forces from territories occupied in the recent conflict" and for "a just settlement of the refugee problem." The resolution was ambiguous in that it did not say Israel must withdraw from *all* the occupied territories. It also called upon states in the Middle East to "live in peace in secure and recognized borders." For the Arabs, recognizing 242 would be tantamount to recognizing Israel's right to exist. The Khartoum Conference of Arabs in September 1967 ruled "no negotiations, no recognition, and no peace" with Israel. But Resolution 242 has remained the basis of argument ever since.

The 1967–70 War of Attrition

Within three weeks after the end of the Six-Day War, Egypt began almost daily attacks against Israeli forces staked out on the east side of the Suez Canal. Israel lost 738 persons, almost as many as in the Six-Day War. The Soviets continued to supply Egypt with weapons and, finally, pilots.

Chaim Bar-lev, the police minister in Peres's Cabinet during my stint in Israel, was chief of staff during the War. In 1969, U.S. Secretary of State William P. Rogers proposed a cease-fire leading to a peace treaty under whose terms Israel would withdraw from almost all occupied territories. On July 30, 1970, Israeli planes got into a dogfight with eight Soviet MIGs piloted by Russian pilots. To utter Soviet humiliation, five MIGs were shot down while the Israelis suffered no losses. Nasser went to Moscow in a plea for more arms, and the Soviets, not wanting further involvement in the volatile Middle East, turned him down. Disheartened, Nasser returned and agreed to a cease-fire, followed by Israel's acceptance on July 31. In September, Nasser died, his dreams of driving Israel into the sea and of pan-Arabism never realized.

The 1973 Yom Kippur War

Israel's war with the Arabs that began on October 6, 1973—Yom Kippur, the Jews' holiest holiday—was its most difficult to that date.

The Soviets had supplied SAMs (surface-to-air missiles) to Anwar Sadat, now in power in Egypt. The U.S. government was in crisis because of the scandals surrounding Watergate and Vice-President Spiro T. Agnew. In part because of an Israeli intelligence failure, Defense Minister Moshe Dayan and Chief of Staff David Elazar disagreed over the significance of Arab actions. Elazar wanted a preemptive strike and total mobilization, but Dayan rejected the proposal. Even as the Israeli Cabinet was meeting, Syria and Egypt capped their long planning with a surprise attack.

For a week the outcome looked bleak for the Israelis. Then Israel went on the counter-offensive, driving into Syria beyond the 1967 lines. Its new nuclear capability also was ominous for the Arabs. Gen. Ariel Sharon's daring charge across the Suez October 17 and his encirclement of the Egyptian Third Army also helped reverse the war, and ultimately, turn the long-festering Israeli-Egyptian relationship toward peace. The Soviets saw the encirclement of the Egyptian army as embarrassing, for they had armed Egypt. The United States pressured Israel into opening up supply lines to the trapped Egyptians. Sadat concluded that the Americans were the only ones capable of restraining Israel, and that Egypt therefore should cast its lot with the United States, not the Soviet Union, thus setting in motion what came to fruition in a peace treaty six years later.

After the 1973 War, the U.N. Security Council added Resolution 338 and reaffirmed Resolution 242. Resolution 338 called for negotiations "under appropriate auspices," which the Arab nations took to mean an international conference. I've never had trouble remembering Resolutions 242 and 338; the UPI number in Jerusalem is not 242-338, but 242-438. Close.

The 1982–85 Invasion and Occupation of Lebanon

For thirteen years, Israel charged, the PLO had used southern Lebanon as a launching pad for rocket and missile attacks on Jewish settlements and kibbutzim in the Galilee. In June 1982, Shlomo Argov, Israel's ambassador to the Court of St. James, was shot and wounded in London, and two days later Israel attacked southern Lebanon. Israel stated that one reason for this "Operation Peace for Galilee" was to stop the rocket attacks, even though there had been none since a cease-fire had been arranged ten months previously.

"For thirteen years a battle for the safety of the residents of the Galilee has been waged . . . shells fired from Lebanese territory. . . ." Defense Minister Moshe Arens told the Knesset later, "We've experienced similar battles in the past. . . . The toll in lives of the early 1950s in the Gaza Strip is what led to the Sinai Campaign [of 1956]. In 1968, 1969, and 1970 there was a terrorist campaign against citizens of the state from Jordanian territory."

Israel had made short thrusts into Lebanon previously. In March 1978, following the hijacking of the Haifa-Tel Aviv bus, the Israelis drove to the Litani River about fifteen miles inside Lebanon. Since then, about 5,500 multinational troops known as the U.N. Interim Forces in Lebanon (UNIFIL) have been stationed in southern Lebanon. They are greatly restricted in what they are permitted to do to maintain peace. But in the summer of 1982, Israelis drove farther and farther north, for a distance of sixty miles, into the southern neighborhoods of Beirut. Often they were greeted by the Lebanese Shiites as the welcome conquerors of the PLO who had taken over their turf. Arafat and the PLO were forced to sail away from Beirut in August in the disgrace of apparent defeat.

In September 1982, Lebanon's youthful new president-elect, Bashir Gemayel, was assassinated. A few days later—with Israeli troops on a small hill only a few yards away, so close that it was impossible to avoid knowing what was going on—Lebanese Christian militiamen stormed into the poverty-ravaged Sabra and Shatilla Palestinian refugee camps in southern Beirut to avenge the death of Gemayel. Hundreds of Palestinians were slain.

The Israelis stayed. And stayed. Soon they began to outwear their welcome and the southern Lebanese people turned on them.

The Israelis began a withdrawal in stages. They pulled out of the Shouf Mountains in September 1983, a full year after the Sabra and Shatilla massacre. Prime Minister Shimon Peres, who took office a year later, saw that stopping runaway inflation and the withdrawal from Lebanon were the two main tasks facing the national coalition government. The Cabinet approved a three-stage withdrawal in January 1985, and five months later, three years to the day after the invasion, the withdrawal was completed. Since then the Israelis have clung to a narrow, three- to nine-mile "security zone" just inside the Lebanese border.

The war could not have been more damaging for Israel:

- Like the Vietnam War for the United States, the Lebanon War was the first Israel had not won. Israel lost more than five hundred soldiers.

- It crushed the infrastructure of the PLO only temporarily and it alienated the Shiites and Druze of southern Lebanon.

- It cost Sharon his job on grounds he shared the responsibility for Sabra and Shatilla, and it almost surely hastened the departure of a weary and saddened Menachem Begin from public life one year later. In three years in Jerusalem, I never saw Begin in public once.

- The war cost Israel a million dollars a day, overheating the Israeli economy just as Vietnam had done to America's.

- It exposed serious weaknesses in the vaunted Israel Defense Forces.

- The war did not have the support of many Israelis. In 1983, 500,000 persons crowded into Tel Aviv in an anti-war demonstration, leading people to observe that more Israelis than Arabs actively opposed the Israeli invasion of southern Lebanon.

"The gravest strategic mistake in the Lebanon war was that the aims of the war were vague, ill-defined, and largely based on deception," said Ze'ev Schiff, military affairs reporter for the respected Israeli newspaper, *Ha'aretz*. He said the war had "an astonishing and painful" effect on the Israeli army.

"You see the change first of all in the eyes of the soldiers and the Lebanese. It's a look that reminded me of the look in the eyes of the American soldiers and officers who knew their chances of winning in Vietnam were less than negligible."

Concluded UPI's Gerald Nadler in 1985: "Israel, which sent a military juggernaut into Lebanon three years ago to destroy the PLO, is withdrawing a broken, demoralized and disillusioned army it may take years to revitalize."

Arab Neighbors

We will discuss the Arab countries that border Israel, although Iraq and others that do not adjoin the Jewish state also have been major players in the ongoing Arab pressure on Israel.

Egypt: Peace At Last

Egypt has been Israel's longest and most persistent enemy, dating back nearly four thousand years to the four hundred years the Israelites spent in slavery there (Genesis 39–Exodus 15). Since the rebirth of Israel, Egypt's rhetoric against the Israelis had been without equal in harshness. Gamal Abdul Nasser, the president of Egypt, asserted, "if the Israelis want war, welcome!" And Egypt and Israel fought several wars. Nasser's successor, Anwar Sadat, made a historic visit to Jerusalem in November 1978, inspiring a chain of events that led to the 1979 Israeli-Egyptian peace treaty. It has proved to be far more sturdy and durable than almost anyone might have dared to hope.

The treaty has survived crisis after crisis—(1) the 1981 assassination of Sadat, one of the "Big Three" architects of the treaty, along with Menachem Begin and President Jimmy Carter; (2) Israel's 1982 invasion of southern Lebanon; and while Israeli troops looked on, (3) the following September's mass slayings of hundreds of Palestinians in the Sabra and Shatilla refugee camps in a wretchedly poor neighborhood of southern Beirut. In protest against Sabra and Shatilla, Egypt withdrew its ambassador from Tel Aviv for the next four years.

Egypt and Israel have failed to implement the forty or more trade, tourist, and artistic agreements accompanying the treaty. They have failed to agree on fifteen tiny parcels of disputed land along the Sinai border, the most important being a pie-shaped piece of beach on the Gulf of Aqaba called Taba. An Egyptian soldier gunned down and killed seven Israeli tourists on a Sinai sand dune at Ras Burka in 1985. But still the treaty survived.

The peace treaty has been helpful to both Israel and Egypt. Under its terms, the Israelis returned to Egypt in 1982 the Sinai Desert they had recaptured in 1967, after capturing it for the first time in 1956 (they returned the Sinai to Egypt then also). For its part, Israel had made peace with its most important Arab neighbor, and gained passageway through the Suez. The part of the treaty dealing with oil has functioned best. When Israel returned the Sinai, it lost half of its oil supply. The treaty provides that Egypt sell oil to Israel which it has done without incident or fanfare.

Egypt is the leading and most powerful Arab country. This assessment has to be tempered, however, by the conclusion of certain qualified observers, chief among whom is Sir John Glubb, for seventeen years commander of the Arab Legion. He has said that Egyptians are ethnically unconnected with Arabs east of the Sinai and that Egypt "cannot be, and never has been, the leader of the Arabs."[10]

Construction of the Suez Canal, completed in 1869, opened the floodgates, so to speak, to Western imperialism in Egypt. The British gradually began to bail out the bankrupt Egyptians by buying Suez shares in 1875 and took control of the country in 1882. The Suez remained under British control for seventy-four years until Nasser nationalized it in 1956 and emerged as hero of the Arabs.

Egypt, with a population of forty-five million, has huge problems. Cairo is a dusty city of fifteen million people, and the population grows at the rate of 750,000 a year. There is a mere handful of traffic lights, thus traffic jams are awesome. That is a microcosm of Egypt's larger problems. The economy is in bad shape. Oil production and tourism, Egypt's two main sources of revenue, have dropped drastically. Presiding over all this is Hosni Mubarak, a man of courage but lacking the charisma of either Nasser or Sadat.

In February 1986 Egypt's conscript policemen rioted, setting fire to luxury hotels and cafes near the pyramids southwest of Cairo, leaving seventy dead and two hundred wounded. One of the hotels was the historic Mensa House, where Roosevelt and Churchill met during World War II. The site afterward was eerie—the burned-out hulks of three luxury hotels, the husks of a hundred burned-out cars, night clubs that had been set afire while shops next-door

---

10. John Glubb, *A Short History of the Arab Peoples* (New York: Stein and Day, 1969), 243.

were left untouched—all within view of the benign and enigmatic Sphinx. There was speculation that Moslem Brotherhood zealots bent on eradicating "western decadence" caused the riot, because the hotels and night clubs that were torched appeared to have been selectively chosen on the basis of whether they had casinos. The government charged later that the cause was exactly what the conscript policemen had said at the time. Drawn from Egypt's lower social strata, they had to live in tents, were paid under $10 a month, and were treated badly; they had rioted when they heard rumors they were going to have to serve a year longer than what had been told them when they were drafted.

Syria: The Chief Adversary

According to Israeli intelligence, President Hafez Assad of Syria has hanging in his office a picture of the great Saladin defeating the Christian Crusaders at Hattin near Tiberias in 1187 (although the Crusaders were not finally vanquished for eight years). The message is obvious. Assad is committed to driving out the latest invaders of Greater Syria—the Jews. And, he is patient. He will take as long as necessary to achieve that goal.

Assad, who took office in 1970, is an air force general who served with Egyptian President Hosni Mubarak in the 1950s when both were bomber pilots. Moshe Maoz, chairman of Middle East studies and politics at Hebrew University, and official Israeli sources describe Assad as a pragmatic, cautious man who would never dash into things in a foolhardy way, but who holds an emotional blind spot of fury toward Israel.

Syria, population 8.6 million, is Israel's chief adversary. Enmity between Israel and Syria dates back to about 1000 B.C. when King David defeated the Syrians in a battle northeast of the Sea of Galilee (2 Sam. 8:5–6). Now, the two nations' population centers— Damascus and Tel Aviv—are within missile range of each other. War talk is frequent. And Syria's leader is one of the most astute in the region.

This is both good news and bad news for Israel. Since Israel is widely acknowledged to be more powerful, it means that Syria is not likely to start a war any time soon. In the meantime, it is probable that Israel and Assad have a subtle, unspoken, unnegotiated understanding that each would deny publicly: Each will leave the other alone—for the time being. On the other hand, once Assad feels that Syria is strong enough to take on Israel by itself, without depending on any of its Arab brethren, he will make his move.

"He's very cautious, cool-headed," Maoz says. "Therefore, when he strikes it will be disastrous for Israel. He will be ready. . . . Israel can do business with him, but only in the short run. In the long run, war."

Most diplomats, Western as well as Israeli, believe that Syria will not move until it has parity—alone, and not in alliance with any other Arab neighbor. In earlier Arab-Israeli wars, Syria joined Egypt and Jordan and took its lumps. Maoz believes Assad hopes to reach "parity-plus-one" with Israel soon, but some Western diplomats believe Syria will not achieve this for five to ten years. Syria is ahead in some areas—it has a larger population and it has modern equipment and larger numbers of equipment. But these diplomats point out that Israel retains an edge.

One Western diplomat told me, "We assume that in a war, Israel would get to Damascus in two or three days and occupy Syria in fourteen days." Israelis disagree. They believe it would be a much harder war.

According to recent Israeli calculations, Israel and Syria each have about 3,600 tanks and 600 fighter aircraft. Syria has an army of 800,000 regular and reserve troops, far larger than Israel's army of 170,000 regulars and 330,000 reserves capable of quick mobilization. Israelis say their aim is to try to limit the Arabs' quantitative edge to 3:1.

Of even greater peril to both nations is the role that each plays as surrogate in the Middle East for its patron, the United States (Israel) and the Soviet Union (Syria). The Soviet Union has armed Syria with highly accurate SS-21 (surface-to-surface) and SA-5 (surface-to-air) missiles, which are capable of hitting targets in central Israel. Syria also has Soviet-made SA-2 and mobile SA-6 and SA-8 antiaircraft missiles. The SA-2 has a range of about thirty miles. On the other hand, the United States now gives about $3 billion a year in economic and military aid to Israel.

67

By and large the Israeli-Syrian border is tranquil. There are occasional incidents, which generally come to naught. Israel shot down a Soviet-made pilotless Syrian drone, an intelligence-gathering aircraft, near the Israeli border in June 1985. Four months later, the Syrians shot a shoulder missile at an Israeli plane over the Golan Heights. In November 1985, Israel shot down two Soviet-made Syrian MIG-23s in a dogfight. Syria moved the SA-6s and SA-8s along its border with Lebanon where it could monitor Israeli reconnaissance flights over Lebanon, but pulled them back in early January 1986.

Given the small size of the two nations and supersonic speed, a Syrian jet can wander over the Galilee in a matter of seconds. The specter of a relatively minor, even accidental incident, or the hasty decision of a low-ranking officer, quickly escalating into a major conflict that would ultimately draw in the United States and the Soviet Union makes the Battle of Armageddon seem like plausible prophecy.

Just as Greater Israel refers to all the land promised to Abraham, so "Greater Syria" historically has referred to Syria proper, Lebanon, Jordan, and Palestine. Interestingly, the Gospel writer Matthew may have reflected this when he said Jesus' fame "spread throughout all Syria" (Matt. 4:24). Indeed, there is some twentieth-century validity to this claim as we shall see in chapter 4. The belief in this destiny is the reason for Syrian troops moving into Lebanon in 1976 and again in 1987 to try to calm that war-ravaged land.

One particularly bitter issue for the Syrians is the Golan, which Israel captured in the 1967 War and annexed in 1981, an action it has not taken in regard to the West Bank or Gaza. About thirteen thousand pro-Syrian Druze live alongside five thousand Israeli Jews there. The Druze are a mysterious offshoot of Moslems.

During Israel's occupation of southern Lebanon, it was possible to stand in an Israeli outpost in the Bakaa and look at a Syrian outpost a few meters away—almost eyeball to eyeball.

There are some signs that Syria is softening its attitude a bit, perhaps fed by a desire "to play in the big leagues" consistent with a perceived role as "Greater Syria." Assad negotiated with the

Reverend Jesse Jackson in January 1984 for the return of Robert Goodman, a U.S. flyer who had been downed in Lebanon. Syria also played a role in July 1985 in obtaining freedom for the American hostages on board the hijacked TWA jetliner.

Jordan: The Friendly Enemy

One of the least-kept secrets in the Middle East is that Jordan's King Hussein, who has borne the burden of leadership longer than any other person in the world, has had many hours of clandestine meetings with Israeli leaders. According to one story, after one such meeting in Tel Aviv, Hussein asked if he might drive up and down Dizengoff Street to watch the night life. Obviously, for either side to acknowledge these meetings would destroy their effectiveness and the possibility of any future meetings.

Jordan and Israel share a common frontier between the Sea of Galilee and the Gulf of Aqaba. Jordan is a poor land. It has one port, at Aqaba on the Red Sea, and its main assets are the beautiful rose-red Petra and the Roman ruins at Jerash.

Despite their formal state of war, a de facto peace has prevailed between Jordan and Israel even longer than the formal peace treaty between Egypt and Israel. There have been almost no incidents across the Jordan River in several years. Traffic flows back and forth daily on the one-lane, sixty-foot Allenby Bridge spanning the Jordan, and Israeli and Jordanian officers on patrol there chat amiably. Significantly, Hussein and Israel share a common opponent: the Palestine Liberation Organization.

As the West carved up the Middle East after World War I, the British created the Emirate of Transjordan in 1921. The British literally created a royal dynasty. Abdullah, who was the son of Hussein, one of the founding fathers of Arab nationalism, was made king in 1946. After Israel's War of Independence, Abdullah annexed the West Bank, a part of Palestine that the Arabs had been able to retain, although the Crown insisted the West Bank had entered into a union with Jordan as a result of a declaration by a majority of Palestinians on the West Bank. In 1950, the union was ratified by an elected parliament with equal representation from both the east and west banks.

A year later, Abdullah was assassinated by a Palestinian on the Temple Mount near the Dome of the Rock. His young grandson, Hussein, was at his side. The boy took the crown at seventeen because his father was not mentally competent. Young Hussein outlived a reputation as a playboy and lover of fast cars and water skis to become widely known and loved as a moderate Arab leader. His fourth wife, Queen Noor, was a beautiful American-born woman, Lisa Halaby. His sons even as teenagers exhibited style and savoir-faire, reflecting generations of good breeding.

Though Jordan is 50 to 60 percent Palestinian, Hussein is not a Palestinian. His grandfather came from the Hejaz, or western part of the Saudi peninsula. Thus, a majority of Jordan's three million people are of a different ethnic background than their monarch.

Some people speculate that actually, Hussein is quite content with the status quo, for if Jordan were to regain the West Bank and its 813,000 Palestinians, they might pose a serious threat to Hussein's crown. A 1986 study showed that 71 percent of all Palestinians on the West Bank favor Arafat as their leader, that 50 percent want a separate Palestinian state, and that only 6 percent want the West Bank to be linked with Jordan.[11]

Hussein has always had an uneasy if not difficult relationship with the Palestinians, especially the PLO and PLO chairman Yasser Arafat. In fact, Hussein's autobiography, published when he was 27, is entitled *Uneasy Lies the Head* (Random House, 1962). It has been said that Hussein keeps on his nightstand a copy of Meron Benvenisti's study on the demographic balances on the West Bank.

The union of Hussein and the PLO held until the 1967 War when in six days Israel captured the West Bank and reunified Jerusalem. The PLO began using Jordan as a base for raids against Israel and climaxed its guerrilla actions by hijacking four airliners and landing them in a Jordanian desert. In what came to be known as "Black September" 1970, Hussein expelled the PLO and Arafat and his guerrillas moved into southern Lebanon.

Fourteen years later, Hussein invited the Palestine National Council, the PLO legislative body, to Amman and several PLO agencies set up headquarters there. Hussein and Arafat began a

---

11. As reported in *The New York Times*, September 9, 1986.

year-long effort to patch up their differences. Their February 11, 1985, accord called for total Israeli withdrawal from the occupied territories in return for comprehensive peace, with peace negotiations conducted in an international conference by a joint Jordanian-Palestinian delegation including the PLO. In return, the PLO would have to accept U.N. Security Council Resolution 242, which, among other things, calls for recognition of Israel. Arafat could not bring himself to do this. Finally, on February 19, 1986, Hussein told his people in a three and one-half-hour televised address that the effort had failed.

"We are unable to continue to coordinate politically with the PLO leadership until such time as their word becomes their bond," Hussein said.

The diminutive monarch of a diminutive country, Hussein always has done the right thing from the perspective of his Arab brethren. He fought alongside Syria and Egypt in the 1967 Arab-Israeli War and entered the 1973 War late and under pressure. He spurned President Jimmy Carter's bid in 1978 to join Anwar Sadat in the Camp David peace process with Israel. Yet, in many ways, Jordan and Israel have similar interests. Hussein and the Israeli leadership share a distrust of the Palestinians. It is possible that Jordan and Israel together could handle a demilitarized West Bank's external affairs while giving the Palestinians their personal rights.

One senses in Hussein's manner and words a gentleness and a deep desire to be a reconciler. He tried to pursue a relationship with the elusive Arafat. He seeks to demonstrate a love of America. He exchanged visits with Syria's Assad in December 1985 and May 1986 in an effort to heal a breach that almost had led their countries into war. He persists in his contacts incognito with Israel. Meanwhile, herds of sheep wander around the half-finished palace that Hussein was building on a high Judean hill just north of Jerusalem.

Lebanon: Israel's Vietnam

As the Middle Eastern states began to emerge in the mid-twentieth century, Lebanon looked the most prosperous and the happiest. Our first acquaintance with Lebanon comes from the Bible—the majestic cedars that grow in the snowy mountains of Lebanon, and two Mediterranean ports that remain in the news to this day, Tyre and Sidon—these the Bible tells us about. Mark 7 suggests that Jesus went there. Earlier in this century, Beirut was the Paris of the Middle East. Now the horror of its wars tears at the memory of past glory and the insouciance.

Lebanon was a small area north of Palestine that came under the French mandate after World War I. It was enlarged eastward at Syria's expense to chip away at Damascus's power and the grand design of a "Greater Syria."

A colleague once described Lebanon in a simple way that also captured its complexity. "Most countries are a people before they become a nation," he said. "Lebanon was a nation before it became a people." That, in a word, captures the essence of Lebanon. Still lacking a strong central government, Lebanon can be compared to fourteenth-century Italy—feudalistic, one people warring against the others. A State Department official says the Lebanese are, in this order, devoted to (1) themselves, (2) their families, (3) their religion and the area where they live—and lastly (4) to Lebanon.

A nation of 3.2 million, Lebanon is comprised of various factions, clans, and militias; at one time it had the largest percentage of Christians of any country in the Middle East. Many of them were Maronites or Melkites, an eastern group that in 1724 identified with Rome and started looking to the pope as their earthly father. The electoral system, established in 1943 and based on the 1932 census, provides that the president always will be a Maronite Christian and the prime minister always will be a Sunni Moslem. By a fixed pattern, the speaker of the House always is a Shiite Moslem.

The proportion of Christians has declined more and more, and eventually Christians held more power than their numbers warranted. All of this gave an artificial dimension to Lebanon.

President Eisenhower sent in the marines in 1958 to calm a civil war. In the absence of a strong central government, the PLO took refuge in southern Lebanon in 1969, set up a government of sorts, and took over the infrastructure. The PLO was very unpopular with the Shiite Moslems and the other southern Lebanese. The civil war that broke out in 1975 has never really ended. The specter of one Lebanese militia fighting another Lebanese militia, and of Lebanese against Palestinians, has proved infinitely worse in reality than anything Israel has done or threatened to do to Lebanon. In the first stages of the civil war, casualties were estimated at more than sixty thousand killed and one million displaced.[12]

In *Richochets*, a movie produced by the Israeli army about its war in Lebanon, one Israeli characterized Lebanon:

> Now it's all perfectly clear. Christians hate the Druze and Shiites, and the Sunnis and the Palestinians. The Druze hate the Christians and the Shiites and Syrians. The Shiites have been [abused] for years so they hate everybody. The Sunnis hate who they're told to. And the Palestinians hate each other, while hating everybody else. But they all have one thing in common: All of them, every one of them, hate the hell out of us Israelis. They'd love to smash our faces if they could. But they can't, because of our army.

All of the wars going on simultaneously—the civil war, the second PLO withdrawal (this time from the port of Tripoli in the north in 1983), the Israeli occupation in the south—all of them ravaged Lebanon.

I made ten or twelve trips into Lebanon during my assignment in the Middle East. One month before my first assignment in Lebanon, in October 1983, 250 American marines had been killed when their barracks at the Beirut International Airport was blown up. I scarcely recognized Beirut as the same city I had known in 1964. The beautiful street leading from the airport was piled with huge mounds of dirt to discourage speeding, bomb-laden vehicles. The twenty-five-story Holiday Inn, the Hilton, and the St. Georges—one of the grandest hotels in the world—stood void along the Mediterranean, their walls scarred by countless shellings; windows were shot out, frames blackened, and the rooms looted. There seemed to be two signs of war everywhere—countless heaps of uncollected garbage and debris, and mounds of raw dirt piled into embankments by bulldozers. Yet, the display windows on Rue Hamra remained filled with high-fashion goods. The Lebanese

---

12. Jimmy Carter, *The Blood of Abraham: Insights into the Middle East* (Boston: Houghton-Mifflin, 1985), 94.

secretaries were dressed in hose and heels every day and businessmen wore suits and ties, quite unlike their counterparts in "Dixie,"
a Lebanese nickname for Israel. It seemed like a non sequitur, a
bizarre contradiction.

To drive through the southern Lebanese countryside is painful.
It is so beautiful—the ageless vineyards and rolling hills are won-
derful. Yet, one can only inch along on most roads, which are
chock full of potholes, a sign that repairs have not been made for
years. On the roads and in the villages, one often sees blackened
patches, the lasting mark of an exploded bomb, or perhaps the
"blister" where tires were stacked and burned in protest.

The Lebanese economy of small, individual entrepreneurs
seems better suited to handling war than corporation-based
economies. During air raids or when a bomb goes off, they
merely close shop, pull down the corrugated metal curtain covering the storefront, go home, and reopen the next day. I and a
colleague, G. Jefferson Price III of the *Baltimore Sun*, witnessed
this persevering attitude firsthand. In the remote Druze village of
Kawkaba near Rashayya, one day in April 1985, as Israeli armored
personnel carriers, tanks, and trucks rumbled by in retreat, we
found a tiny grocery with French cheeses and delicacies. The
store was better stocked, and its food cheaper, than the small
groceries in our Jerusalem neighborhood.

A dominant feature of southern Lebanon is six thousand-foot
Jabal Barouk, the highest peak in the area. A big bunker and a forest
of communications aerials and saucers decorated its flat top during
the Israeli occupation. From the top, one can see Beirut twenty
miles to the northwest with the naked eye, and radar easily picks up
Damascus thirty miles to the northeast. It was costly for Israel—
and probably for the United States—to give up Jabal Barouk. From
there, Israeli soldiers boasted their sophisticated electronic surveillance gear was capable of detecting the movements of every Syrian
soldier "day and night," and the takeoff of any airplane in northern
Iraq. The young commander refused to admit it, but in all likeli-
hood Israel gave the United States the data it gathered from moni-
toring the Soviet Union. When the Israelis left Jabal Barouk, they
blew up the bunker—where I had eaten lunch with the Israelis

only a few weeks earlier—and reassembled their gear on the slopes of Mount Hermon inside Israel, 2,400 feet lower.

In one of the situations that makes sense only in the Middle East, while Israeli military convoys headed home from southern Lebanon, an almost equal number of Lebanese vehicles headed north, laden with Israeli goods. Ironically, businessmen in Lebanon and Israel kept up a booming trade across the border—between $5 and $6 million a month—during the occupation. Lebanese Christians ignored orders from their government and the PLO and bought agricultural equipment, medicine, canned food, electronic devices, and roses. The Lebanese, however, were much less successful in selling their goods in Israel.

Anti-Semitism

Fifty years after the Nazi Holocaust took the lives of a third of all the Jews in the world, there is a strong sense that anti-Semitism is rising once again. I offer little data, rather an intuition.

In 1986 former U.N. Secretary-General Kurt Waldheim was elected president of Austria despite allegations that as a young army intelligence officer during World War II he was in an outfit that ordered the deportation of Greek Jews. The United States found the evidence adequate enough to bar him from American shores.

The leader of the West Berlin Jewish community said in 1986 that anti-Semitism in West Germany was stronger then than at any time since Nazi Germany.

It recurs repeatedly in the United Nations, the same body that approved partition of Palestine and the creation of a Jewish state in 1947. Nowadays, however, the Arab states, Third World countries, and the Soviet bloc consistently vote against Israel. Many of the resolutions, it must be acknowledged, contain appropriate criticism of Israel; the problem is that the U.N. demands behavior of Israel it does not require of almost any other nation.

In 1986, the United States vetoed a Security Council resolution saying that Israel had desecrated the Temple Mount by allowing the visit there of several Knesset members. The resolution would have passed 13-2 otherwise. In 1985, the General Assembly approved (86–23) a resolution accusing the Jewish state of war crimes and urging other nations to isolate Israel in diplomatic, trade, and cultural relations because it is "not a peaceful state." Earlier in the year, the Assembly voted 88–13 to urge other nations to stop giving nuclear assistance to Israel because it had bombed the Iraqi nuclear reactor four years earlier. By overwhelming majorities it has passed resolutions condemning Israel for annexing Jerusalem and the Golan Heights and for the "pillaging of archaeological and cultural property."

The Security Council, however, voted to condemn the 1985 Christmastime terrorist attacks on El Al in the Rome and Vienna airports.

The Security Council, with the United States abstaining, voted 14–0 to condemn Israel for its 1985 bombing of the PLO headquarters in Tunis. In 1984, the United States vetoed a Security Council resolution that would have passed 14–1, calling on Israel to "strictly respect the rights of the civilian population" in its occupation of southern Lebanon.

The most offensive step, to Israel, was the passage of the U.N. resolution equating Zionism and racism in 1975. On the tenth anniversary of that resolution, President Herzog said: "Racism is the absolute opposite of everything that the people of Israel stand for—the Jewish tradition, the Torah, Jewish history, from all of which Zionism derives."

3

The Problem Within

If you walk in my statutes and observe my commandments and do them, then I will give you your rains in their season, and the land shall yield its increase, and the trees of the field shall yield their fruit.
—Leviticus 26:3, 4

Cursed be he who perverts the justice due to the sojourner, the fatherless, and the widow.
—Deuteronomy 27:19

No matter how serious Israel's security situation is, as President Chaim Herzog has frequently said, it is not Israel's No. 1 problem. "The danger in our society is internal, not external, and only we can uproot it."

These words are worth noting because they were spoken not by one who loathes Israel but by one who loves Zion, not by a "dove" but by a former military intelligence officer and chronicler of Israel's wars. They were spoken not by a skeptic but by a man steeped in the Torah, the son of a former chief rabbi of Ireland.

On the thirty-seventh anniversary of the independence of modern Israel, Herzog elaborated: "It is our internal problems that give me particular cause for concern. Extremism still flourishes and to our sorrow, marginal elements in our society—particularly young people—have become captives of strange, violent doctrines held by fanatical groups, alien to the true spirit of Israel. On the margins of our society we hear advocacy of racist concepts and of actions that contradict the Torah and tradition of Israel and the values of our society."

The Torah declares frequently that the Israelites were to show

77

justice and mercy toward "the widow, the orphan and the alien" in their midst, sometimes phrased "the widow, the fatherless and the sojourner" (Exod. 22:21, 22; Deut. 10:18; 14:29; 16:11; 24:19, 20; 27:19). It is clear who the "alien" is today: the Palestinian. The tradition of Israel was certainly one of being an ethical beacon to the world. Yet, it is sadly all too apparent that there has been a flouting of that biblical mandate and tradition, a dangerous skid morally. It is all the more sad because Israelis are a people who know pain and their country was reborn almost literally in the ashes of the Holocaust, one of the most grievous events in history. There is a remarkable parallel psychologically: The victim of child abuse often becomes a child abuser; the child of an alcoholic often becomes an alcoholic. But these psychological truths do not justify child abuse or alcoholism any more than the Holocaust justifies Israeli behavior against the Palestinian.

U.S. President Jimmy Carter said repeatedly the No. 1 responsibility of a nation's leader is to protect the national security. But is it? What good are secure borders if the society contained therein is oppressive and harsh? Is not the No. 1 responsibility of a nation to obtain justice and mercy for its people?

As Herzog told the 11th Knesset in his inaugural address:

> Has not the ancient Torah of Israel decreed, "Judges and officers shalt thou make thee in all thy gates," following which it says, "Justice, justice shalt thou pursue, that thou mayest live and inherit the land" (Deut. 16:18, 20). But two days ago we read in the weekly [Torah] portion: "Behold, I have taught you statutes and ordinances . . . observe therefore and do them; for this is your wisdom and your understanding in the sight of the peoples, that, when they hear all these statutes, shall say, "Surely this great nation is a wise and understanding people" (Deut. 4:6).[1]

Israel's "problem within" manifests itself in a variety of ways, some overt and aggressive, others subtle and elusive. One problem, that of the Occupied West Bank, is so comprehensive that we will treat it separately in the next chapter.

---

1. In a speech to the Knesset, August 13, 1984.

Retaliation

The constant fear of war and terrorism has been devastating to the Israeli psyche. It has led to retaliation often worse than the acts of terrorism itself.

On a Sunday afternoon in October 1984, I stood on our balcony and noticed a disturbance on the main Jerusalem-Hebron road that passed a block from our apartment. An old and dusty Arab bus, easily identifiable because of its green-gray markings (contrasted to the spanking new red-and-white Egged buses), had stalled on the incline of a small hill and a crowd was gathering. Sensing something, I sprinted to the scene. A Palestinian young man lay in a pool of blood in the middle of the street, his whitened skin indicating profound shock. He was obviously near death. The bus had a gaping hole just above the middle door. I quickly concluded a bomb had gone off inside it, but an Israeli reporter friend whispered to me that it appeared someone had fired an RPG (a rocket-propelled grenade) into the bus from the outside. Nine others were wounded, but I marvelled that fifty or sixty Arabs were not killed. Israeli police combed the scene.

Later, the sad facts came to light. A week earlier two Israeli college students, a young man and a young woman, had been strolling in the woods near the Cremisan Monastery west of Bethlehem. It was Arab land in the Occupied West Bank. Someone, probably an Arab, accosted them and killed them. A nineteen-year-old Israeli soldier heard about the killings and vowed to get revenge. He stole an RPG from an Israeli army arsenal and on that Sunday afternoon climbed the hillside along the street, hid behind bushes, and waited for the Arab bus to come. Then he fired the rocket at close range. The victim was an honor graduate student in engineering. *The Jerusalem Post* reported that the young soldier told the judge: "Innocent Jews are being killed indiscriminately, and I can't stand it any longer."

This Israeli pattern of reacting with vengeance is all too common. There probably have been *more* Arab victims of Jewish terrorism than Jewish victims of Arab terrorism. This is due to a harsh interpretation of the principle of retribution. When Jesus referred to the Old Testament notion of "an eye for an eye, and a tooth for a

79

tooth" (Exod. 21:24 and Matt. 5:38–42), he probably meant that if someone pokes your eye, you may not take *more* than an eye in return. In other words, a *limit* is set on punishment, not a starting point. But some Israelis have interpreted this biblical ordinance to mean that if an Arab takes one Jewish life, they may take *many* Arab lives. This excessive retaliation marks the Israelis' chief mode of response to their Arab problems.

On Yom Kippur 1985, the Jews' solemn Day of Atonement, three Jews were taken hostage for hours on their yacht moored off Cyprus and finally shot to death. A select group of the PLO called Force 17 quickly claimed responsibility. One week later, Israeli warplanes flew thirteen hundred miles across the eastern half of the Mediterranean and bombed PLO headquarters in Tunis— killing seventy-three. Thus, it was not three lives for three lives, but *seventy-three* lives for three. Defense Minister Yitzhak Rabin told reporters, "The long arm of the I.D.F. can reach wherever terrorist forces are deployed."

Ten days after a suicide bomber crashed into the marine barracks at the Beirut Airport and killed more than 250 Americans in 1983, another suicide bomber broke through the lines and hit Israeli military headquarters in Tyre, southern Lebanon, killing sixty-one. Israel immediately reinstituted its air raids, and in the two years that followed, its warplanes bombed targets in southern Lebanon thirty times. Almost always the Israeli air raids were bloodier than the Arab terrorist attacks that provoked the raids. The raids continue. Israelis contend that they employ precision bombing designed to hit only the camps of the Palestinian armed struggle; but they charge the Palestinians target cities and civilians at random. They also contend that it is not only how many are killed, but who, and what reasoning is behind it. Officially, the Israeli army says merely that it will attack terrorists wherever and whenever it wishes with means of its own choosing.

That was illustrated with particular vengeance in the Palestinian hijacking of an Israeli bus on the coastal highway near the ancient Philistine cities of Ashdod and Ashkelon in April 1984. Four Palestinians commandeered a bus carrying thirty-four passengers around dusk, and speeded down the road until it was forced onto a side road and stopped at Deir el Balah in the Occupied Gaza Strip.

Israeli troops stormed the bus just before dawn while still under the cover of darkness. The official I.D.F. announcement said one Israeli passenger and two of the hijackers were killed during the rescue operation and that the other two hijackers died en route to the hospital. At 8 A.M., the army bulldozed the homes of the four guerrillas. The pro-Marxist Popular Front for the Liberation of Palestine, a PLO group, claimed responsibility for the hijacking, saying "armed struggle will escalate to achieve the right of self-determination for the Palestinian people."

There the matter lay for a few days. Then *Hadashot*, a new and aggressive Israeli tabloid newspaper, said it had a picture showing Israeli soldiers leading away one of the guerrillas unmarked and apparently unhurt. The implication clearly was that the two guerrillas had been led away and beaten to death. When *Hadashot* disclosed that Defense Minister Moshe Arens had ordered an inquiry, the military censor closed down the newspaper, saying the paper had not complied with the law that all news reports dealing with security matters must be reviewed before publication.

Sixteen months later, Brig. Gen. Yitzhak Mordechai, the army's chief paratrooper, was acquitted of charges of violent behavior while interrogating the two guerrillas. An army disciplinary court said the injury caused to the two guerrillas was "not unreasonable." The story did not end yet. More than two years after the hijacking, Shimon Peres, the new prime minister, and Yitzhak Shamir, prime minister at the time, claimed national security as their reasons for opposing an investigation into the killings. Shamir refused to reveal whether he knew about the bludgeoning or approved it saying only "I knew what a prime minister had to know, and I acted accordingly."

The question I asked the Israeli Foreign Ministry was whether the Israeli air raids were themselves terrorist acts. "You ask that question every month," the spokesman replied. "We'll set up an appointment," he said, thus dismissing my query but not dealing with it.

I once asked the Foreign Ministry to demonstrate logically and specifically that Israel's retaliations had halted terrorist attacks. The spokesman pointed out there had been no successful attacks on El Al recently. But Israeli journalist Mark Lavie returned, "You are mixing apples and oranges, . . . it was security measures not retaliation that stopped attacks on El Al."

Collective Punishment and No Due Process

The same spirit of retribution spills over into the infliction of punishment in ways that violate every sense of justice and due process.

During an eighteen-month period in 1984–85, in a fresh outbreak of attacks, seventeen Israeli Jews were killed. Their deaths provoked the Cabinet into reviving British Mandate practices of "administrative detention" (a euphemism for jailing without formal charges or trial) and deportation on security grounds. Within a month Israel had jailed fifty-five Palestinians without charges. At the time, Police Minister Chaim Bar-lev estimated there were 7,700 Palestinians in Israel's prisons—3,359 for security reasons and 4,391 for criminal reasons. *Davar*, the Histadrut labor federation newspaper, warned that this rash reaction would feed "Israeli Nazism."

The Israelis frequently have resorted to collective punishment in dealing with the Arabs, that is, punishing all for the sins of a few. In the 1983 bombing of an Israeli bus in western Jerusalem, two Arabs were given life sentences but a third suspect was not found. Almost four years later, Israeli soldiers went to his family's home in Ramallah and blew up the top part of the house where his bedroom was located—even though his family protested that the young man had not been there for more than two years; he never has been formally charged.

"If the terrorism is not organized, the punishment of the families of the terrorist is very effective," said Bar-lev, the chief of staff in the War of Attrition. "When families learn it will cost them their house or they will be expelled, they tend to take their youngsters into their own hands." But the theory is applied only to the Palestinians. The house of an Israeli suspect is never destroyed, no matter how grievous the crime. The destruction of citrus groves and houses along the highway is often cited as another example of collective punishment; they were destroyed not because of any acts by the owner but merely because they might be used by commandoes or guerrillas. Collective punishment is not administered infrequently. It is imposed all the time. But there are perhaps even more ominous signs of the "problem within."

Hardening Attitudes and Meir Kahane

American-born Rabbi Meir Kahane carried his reputation for violence and hate from the Jewish Defense League in New York in the 1960s to Israel's Arab communities in the eighties. He advocates expelling all Arabs from Israel and the West Bank. His cry is, "Compensation for their property—and then out."

Kahane is a small man who characteristically wears a gray suit with a white shirt open at the neck. A cadre of young men wearing yellow T-shirts adorned with the sign of a fist surround him. He speaks Hebrew and English equally impeccably, and his speeches are laced with Scripture. "We have the same skin and blood . . . and the same intelligence," he says. "The difference is that 'we are the chosen people. . . .' the Bible said it," he affirms, waving a copy of the Scriptures.

For a long time, most observers overlooked him. But in the 1984 national elections, he got 22,500 votes, enough to gain him a seat in the Knesset. A few days later, he gave a speech in Beit Agron, Israel's equivalent of a national press building. There was standing room only. He boasted that in the next election he would win 100,000 votes, or five seats, from people who now felt free to support him.

After the election he became more strident. The next day he went on a victory march through the Old City kicking at Arab shops. He urged the handful of Jewish women married to Arabs to leave their spouses. He tried to march into Umm el-Fahm, the largest Arab city in Israel, but Israeli police turned him back. He used Knesset stationery to write hundreds of Arabs and urge them to leave Israel. A pistol at his side, he marched into Dheisheh Refugee Camp on the West Bank and prayed near a mosque, as he put it, "to let the inhabitants know there will be no more stone-throwing against Jews."

There is a bit of the Old George Wallace in him, often condemning the press but letting them know with a sly glance that he doesn't mean what he is saying. UPI was notified it would not be welcome at any more of Kahane's events because he had been insulted by a young member of my staff. When I personally apologized for whatever slight he felt, Kahane warmly let me know there was no problem.

The Israeli press quietly imposed a de facto embargo on Kahane's frequent news conferences. Then Kach (the name of his party, a Hebrew word meaning "thus") representatives started calling to ask for a commitment that someone would cover what he had to say. Kahane, in a curious mixing of loyalties, fought State Department efforts to strip him of his U.S. citizenship after he had been elected to a foreign parliament.

In a written statement, Kach asked: "Is Rabbi Kahane merely a 'fringe element' in Israeli politics, as some have thought to portray him—or is Kahane in fact on the verge of becoming a major force in Israel? Why are so many Israelis turning to the Right?"

The attitude of hate is hardly restricted to Rabbi Kahane. Officials of the Israeli government *always* refer to the "terrorist PLO"—so much so that it is spoken as one word. At one Foreign Ministry briefing calling for a relaxation of tensions in then Israeli-occupied southern Lebanon, I asked the spokesman whether Israel's constant use of "terrorist" served only to heighten emotions. He brushed aside the question.

On the initiative of Knesset member Abdel Wahab Darousha, the Knesset's education committee held a discussion in January 1986 on how the Israeli media portray the Arab. Darousha said the Israeli press emphasizes the negative—when an Arab suspect is arrested for murder or rape, his Arab background is emphasized, he said, but when a Jewish suspect is arrested, his Jewishness is not stressed. The Israeli press, he accused, disregards the positive—the contribution of Israeli Arabs to the country is ignored. And, he added, the Israeli press indulges in generalization, characterizing Arabs as murderers and rapists. The Israeli press, in fairness, often is very aggressive in criticizing or ferreting out wrongful behavior on the part of the government.

Is it any wonder that children in every part of Israel are infected with fear of Arabs, feelings that graduate into hatred when they become young adults? What does this indicate for the next generation? The next forty years?

Haifa University's Center for Children's Literature found, in a three-month study of 260 children in Haifa's Carmel section, a deep fear of Arabs. One sixth-grader wrote, "I'm scared to death of Arabs, because of what my mother told my father—that even if an Arab is your friend, if you turn around to leave, he'll shoot you in the back."[2] The survey, however, followed the kidnapping, torture, and slaying of an Israeli boy, Danny Katz, by three Arab youths. In Eilat, ninth-grade students called for killing and torturing terrorists in prisons, including castrating them and cutting off their fingers.[3]

A study by Daniel Bar-tal of Tel Aviv University's School of Education shows that 50 percent of the literature dealing with Arabs in grades 1–8 in Israeli schools puts them in a bad light. The Van Leer Research Institute in Jerusalem found that 25 percent of Israeli Jewish teenagers are "consistently antidemocratic" and "racist" in their views toward Arabs. It said 40 percent of Israeli teens favored granting civil rights to Arabs as a reward for complying with Israeli law and restricting the rights of those who do not. It further said 50 percent hold antidemocratic views when talking specifically about their relations with Arabs.

I have witnessed a most subtle Israeli manipulation of the Arab culture in something that appears to be relatively minor. Two decades earlier I had participated in the late Joseph Free's ninth and final archaeological excavation at Dothan on the West Bank. We also visited many places in Israel, including Hebron. When I returned to Israel on assignment, I heard Israelis speaking about do-THAN and he-BRON, accenting the last syllable in modern Hebrew fashion. But I was sure that the pronunciation was

---

2. As reported in *Ha'aretz*, January 30, 1985.
3. As reported in *Ha'aretz*, May 23, 1985.

DO-than and HE-bron when I was there in 1964. Eventually I made return visits to both places, which are Arab communities, and found that, sure enough, the local people still say DO-than and HE-bron. The Israelis have tried to tell the Arabs how to pronounce their own names.

Incidentally, if modern Hebrew uses the same pronunciation that the ancient Israelites did, then 99 percent of Western Christians fail to pronounce the proper names of the Bible correctly, not accenting the last syllable.

Isolation

One evening, my wife and I were invited to dinner at the home of a foreign diplomat. An Israeli couple and an Arab couple also were guests. The Israeli man and the Arab man both belonged to the same profession and had had some contact with each other. As the evening wore on, and the conversation moved to the Jewish-Arab conflict, the Israeli man demurred while our host kept urging him to express his opinion. Our host persisted, and finally the Israeli began to speak forthrightly. The evening ended with even a small measure of rapport. The Israeli, although he was a sabra, said that he had never had such a candid conversation with an Arab. But the next day, the man's wife called my wife and expressed her unhappiness at the evening's course of events. She felt the host had pressed her husband too much to get him to talk about the conflict.

Social psychologist John E. Hofman of Haifa University has studied the relationship between Jews and Arabs. Hofman says: "It must be clear to anyone with some insight into the Israeli scene that contact between Jews and Arabs, when it occurs at all, is confined to highly formal and constrained conditions—at work, in the market place, in government offices, in gaols, and so forth. Even then, the meeting is seldom between status equals, but rather between Jewish foreman and Arab worker, Jewish housewife and Arab peddler, Jewish official and Arab petitioner, Jewish guard and Arab prisoner. . . . One rarely finds Jews and Arabs fraternizing in restaurants, inviting one another over for coffee, or joining together for any number of

The author interviews Labor Party leader Shimon Peres before the 1984 national elections. Peres went on to become prime minister. A photo of David Ben-Gurion, the first prime minister of Israel, hangs above Peres. *Photo by Jim Hollander.*

The author interviews Israel Prime Minister Yitzhak Shamir in May 1984 (above) and U. N. Secretary-General Javier Perez de Cuellar (below) in Qana, southern Lebanon, during the Israeli occupation.

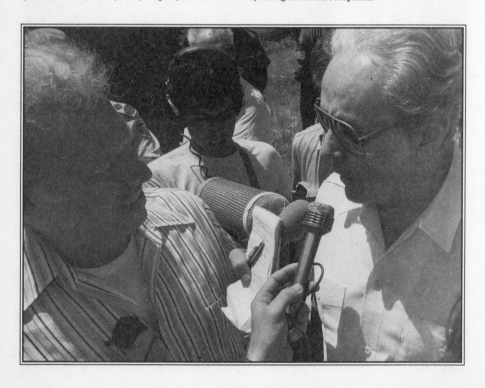

REUTERS BETTMANN

An Israeli soldier holds his M-16 rifle in grief at the grave of one of twelve comrades killed by a suicide car bomber in a Shiite village in southern Lebanon, March 1985. The next day, Israel raided another Shiite village and killed twenty-four Lebanese guerrillas. *Photo by Jim Hollander.*

REUTERS BETTMANN

Two Jews plant grass while, in the background, are several unfinished apartment buildings in the West Bank Orthodox Jewish settlement of Emmanuel. *Photo by Havakuk Levison.*

REUTERS BETTMANN

Palestinians stand alongside their demolished house in the West Bank village of Tzafa, ten miles north of Jerusalem. The Israeli army arrested thirty members of the radical Popular Front for the Liberation of Palestine and then destroyed the homes of five squad members. The army said the squad was responsible for shooting an Israeli soldier, killing a suspected Arab collaborator, and planting a grenade on a truck. *Photo by Jim Hollander.*

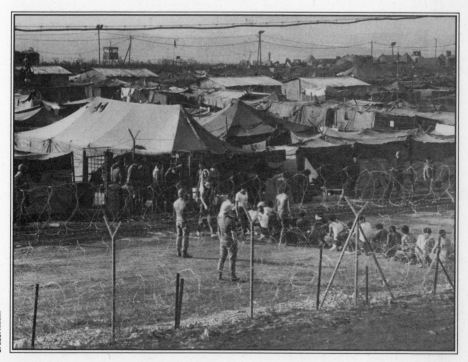

UPI/BETTMANN

Israeli Defense Forces stand guard over Lebanese prisoners at Ansar Detention Camp in southern Lebanon, when many prisoners were moved into the open as new quarters were prepared. This photo was taken in August 1983, over a year after the camp was opened.

The author outside PLO Chairman Yasser Arafat's headquarters in Tripoli, Lebanon, in late 1983, a few days before Arafat's expulsion from Lebanon. *Photo by Jim Hollander.*

REUTERS BETTMANN

An armed Israeli border guard checks the identity card of an Arab man as an Israeli paratrooper stands at the ready during a security sweep through the Arab market section of the Old City in East Jerusalem. *Photo by Havakuk Levison.*

REUTERS BETTMANN

Two ultra-Orthodox Jews walk in the Mea Shearim neighborhood of Jerusalem as a tour group gathers underneath hanging laundry to discuss the unique area. *Photo by Jim Hollander.*

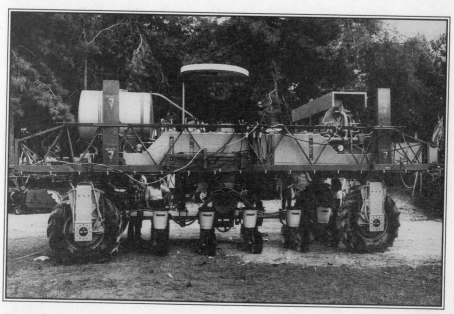

A square four-wheel "Merhav" tractor developed by Israel in the old Philistine city of Ashkelon, in a factory that once made tanks. But the prophecy of Micah that they would "beat their swords into plowshares" has only partly come true.

REUTERS BETTMANN

Two ultra-Orthodox Jewish boys stand in a burned-out bus shelter near the central Jerusalem bus station. Ultra-Orthodox burned the shelters and defaced advertisements that were displayed in them because they considered the ads lewd and offensive. *Photo by Jim Hollander.*

"If We Go in the Way of the Torah . . . There Will Be Plenty"

By Wesley G. Pippert
United Press International

JERUSALEM (UPI)—Israel's two chief rabbis, in a rare interview, condemned terrorism and said they do not believe the modern Jewish state has become secular and is spawning violence.

The rabbis also said in wide-ranging comments they are "totally opposed" to U.S.-born Rabbi Meir Kahane's militancy but stopped short of reprimanding him.

God is punishing Israel through its current economic crisis for having gone "just a bit wrong," the rabbis said, but they believe the nation remains committed to justice and righteousness.

"The ideals of the Bible are the ideals to this day," one said. He did not elaborate as to what had gone "a bit wrong."

Seated side by side at a cluttered desk in their office next to the Great Synagogue, the Ashkenazic chief rabbi, Avraham Shapira, 67, and Sephardic chief rabbi, Mordechai Eliyahu, 56, alternately answered prepared questions in Hebrew in a half-hour interview with United Press International.

In general, Ashkenazi Jews are from Europe and Sephardic Jews from Arab countries. Sephardim now are slightly more numerous in Israel.

The Chief Rabbinate was created in 1921 by the British mandate to deal with religious and family matters, such as divorce. Shapira and Eliyahu were elected in 1983 to ten-year terms.

The rabbis were asked how modern Israel measures up to the oft-repeated biblical mandate to care for "the widow, the orphan and the stranger" and the Psalmist's marriage of righteousness, peace, mercy and truth.

"This has been the aspiration of all the people of Israel since Creation. It exists as an aspiration today as well as no less than before," Shapira, a sixth-generation Jerusalemite, said.

"The ideal of every Jew in the country, everywhere, is justice and one may say the entire land relies on the Bible . . . lives by the Bible."

Eliyahu said the eating of kosher food even though it is more expensive, and the observance of the Jewish holidays show that Israelis as a whole are not secular.

"I do not ignore the fact that here and there there are some people who have opinions against (religion) but those are very few," he said. "Most of the nation is comprised of people who love tradition, keep it, love the Torah and try as much as they can to fulfill the laws and rules of the people of Israel."

Eliyahu said, "the hand of God" has been evident throughout modern Israel's history, including success in war, and even in punishing Israel through the current high inflation and growing unemployment.

"In the entire world the heads of economy are Jews. Here in Israel we see that they are unsuccessful," he said.

"This has a great moral for us. Part of the people of Israel do not believe in God, do not believe that in the land of Israel there is special providence—here we are in a king's palace—here we must conduct ourselves better than anywhere else in the world.

"The moment we go just a bit wrong, we immediately get our punishment. We are shown, where is your wisdom, your expertise? A bad economic situation is our punishment.

"If we go in the way of the Torah and of reverence, there will be plentitude of everything," Eliyahu said.

The rabbis said the terrorism by Jewish settlers was a reaction against Arab violence, and said they welcomed co-existence as long as Arabs obey the law.

recreational activities."[4] He says the percentage of Jews who claim they have an occasional opportunity to meet socially with Arabs has not exceeded 30 percent in a long series of surveys.

In my own experience, rarely were Israelis and Arabs invited to the same function. Churches and diplomats, who surely ought to be reconcilers, especially lacked courage. They never mixed their groups. The British, French, and Italians have separate parties for the Israelis and for the Arabs on their national days of celebration. "Oh," the wife of one consul replied with feigned horror when my wife asked why she didn't have just one party. "It just isn't done."

It was done, however, by journalists and the U.S. Consulate, who, whatever their other flaws, were courageous. When a foreign correspondent was newly arriving or departing after a tour of duty, Israeli and Arab colleagues alike were on hand for the party. The Americans decided a few years ago to break the diplomatic rigidity and have one Fourth of July party for Israelis, Palestinians, and the various clergy. The first year, only a few Arabs came, and one could see the tentativeness in their behavior. Each year a few more came; gradually, breakthroughs occurred. It was a delight to see—Israelis and Arabs engaging in friendly, if reserved conversation, and the clergy in their regalia providing the backdrop. But this mixing occurred, unfortunately, far too infrequently.

One study showed that few Arabs from east Jerusalem ever ventured into Jewish west Jerusalem, and, in fact, some Arab students did not know where the main drag, King George Street, was located. When I asked about this, Mayor Teddy Kollek replied that in New York probably few children from The Bronx ever make it into other parts of the city.

Fleeting Memories

Despite the horror of the Holocaust, many Israelis refer patronizingly to the victims of Auschwitz and the other camps as "soaps." They say bluntly that the Jews did not resist the Nazis strongly

---

4. "A Social Psychological Perspective on Relations Between Jews and Arabs," an unpublished manuscript in the library of the University of Haifa.

enough. This may represent an attempt to deal with the grotesque by a flip remark; it may also mean that the Holocaust already is receding in the Jewish people's minds.

"Terrible ignorance exists about the Holocaust," says Avraham Anavi, principal of Municipal High School D in Tel Aviv. Sensing that, *Hadashot* newspaper went to four Tel Aviv area high schools and asked the students what they knew about the Holocaust. A twelfth-grader wrote: "I don't know if the oriental Jews were also harmed in the Holocaust. We didn't study that. I never gave any thought to the meaning of the Holocaust. Conceptually, I have never considered it." One tenth-grader wrote: "'The Holocaust didn't happen during the war. It was in Germany. The Jews started to grab good jobs, and the Germans started getting envious so there was an upheaval.'"[5] The Hebrew word the student used for upheaval, *mahapakh*, is the same word used to describe Menachem Begin's victory in the 1977 national elections. In the student's mind, the Holocaust was no more than an elaborate Israeli shrug.

Israeli leaders, presumably concerned about this lack of knowledge of the Holocaust, began waging highly publicized campaigns to find Josef Mengele and to try John Demjanjuk for Nazi war crimes. Mengele's body was found in South America, and Demjanjuk was extradited from the United States to stand trial in Jerusalem. The publicity brought back memories of the Holocaust with a bitter vengeance.

Censorship and Militarism

Any nation that has been involved in as much war and spends as much on defense as Israel does suffers from the threat of a militaristic society.

As we have noted, Israel retaliates regularly with force to any provocation. It is the world's No. 15 arms importer and the No. 22 arms exporter, although it doesn't differ from its Arab neighbors in this respect. Safran, who fought in the 1948 War, recalls the wholesale curtailment of liberties imposed on the Arab minority in the first fifteen years of the state. Yet, he does not believe

---

5. As reported in *Hadashot*, April 17, 1985.

that Israel has become militaristic. The army remains largely a civilian army of reservists who go on active duty for short periods. Despite the large number of ex-generals who go into politics—10 percent of the 120 members of the Knesset are former senior military officers—civilian control of the military never has been challenged. In fact, the widespread draft has helped in Israel's melting-pot process.[6]

Likewise, Israel has a censorship but has not used it excessively. Every foreign correspondent agrees to submit stories to the military censor. Generally, the only stories that the censor actually wants to examine are those dealing with Israel's military capability, the timing of operations, and terrorist attacks against Israelis that are under way. Only one correspondent has had his or her credentials yanked. A reporter for one of the American networks did a revealing story about Israel's nuclear reactor in Dimona, and when the censor objected, he flew to Cyprus and broadcast the story. The censor killed stories we had done about the U.S.-Israeli naval maneuvers and about the timing of the dismantling of Israel's electronic surveillance gear from the top of Jabal Barouk during the withdrawal from Lebanon. The censor also embargoed the details of any stories about the Israeli bus that had been commandeered on the coastal highway in April 1984.

Generally, if we transmitted these stories without submitting them to the censor, we were given a written warning in Hebrew, but that was the end of it. Sometimes, the stories were halted as we were transmitting them—the printer just stopped printing. Most foreign correspondents assumed their telephone calls also were tapped. It would be too time-consuming—and consummately boring—for a censor to listen in on telephone calls and to read every story filed. We surmised that certain words, such as "terrorist" or "bomb" or "nuclear," triggered an electronic mechanism that alerted the censor.

Israel's newspapers are also subjected to censorship. Some of it is formal, but there also is an informal censorship the editors themselves impose, such as the decision not to cover Meir Kahane.

In October 1986, the London *Sunday Times* ran a detailed

---

6. Safran, 317–330.

story about Israel's nuclear capability in Dimona, complete with sketches. The story was based on information from Mordecai Vanunu, an Israeli Jew. The member of a family that had come to Israel from Morocco in 1963, Vanunu had worked on nuclear research in Dimona, was apparently fired because of his friendships with the Arabs, and left Israel. Soon after the story was published, Vanunu mysteriously turned up in custody in Israel and was charged with espionage and treason.

Sloth

I had assumed, in my naïveté, that since Israel was a young, lean, aggressive country, its craftsmanship would be superb and skilled. How wrong I was. Instead, I found a country in which there is inordinate laziness and sloppiness, and a flood of Byzantine-like paperwork not unlike anywhere else in the Middle East.

One of my first professional decisions in Israel was to move UPI's main bureau from Tel Aviv to Jerusalem. I made this decision for reasons directly related to the news coverage—Jerusalem was the seat of most governmental offices, including the prime minister and the Knesset, it was closer to the West Bank, and it was the location of many religious shrines. From a political standpoint, this decision should have made the Israelis happy because it fortified their contention that Jerusalem is their capital city.

UPI did not receive one word of criticism from its clients in the Arab world for this decision. But we also did not receive one bit of help from the Israeli government in making the move. The transfer took months to accomplish when weeks or even days, at the most, should have been necessary. Weeks passed before we got an extension of our lines so that we could send and receive copy in Jerusalem. And it took additional weeks for a modem to be installed so that we could transmit automatically without having to place a telephone call to our Tel Aviv bureau and make manual switches. Even from then on, our lines failed on the average of once a week, sometimes keeping us from sending or receiving copy for days at a time. To reinforce my belief in the reality of evil, the lines generally failed Friday afternoon, meaning no technician would be available to fix them until after Shabbat—

Sunday morning. Then, it would require a new call, and a wait of a few hours—or days. I once went an entire week with no telephone service, having to scamper to a neighbor's office whenever I needed to make a call.

No amount of protests or pleas to the Communications Ministry or other officials helped. It was my biggest frustration in Israel, a country supposedly skilled in hi-tech and electronics. By contrast, in war-torn Beirut, I discovered while on my brief assignment there that one could get telephone or line service the same day. In Israel, I don't think a single thing happened easily, simply, or on the day I wanted it. Always I heard: "impossible" or, "not today" or, "early next week," which often turned out to be the week after next. These were not merely my experiences. I have seen utterly calm and phlegmatic adults explode and lift their fists in rage at some of the incompetence.

While we were installing the lines in our office—at last!—technicians nailed a couple of short boards to the wall to hold the connections. At the esthetic least, the boards should have been nailed so that they were level, but they were not even approximately level. In my exasperation I nailed a third board above the two to show the technician how uneven the boards were. He simply shrugged in disinterest.

Israel observes a large number of holy days. There is quite a list:

- Rosh Hashanah—the start of the Jewish New Year
- Yom Kippur—ten days later, the solemn Day of Atonement
- Succoth—the Festival of Tabernacles at harvest time
- Hanukkah—the Festival of Lights somewhat parallel in timing to Christmas. It is an eight-day celebration of the Maccabean liberation of ancient Israel from the Syrian Greeks in about 160 B.C.
- Purim—the fun-loving holy day, commemorating deliverance of Jews in the time of Esther
- Passover—a weeklong observance when no leavened bread is eaten (and when all bakeries close)
- Shavuot—the Feast of Weeks, celebrated also by Christians (Pentecost)

In addition, there are national holidays, Holocaust Remembrance Day, and in May, Independence Day.

Israelis don't observe just the holy day itself but generally the previous day as well. We arrived in Israel in September, just before the Rosh Hashanah and Yom Kippur holidays, which that year came on Thursdays. Thursday and Wednesday were thus effectively omitted from both the weeks. Since very little business is ever done on Friday mornings because of the start of the Shabbat, those weeks were effectively over by Tuesday night in terms of getting anything done.

When I first arrived in Israel, my Israeli office manager accompanied me to Tel Aviv to apply for a "B1" visa, which would allow me to work in Israel. It was the day before a holy day. We arrived at the tax office about 10 A.M. After a due wait, an official summoned us to his desk. After speaking with us a while, he suddenly excused himself and left his desk. We assumed he had gone to check on something. Five, ten, fifteen minutes passed, and he did not return. Finally, exasperated, I asked another worker in the office where he had gone. "Oh," she said, "he went home to start his holy day."

Ohad Gozani, my astute sabra colleague, theorizes that the hard-work ethic of the Israelis was a casualty of the 1967 War. Israel captured the West Bank, Gaza, and the Golan Heights in that war, thus making available an abundance of cheap Arab labor. One seldom sees Israelis doing menial labor nowadays. Arabs are even employed as construction workers at West Bank Jewish settlements that Arabs believe are encroaching on their land! Even an official in Rabbi Kahane's Kach Party was using Arab construction workers to build his house in Kiryat Arba.

Every morning as I left our apartment, I got caught up in rush-hour traffic headed into Jerusalem. Almost all of the traffic were older cars with blue license plates indicating they were from the West Bank. These were mainly Arabs on their way to work in Jerusalem as waiters, janitors, and construction workers. At night, these same people formed the outward bound rush-hour traffic. The same was true in Tel Aviv.

Israel prohibits West Bank Arabs from staying in Israel overnight. There is almost no unemployment on the West Bank now, but this is true at some cost to Israeli industriousness. The State Employment Service found in 1984 that some unemployed Jews refused to take manual jobs and *The Jerusalem Post* quoted a labor-exchange director as saying "no amount of Zionist rhetoric" could persuade them.

If this sloth is allowed to infect the vaunted Israeli army, then dark days may lie ahead. There is evidence this is happening.

During Israel's 1982 invasion of southern Lebanon, 297 Israeli soldiers were killed up to the time of the cease-fire. An IDF general revealed later that of this toll, thirty-four were killed when an Israeli *Phantom* jet mistakenly bombed the headquarters of an Israeli armored brigade. Two or three other Israeli soldiers were killed when two columns of Israeli tanks fired at each other. In shocking terms, this meant that more than one in ten of Israel's casualties in the Lebanon invasion was at the hand of Israelis themselves. The military censor prevented publication of the disclosure.

On November 4, 1983, a suicide bomber rammed Israel's military headquarters in Tyre, southern Lebanon, killing sixty-one Israeli soldiers and Lebanese. This happened only a few days after the October 24 suicide bombing of the U.S. marine barracks in Beirut—which should have served as a stark warning to the Israelis to tighten up. Rather, an investigation revealed that slackness contributed to the loss of life in the November 4 bombing.

President Herzog spoke out in dismay. "As a result of negligence and lack of discipline some Israeli soldiers were killed in Lebanon in the past year," he told students in Upper Nazareth. He also said that as a result of negligence, fifteen-thousand persons had been killed in traffic accidents since 1948 compared to a smaller number killed in the Israeli-Arab wars.

A study by the National Insurance Institute in Israel showed that one of ten Israelis lives below the poverty line, which caused *The Jerusalem Post* to comment: "The myth that Israel is an egalitarian society has been thoroughly shattered by the study on income distribution."[7]

During our first year in Jerusalem, we moved from one apartment to another. When the movers arrived on the appointed day,

---

7. As reported in *The Jerusalem Post*, September 9, 1985.

it was raining. One man, an Israeli, appeared to be in charge; and a couple of Palestinians were working for him. One of the Palestinians, so slight he weighed probably less than one-hundred pounds, began carrying the refrigerator on his back while the husky straw boss stood idly by, almost snapping his fingers for the Palestinian to hurry. My wife was shocked, and pointed out to the Israeli how the other man was overexerting himself.

She asked who was the owner of the company. "I'm the owner," the Israeli replied, grinning. "Aw, he can do it." Had not my wife stopped him, the boss would have instructed the workers to carry our sofa uncovered through the rain.

Sloth—and insensitivity.

Blessing or Cursing

The Jerusalem Post publishes each week a commentary by Rabbi Pinchas Peli of Ben-Gurion University in Beersheba on the assigned portion of the Torah. One particular week his text was Leviticus 26, which deals with blessings and cursings. He wrote:

> Notwithstanding the long-standing special relationship between God and his chosen people, Israel does not enjoy special privileges. No protekzia. The blessing Israel is to receive is conditional. . . . [quoting Leviticus] "If you follow my decrees and are careful to obey my commandments, I will send you rain in its season" and all other blessings that follow (26:3–13). "But if you will not listen to me. . . . and if you reject my decrees. . . . then I will do this to you," and a long list of curses follows (26:14–39).

The commandments had to do not merely with wrongful worship but with the sins of injustice and the failure to obey the prophetic mandate to care for the widow, the orphan, and the stranger. These are commandments which Israel today must consider and ask itself some tough questions.

4

The West Bank
Judea and Samaria

So Joshua defeated the whole land, including the hill country. . . .
—Joshua 10:40

The West Bank is jammed between the state of Israel and the Jordan River, its ancient landmarks worn by time and conflict. It is about the size of Delaware, shaped like a giant backward B. The belt buckle of the B is East Jerusalem.

The West Bank is rich in biblical history. Bethlehem, where Jesus was born; Hebron, where the patriarchs are buried; Nablus near the site of old Shechem, the capital of the northern kingdom; Dothan, where Joseph was dropped in a pit—all of these are located in the West Bank. But in its recent history, the population of the West Bank has been almost totally Arab. And therein lie the seeds of conflict.

One catches occasional glimpses of that conflict in a drive through the terraced vineyards and jagged rocks of the West Bank: A new, fortress-like Jewish settlement overlooks an old Arab village; an Israeli military vehicle rumbles along, weapons at the ready.

A drive on Nablus Road, the main thoroughfare north from Jerusalem, starts in the suburb of Sheikh Jarrah. Off to the west is Nabi Samwel, where the prophet Samuel is buried (1 Samuel 28:3), the highest point in the area; in the east are the apartment buildings of the French Hill neighborhood. The drive continues north past Jerusalem's relatively inactive Atarot airport (where Lilli Shalit's Palestine Airways planes landed in Israel's early days) and on through the Christian Arab town of Ramallah and its smaller Moslem twin, El Bireh. They say that on a clear day you can see the

Mediterranean thirty-two miles west, but I never have. But I have seen Israel's highest building, Shalom Mayer Tower in Tel Aviv.

Farther along, there are some harrowing hairpin curves, then the lush expanse of a small plain, and on to Nablus, the biblical Shechem and now one of the two largest cities in the West Bank. This ancient city is nestled in the valley between Mount Ebal and Mount Gerizim, the mount of blessing and the mount of cursing (Deuteronomy 27). Farther north is Dothan (DO-than), where I took part in a dig in 1964; and just across the way to the west, is a new Jewish settlement called Dotan (do-TAN). This is biblical Samaria, an area that was somewhat hostile to the Jews in Jesus' day and gave rise to his parable about the Good Samaritan (Luke 10:29–37), although according to the Gospel account the act of mercy took place on the Jericho-Jerusalem road where an unused, roofless inn marks the spot.

A drive south of Jerusalem on Hebron Road, the main thoroughfare, is slightly less rugged. One swings past the new neighborhood of Gilo, and past Bethlehem, Christ's birthplace and now almost a suburb of Jerusalem. This is old Judea, and a sign over the police station just off Manger Square says "Subdistrict of Judea" (as in Matthew 2:1). The blacktop continues on past the Dheisheh refugee camp and Solomon's Pools (although actually not nearly that old), along a curving highway to Hebron, the other large city in the West Bank and the burial spot of Abraham, Isaac, and Jacob.

Before 1967, the West Bank had a population of about 750,000—except for a handful of westerners, all Arabs. There had been a community of seven hundred Jewish families in Hebron, but they fled in 1929 when Arab rioting killed sixty-three of their members. Within six days in June, the West Bank as well as the Gaza Strip, Sinai, and the Golan Heights came under Israeli control. Israel annexed the Golan in 1981 and returned the Sinai in 1982, but the West Bank and Gaza remain under military occupation to this day.

The capture of the Delaware-sized West Bank satisfied two sharply differing quests for Israel. Geographically, the West Bank fleshed out Israel, giving it a much more rectangular shape and rendering it much more defensible. Religiously, to the Jews, the

97

West Bank is part of the Promised Land and thus conquering it went a long way toward fulfilling that promise.

Menachem Begin retrieved the ancient biblical names of Judea and Samaria. But to most Israelis and the rest of the world, however, Judea and Samaria are the Israeli-occupied West Bank. The Israeli military established something rather erroneously named the "Civil Administration in Judea and Samaria" to administer the occupied territories. It may have been called civil but it was military.

Life in the Occupation

When I made my first trip to the West Bank as a working reporter, I went with Captain Ofra as my escort. She threw a submachine gun in the typically all-white Army Peugeot before we departed and I rode along with a gun under my feet. With a jolt I became aware of what it is like to live under military occupation.

Almost immediately after the 1967 War, life changed abruptly for the Arabs on the West Bank. They began living in the constant presence of Israeli soldiers. It is difficult to go far in the West Bank without encountering the Israeli army.

Almost daily, Arab boys resort to the form of protest used in an earlier day by a young Hebrew boy named David against one of their predecessors, the Philistine Goliath—stone-throwing. Their older brothers graduate to something more sophisticated. They throw a Molotov cocktail (a container of gasoline with a lighted wick) or they set a homemade bomb at a bus stop or along a roadside. Then the Israelis retaliate, as we described in chapter 3. American television cameras have recorded some instances in which Israeli soldiers pistol-whipped West Bank Arabs or slapped them around.

Perhaps more insidious, the West Bank Arab, often poorly educated, had to start coping with a maze of laws—Jordanian law, since legally the West Bank remains part of Jordan; left-over Emergency Regulations from the period of the British mandate (1921–1948); and Israeli military regulations, of which there are more than eleven hundred, often printed only in Hebrew. Many matters pertaining to the West Bank are handled with civil Israeli law in Israeli courts. But West Bankers have to obtain Jordanian passports or educational certificates from Amman. The Jewish settlers living on the West Bank, of course, are exempt from all this. They are subject only to Israeli law.

Ibrahim Mattar, an American-educated Palestinian economist, says that many of the military regulations severely restrict West Bank agriculture. The Arab farmer is accountable for the regulations even though he may not be able to read them. The rules govern the exporting of tomatoes and other vegetables that form the bulk of the West Bank produce. Or, the rules may prohibit the growing of grapes and plums without a military permit. The obvious effect of the rules is to give a huge trade advantage to Israeli farmers at the expense of West Bank Arab farmers. There is a huge trade imbalance. Only 3 percent of Israel's imports come from the West Bank and Gaza, but 90 percent of the West Bank-Gaza imports come from Israel.[1]

Palestinians on the West Bank drive cars with blue or green license plates that clearly distinguish them from the Israeli cars with their yellow plates. Israeli soldiers can easily identify the blue or green plates in order to stop the cars and check the occupants' registration papers.

It is always an effort to travel between Jordan and Israel. From Israel, one may take a roundabout flight to Cairo, overnight at the airport, and then fly on to Amman. Or, one may take the much more direct route of using one of the Jordan River bridges. But crossing that sixty-foot, one-lane Allenby bridge takes one hour, spent mostly in red tape.

For Arabs, the process is infinitely more exacting and lengthy, often to the point of ignominy and insult. Since the West Bank was part of Jordan in reality up to 1967, there is much trade between the two sides; Arab people are continually going back and forth across the Allenby and Adam bridges. Rules about permits and passports and special cards change constantly, so that it is a hassle for anyone, especially if you are an Arab. Hundreds of trucks, carrying watermelons and grapes and other vegetables and fruits, start lining up after dawn. Clusters of Arabs, some businessmen or

---

1. Benvenisti, 10–11.

mothers with small children, sit on rough benches in what looks like a massive carport, with only a corrugated tin roof protecting them from the blazing sun.

A noted Arab Christian evangelist, Anis Shorrosh, a native of Nazareth and now a U.S. citizen, said he was stopped while crossing the Allenby and searched by Israelis for more than an hour once—even though he had made the crossing twenty-four times and was acquainted with the officials. The Israelis confiscated his copies of his biography *The Liberated Palestinian* which draws its title from his conversion and not politics.

A 1981 study of 185 Israeli and 128 Palestinian eleven-year-olds on the West Bank revealed a high anxiety level, far higher than that of children sampled in the United States. Finnish psychologist Rai ja-Lena Punamaki found that when asked whether wars were always necessary, 72 percent of the Israeli children and 81 percent of the Palestinians said yes. But only 54 percent of the Americans said yes. The study also included drawings of such topics as "what happened in school today?" Jewish children's answers were ordinary, such as "nothing special" or "the teacher was angry because I didn't do my homework." But Palestinian children almost without exception injected violent events: "Soldiers burst into the classroom and sprayed us with gas" or "we threw stones at the soldiers."

In 1984, a report to U.N. Secretary-General Javier Perez de Cuellar had made much the same point, saying the Jewish settlers on the West Bank form a "privileged class" that adversely affects the Palestinians. The U.N. General Assembly's Special Committee on "Israeli Practices Affecting Human Rights" in Occupied Arab Territories said in its seventeenth annual report in 1985 that in the occupied territories, there is "a continuing deterioration in the level of respect for the human rights of the civilian population." The General Assembly condemned Israel for its "collective punishment, mass arrests, and ill-treatment and torture" of Arabs in the Occupied West Bank.

In September 1985, the Israeli press reported rumors of a series of humiliating and degrading acts to which Israeli soldiers had subjected Arabs on the West Bank. In Hebron a soldier allegedly tried to make an Arab man kiss the rear of a donkey. In Gaza, soldiers were reputed to have made Arab youths drop their pants and dance before the soldiers would return their identity cards. In Jenin, *Ha'aretz* newspaper said, there was a complaint that soldiers forced elderly persons to stand on one foot with their hands in the air. Army Chief of Staff Moshe Levy conducted an inquiry into these rumors. The army refused to say which or how many incidents actually took place—although it apparently found no evidence of the donkey incident—and reported that all of the irregularities had been dealt with.

"I Also Pay the Price of the Holocaust"—an Arab

Raja Shehadeh, a young lawyer from Ramallah, has written a searing account of what befalls the Arabs in a book entitled *The Third Way: A Journal of Life in the West Bank* (London: Quartet, 1982). "Sometimes, I think I am the victim of the victims of the Nazis. Fate has decreed that I also pay the price of the holocaust," he writes. "I have the horrible suspicion that I am more aware of the concentration camps, think about them more and dream about them more than the average Israeli of my age does."[2]

In fairness, it must be pointed out that life has improved in many ways on the West Bank under Israeli occupation. Unemployment is 3.6 percent, half that for Israel. Pinchas Wallerstein, a resident of the Jewish hilltop settlement of P'sagot, north of Jerusalem, and chairman of the Benjamin Regional Council of Settlements, has estimated that 120,000 Arabs—that's one in seven Palestinians on the West Bank—work in Israel. Benvenisti estimates that ninety-four thousand Arabs on the West Bank and Gaza work in Israel.[3]

During Jordanian rule in 1964 while I was studying at the Near East School of Archaeology on the Mount of Olives, I used to walk to the Intercontinental Hotel a few blocks away to eat what was then a delicacy, ice cream. An Arab man was a waiter in the restaurant. Twenty years later on a return visit one afternoon, I found the waiter still working there. "How are things now?" I asked. "Oh,

---

2. Shehadeh, *The Third Way*, 64.
3. Ibid., 8.

much better," he said. "I would never want to go back" to the period of Jordanian rule.

A prominent Arab lawyer once acknowledged to me that despite his protests about the administration of justice on the West Bank now, it is an improvement over what it was under Jordanian control.

Palestinians and University Education

The Palestinian universities on the West Bank serve a dual purpose. Each is at once an educational institution and a political weapon. This presents a serious dilemma for everyone concerned. For the Palestinians, since many of the municipalities have been taken over by the Israelis, the universities remain their only political arena. Because many of the political activities on campus espouse the PLO, the Israelis, who sponsored and encouraged the opening of the universities, close down the campuses with some frequency. Educators face the problem of trying to operate an academic program despite these interruptions. If a campus is closed down for a sizeable portion of the year, the educators must give up substantial parts of their vacation period in order to make up for lost time and meet academic goals, such as being able to qualify their students for graduate schools.

Several of the universities have religious sponsorship. Bethlehem University, which has about fifteen hundred students, is sponsored by the Vatican. Bir Zeit University, near Ramallah, with twenty-five hundred students, has Methodist leadership. Najah University near Nablus has a student body of thirty-three hundred. Islamic University in Hebron, of course, is Moslem, with about fifteen hundred students. The al-Azhar University at Gaza has about twenty-five hundred students.

In the long run, and most significant of all, the universities are helping make the Palestinians the best educated people in the Arab world. These students are likely to provide the leadership and the wherewithal to mount a fight for Palestinian freedom in the decades ahead. (See also p. 177.)

The number of Arab workers without any schooling decreased in the last twenty years from 30 percent to 4 percent while those with more than a high-school education rose from 2 percent to 12 percent, the study said. These changes are remarkable but a considerable gap remains between Arabs and Jews. By contrast 31 percent of the Israeli Jewish workforce have more than a high-school education.

About a quarter of the West Bank's employment as well as gross domestic product involves agriculture and more than 48 percent of the employment and gross domestic product involves services, highly menial.[4]

The Mayors

The most famous mayor in the world at Christmas time is Bethlehem's Elias Freij, an articulate, courteous, moustached man who fits the Arab tradition of mayors coming from an eminent family. Invitations to his Christmas party—even the Israeli prime minister goes—are considered a prize. I consider it a valued compliment that when Freij learned I was finishing my assignment in Israel he told me that we must have lunch together.

Freij is a Greek Orthodox Christian in a town that is about half-Christian and half-Moslem. In Bethlehem, one also sees a Freij money-changers shop, a Freij souvenir shop, and other stores with the family name. His office overlooks Manger Square. He tools around Bethlehem in his Mercedes.

One of the mayors often seen with Freij at parties is Hanna Atrash, the mayor of Beit Sahour, a couple of miles east of Bethlehem. When I got a beeper message assigning me to go to Beirut in November 1983, I was sitting in Atrash's office talking about the faithful who had said they saw a vision of the Virgin Mary in the church on the site in Beit Sahour where tradition says Joseph and Mary and the baby Jesus stopped for a drink of water enroute to Egypt. Atrash's wife had seen the vision but he hadn't.

Among the Palestinians, the Arab mayor probably has provided the chief competition to the Palestine Liberation Organization for indigenous leadership. An Arab mayor, especially in

---

4. Benvenisti, 7.

towns and villages, traditionally comes from one of the town's most eminent or wealthy families, the *hamulas*, such as the Masri family in Nablus or the Freij family in Bethlehem or the Shawwas in Gaza. Israel has erred by giving a sort of de facto recognition to Arafat by continually denouncing him. It has missed a golden opportunity by not dealing with the mayors. Moshe Maoz of Hebrew University, in his *Palestinian Leadership on the West Bank* amplifies the belief that Israel has missed opportunity after opportunity to capitalize on the grass-roots leadership of the mayors.

It was under Israeli rule that the mayors became agents of Palestinian nationalism, and, ironically, that the mayors became radicalized. The first years following the 1967 Six-Day War when Israel took control were relatively quiet. Many municipalities went ahead with finishing the municipal infrastructure and providing municipal services, such as water, sewage treatment, and libraries. There was only sporadic violence or guerrilla activities. Maoz points out that Israeli policy was to forbid any Arab political activities and to curtail the establishment of West Bank leadership, whether from within Palestinian nationalism or of the sort loyal to Jordan.

Israel held mayoral elections on the West Bank in 1972 and again in April 1976; to their astonishment, in the second election a group of radical Palestinian nationalists was elected—Bassam Shakaa in Nablus, Kharim Khalaf in Ramallah, Fahd Qawasma in Hebron. Others, like Rashad Shawwa in Gaza and the moderate Freij, were reelected. As the ruling Likud bloc planted more and more Jewish settlements on the West Bank, the radicalization continued. In 1981, Jewish settlers tried to kill three Palestinian mayors but succeeded only in maiming two of them. Finally, in 1982 the Israeli army, acting in its capacity as the occupying force, fired most of the popularly elected mayors. The pragmatic Freij was one of the few Palestinians to remain.

In December 1985, the Israeli army selected Zafer Masri, the scion of a well-known Palestinian family and cousin of Jordan's foreign minister, as mayor of Nablus. Three months later, he was dead, victim of a Palestinian assassin's bullet. Tens of thousands marched in the streets in mourning him. Masri exemplified both the continuity and fragility of the Arab mayor.

The Palestine Liberation Organization

It was the late spring of 1964 and I was just finishing a term with the Near East School of Archaeology. Half of our time we spent in an excavation at ancient Dothan on the West Bank. The other half we attended classes on the Mount of Olives in East Jerusalem. At that time both the West Bank and East Jerusalem were under Jordanian control. Unbeknownst to me, elsewhere in East Jerusalem, an announcement was made at a Palestinian Congress as a follow-up to a decision by the first Arab Summit Conference in Cairo that January to establish the Palestine Liberation Organization (PLO).

About sixteen years had then elapsed since (1) the Arab governments had turned down the 1947 U.N. Palestine partition resolution on grounds it was unjust, inequitable, and injurious to the Palestinian people, and (2) the 1948 Israeli War of Independence in which the Israelis gained an even larger piece of ground than allocated under the partition. During this period the Palestinians had relied on the Arab states for help, but had not regained one *dunam* (a quarter of an acre) of land from the Israelis. Hundreds of thousands of Palestinians remained refugees. Egyptian leader Nasser shouted, "if Israel wants war, welcome!" War had taken place in 1956, but no land was regained. In fact, Nasser had opened the Gulf of Aqaba to Israeli shipping.

Against this bleak background the Palestine Liberation Organization came into being. Later, Jordan's King Hussein said the PLO had been established "for the political purpose of regulating the Palestinian voice under one organization which would speak for it with the purpose of keeping the Palestinian issue alive in the world arena and for the declared purpose of liberating Palestine."[5] But one thing loomed large in print for the Israelis: The Palestinian National Charter of the PLO declares, "Armed

---

5. An address to the nation of Jordan, February 19, 1986.

struggle is the only way to liberate Palestine" (Article 9) and "The liberation of Palestine, from an Arab viewpoint, is a national duty and it attempts to repel the Zionist aggression against the Arab homeland, and aims at the elimination of Zionism in Palestine" (Article 15). To Israel, this means the PLO's goal is to exterminate the Jewish state and to do so by terrorist attacks. The main organization within the PLO was Fatah, which Yasser Arafat has led over the years. Fatah moderated over the years, as the decline in guerrilla attacks indicates. Other factions more radical than Fatah included the Popular Front for the Liberation of Palestine and the Democratic Front for the Liberation of Palestine. The P.F.L.P. was headed by Dr. George Habash and the D.F.L.P. by Nayif Hawatmeh. Both men are Christians.

The first leader of the PLO was Ahmad Shuqairi, who was described as "a deferential, if demagogic, professional politician."[6] He shouted that the Palestinians would drive the Israelis into the sea. Yasser Arafat, an educated petroleum engineer, became chairman in 1969 and has served since then.

I observed Arafat at close range in Tripoli, Lebanon, in 1983 when the PLO once again was being expelled from a brother Arab nation. Foreign correspondents made daily taxi trips from Beirut to Tripoli to see (1) whether Arafat was still alive, for he was being targeted daily by the Syrians and a PLO rebel named Abu Moussa, and if so, (2) whether he was still in Tripoli. Every day about noon, he drove up to a plain building on a messy side street in a poor neighborhood of Tripoli and held a news conference.

He showed serenity, certainty, and then, a measure of kindness. Wearing his trademark—peaked cap and black and white scarf tucked in his olive jacket—his natty dress surprised me. He handled hostile questions easily, his smile never leaving his face. One day, a woman quickly made her way to him in the crowded room. She threw her arms around him and laid her head on his chest and sobbed. He put his hands on her cheeks, almost

---

6. David Hirst, *The Gun and the Olive Branch* (London: Faber and Faber, 1977), 280. Hirst is a long-time Middle East correspondent for *The Guardian* in England.

tenderly, and looking into her face, said something to her softly. Then he kissed her forehead. Then a second woman did the same thing, and a third. A few moments later, surrounded by his young loyalist fighters, Arafat worked his way out of the door. Some boys rushed up to him calling him by his nickname, "Abu Amar," which, loosely translated, means "founding father." As if he had all the time in the world—instead of perhaps hours—he playfully showed them how to make V-for-victory signs with their fingers. Then he got in his dusty Chevrolet and was driven off, still smiling.

I had finished my assignment and had returned to Jerusalem by the time a few days later when Arafat and his fighters sailed away from Tripoli. Each night before his departure, the telephone in my apartment rang about 1 A.M. It was a *golem*, which is a special announcement by the Israeli army phoned to correspondents. It stated that the Israeli navy had shelled Tripoli, probably not so much wanting to hit Arafat as to scare him.

Time and again the wily Arafat has survived challenges from within and without. He was expelled from Jordan in 1970, from Beirut in 1982, from Tripoli in 1983. By February 1985, he was joined with Jordan's King Hussein to work on establishing a joint Jordanian-Palestinian negotiating team, an effort that collapsed one year later with Hussein blaming Arafat. Yet Arafat carries on. But many Israelis say Arafat has hurt the Palestinian cause more than he has helped it.

As the list of guerrilla attacks in chapter 2 indicates, the PLO has used armed operations, especially during its first decades. *Fedayeen*, or commandos, with a particular religious fervor, carried out the attacks, often using Jordan as a launching pad. As Hirst put it, "It was Fatah's aim to draw the Arab peoples, rather than their governments, into the kind of 'popular liberation war' which they *could* win."[7] This was yet another of the peasant wars that have characterized the twentieth century, creating a new and terrible kind of modern war called terrorism.

Moshe Maoz suggests, however, that the PLO was not very successful in the first few years in creating a revolutionary situa-

---

7. Ibid., 275.

tion in the West Bank.[8] He attributes this to the inclination of the local population on the West Bank who wanted to lead normal lives, and to the force of the occupying Israeli military. In Black September 1970, after the PLO hijacked four airliners, flew them to a Jordanian desert, and blew them up, in fury, Hussein expelled the PLO with a resultant loss of power and prestige for the organization. The PLO quickly reassembled in southern Lebanon.

In 1972, the Palestine National Council met in Cairo and voted to mobilize and arm the masses, to organize trade unions, to develop national productive projects so as to try to use the Palestinian workers locally, to develop national economic and cultural institutions, and to provide assistance in education and welfare.

The 1973 Yom Kippur War, although won by Israel, raised serious doubts about Israeli military invincibility, and thus greatly promoted the status of the PLO. In November 1974, amid some of the PLO's worst guerrilla attacks against Israel, Arafat spoke to the U.N. General Assembly and said, "I have come bearing an olive branch and a freedom fighter's gun." A few days later, the General Assembly passed a resolution recognizing the PLO.

The Arab League, which was founded in 1945 in a desire for greater Arab unity, designated the Palestine Liberation Organization in 1974 as the sole legitimate representative of the Palestinian people. Later that year, the U.N. General Assembly passed Resolutions 3236 and 3237 recognizing the PLO as the representative of the Palestinian people. The PLO has offices or embassies in ninety countries. Israel and the United States are the main nations not recognizing it.

According to a survey by *Al Fajr* newspaper in East Jerusalem, more than 70 percent of those polled on the West Bank regard PLO Chairman Yasser Arafat as their leader; only 3 percent looked to Jordan's King Hussein.[9]

The PLO is more than a political or guerrilla organization. It has an array of bureaus and departments, roughly comparable to a

---

8. Moshe Maoz, *Palestinian Leadership on the West Bank* (London: Frank Cass, 1984), 112.

9. As quoted in *The New York Times*, October 23, 1986.

formal government. Its worth is estimated from $2 billion to $14 billion, with bank accounts in Switzerland, West Germany, Mexico, and the Cayman Islands. It has real estate holdings of hotels and office buildings in the Middle East, and farms and ranches in the Sudan, Somalia, Uganda, and Guinea. It reportedly owns shares in a Belgian charter and Maldive Airways.[10] Major oil-exporting Arab states were instructed at the 1978 Arab summit to donate a total of $300 million a year to the PLO.

The Future

One of the long-range problems the PLO faces is that of leadership, either as an alternative or successor to Arafat. George Habash of the P.F.L.P. and Nayif Hawatmeh of the D.F.L.P. always pose harder-line, Marxist threats to Arafat within the PLO.

Two persons were designated by the Israelis as acceptable choices to sit on a joint Jordanian-Palestinian delegation to negotiate with Israel. They are Hanna Siniora, fifty, a pharmacist and publisher of *Al Fajr*, who attended Marin (Calif.) Junior College, and Faiz Abu Rahmeh, a lawyer and past president of the Gaza bar association. But neither man seems especially connected to the present leadership of the PLO.

Some of the most effective and most articulate Palestinian leaders have passed the time of active leadership. We have cited Edward W. Said, fifty-two, a professor of literature at Columbia University and a member of the Palestine National Council. The elder statesman of the Palestinians was Anwar Nuseibe, former Jordanian Defense Minister and owner of the East Jerusalem Power Company, who ranked with Abba Eban as one of the most erudite English speakers in Israel and the West Bank. Many of the mayors probably are past the point of assuming leadership as well. Bassam Shakaa has been deposed as mayor of Nablus, his legs shot off. Zafer Masri, his successor as mayor of Nablus, was assassinated. Rashad Shawwa of Gaza also has been deposed. The pragmatic Elias Freij of Bethlehem seems content to be a prominent mayor.

---

10. Marvin Scott, "What Is the PLO Worth?" *Parade,* Sept. 21, 1986, 17.

It remains unclear as to who the new generation of leaders will be. Jonathan Kuttab and Raja Shehadeh are two outstanding young lawyers on the West Bank. Shehadeh, of Ramallah, is the son of the late Aziz Shehadeh, head of the biggest law firm on the West Bank. Kuttab, of East Jerusalem, is the son of a Christian minister and was educated in the United States at Messiah College and the University of Virginia law school. Both have been active in defending human rights cases and are cofounders of Law in the Service of Man, a human rights organization. Another possibility is Sari Nuseibe, a Palestinian intellectual who lives in Jerusalem's Old City. Nuseibe told my colleague James Dorsey that he favored Israel annexing the West Bank because it would require the Jewish state to grant full rights to the West Bank Palestinians.

What lies ahead? Shehadeh's journal of life on the West Bank is entitled *The Third Way*, ironically drawn from the Holocaust, from the wisdom of the Treblinka concentration camp.

> Faced with two alternatives—always choose the third, between mute submission and blind hate. . . . I choose the third way. I am Samid. (The word means "the steadfast," "the persevering.")

Kuttab says much the same thing. "Nothing has changed," Kuttab told the national convention of the American-Arab Anti-Discrimination Committee in Washington, D.C. in 1987, "but now we know it . . . (and) that new knowledge has had revolutionary implications. It gives us energy, vitality, and hope for the future. We now know no one will save us but ourselves."

Kuttab says the Palestinians now understand the weaknesses of the Israeli system "and no longer are we overawed by the Israeli superman. . . . we know their failings, their weakness and have an understanding of those forces that are able to overcome them." In this climate have mushroomed new cooperation—of non-violence (which we discuss in chapter 10) and of grass-roots cooperation.

The Refugees

During the 1948 War, either because the Arabs ordered them to, or out of fear of the Israeli army, many Palestinians fled their homes and became refugees. Their plight is tragic; just as the Palestinians symbolize the Arab-Jewish problem, the refugees symbolize the Palestinian problem.

They abandoned their houses. Some were left vacant, and you see them even yet on the western slopes leading into Jerusalem, fine old Arab houses with the distinctive Mediterranean lattice-work, now empty and void as they have been for decades. Others were taken over by Israelis. Our first living quarters in Jerusalem in the mixed neighborhood of Abu Tor was a reno-vated Arab apartment with remarkable wood shelving and cabi-nets, the work of the cabinetmaker for the king of Jordan. In Amman, Jordan, I heard one upper middle-class Arab woman remark that she had returned to Jerusalem recently and had gone by the house that once was her home. An Israeli family now lives in it.

Initially, the Red Cross and the American Friends had cared for the refugees. The U.N. General Assembly established the United Nations Relief and Works Agency in 1949 to take over the re-sponsibility. About nine hundred thousand Palestinians had been listed as refugees, but UNRWA's first census corrected this to seven hundred fifty thousand.

According to UNRWA, in 1987 there were 766,973 Palestinian refugees in UNRWA camps and 1,434,150 not in camps for a total of 2,201,123 refugees. Of these, 373,586 were in the West Bank and 445,397 were in the Gaza Strip. There are twenty refugee camps on the West Bank, eight in Gaza, twelve in Lebanon, ten in Jordan, and ten in Syria.

The refugees have freedom of movement with one big excep-tion—they may work in Israel proper but may not live there. UNRWA provides education and health care. It operates eight vocational training centers, with two-thousand Palestinians study-ing in the training centers at Kalandia and Ramallah in the West Bank and at Gaza.

I visited the camp at Dheisheh, with a population of six thousand, in late 1984. Dheisheh is located just south of Bethlehem on the east side of the Jerusalem-Hebron highway. The Israeli army has shut off the main gate and all passageways between the camp and the main Jerusalem-Hebron highway with barbed wire and barrels filled with concrete. The army said it took this action because some residents of the camp threw stones at Israeli vehicles on the highway. Across the road, the Israeli army maintains a short, squat lookout tower.

At the time of my visit, Rabbi Moshe Levinger camped alongside the road in an orange van in hopes of frightening the Dheisheh residents against throwing stones at yellow-plated Israeli vehicles. Several generations of Palestinians reside in the camp; the elder residents tell of leaving their homes a few kilometers away nearly twenty years ago and having never returned. Their lively children have known no other existence.

The Israelis contend that what happened around 1948 was a massive exchange of people, and that the number of Palestinians who were displaced from what is now Israel just about equalled the number of Jews who moved from Arab countries into Israel. In 1948 there were about eight hundred thousand Jews living in Arab countries; most of them now live and have been assimilated in Israel. The Israelis contend the other Arab countries have made no effort to resettle or assimilate the Palestinian refugees.

With UNRWA approval, in November 1985 the Israeli army bulldozed much of two largely vacant camps just north of Jericho. The camps looked like a huge collection of tiny, crude cardboard boxes to passersby on the Jordan Valley road. About one-third of Aqabat Jabar and most of Ein Sultan were destroyed, about five thousand empty houses in all. Left were homes where people were living, the trees, a mosque, and schools. The twenty bulldozers did their work in a few hours. A mere tap at one of the houses turned it into a pile of dirt with a thick cloud of dust hanging overhead. The spring rains would dissolve the clods and leave the destruction looking like a plowed field.

Between forty-five thousand and fifty-thousand persons had lived at the camps between 1948 and 1967, making them together one of the biggest cities in Jordan. By 1985, only about twenty-six hundred refugees remained at Aqabat Jabar and six hundred at Ein Sultan. Rabid animals and drug traders used the empty houses, an UNRWA worker said, and the Palestinian population welcomed the destruction.

Jewish Settlements

Establishing settlements is a century-old method that Jews have used to reclaim land in Palestine. The oldest settlement is Petah Tikva, organized in 1878, a thriving city just northeast of Tel Aviv. Even before statehood was proclaimed in 1948, the Etzion block of Jewish settlements was established halfway between Hebron and Jerusalem. The four settlements came under severe attack in the War of Independence, were captured, and did not revert to the settlers until after the 1967 War.

Gush Emunim (Hebrew for "Block of the Faithful") is the movement that now fosters settlements; it boasts eighty thousand to one hundred thousand followers. After the 1967 War, Israelis began establishing Jewish settlements in the West Bank. Now, at least 120 Jewish settlements have been established and an estimated 65,000 Jewish settlers live in them. More than 100 of them were established under Menachem Begin's premiership, 1977–83. Prime Minister Shamir refers to them as "facts," that is, proof of the Jewish return to the land. A higher birth rate has increased the Arab population on the West Bank to 813,000, meaning that the West Bank is still 90 to 95 percent Arab.

The typical settlers are, in some ways, much like the American frontiersmen of the nineteenth century—tough, sturdy, persevering, taking the law into their own hands. Many are American-born and raised and many are well-educated. More than three-fourths of all American Jewish settlers have college degrees; one in ten holds a doctorate.[11] A large number of the settlers are observant Jews. Of the American Jews in settlements, 69 percent are Orthodox.[12] There is much greater zealousness among the

---

11. Chaim Waxman "American Israelis in Judea and Samaria: An Empirical Analysis," *Middle East Review*, XVII: 2, Winter, 1984–85, 49.

12. Ibid.

Jewish settlers than among their Israeli kin, which they themselves recognize.

"The general atmosphere in Israel as a result of (the war and
occupation of) Lebanon tends toward cynical expression and a
sort of nihilism and despair," says Daniella Weiss, a sabra and
former English teacher, now general secretary of Gush Emunim.
We talked in her home in Kedumim Settlement in Samaria. The
house, decorated with paintings and silver, was as aesthetic and
comfortable as most upper middle-class homes in America, I
think.

She added: "In the settlements, you will see the opposite. You
won't see the same pessimism and despair. . . . We want to see
ourselves as continuing the national stream of Zionism. This is
what we believe in. This is what we are building."

Arab villages are located in the valleys next to the farm land
because many Arabs till small plots of ground. Jewish settlements
for the most part are located on hilltops. There, the settlements
serve as lookouts on any hostility, their fortress-like stone buildings with massive walls and narrow windows making them appear
more like a military outpost than a community. Many settlers
commute to Jerusalem and Tel Aviv and do not need to use land
for agricultural purposes. And, being situated on the hilltops
serves to maintain a certain distance from the Arab villages. There
is no social contact between the Arab villagers and the Jewish
settlers—none. But there are two big exceptions to the pattern of
keeping Jewish settlements segregated from the Arab villages, in
Hebron and Nablus, as we shall discuss later.

Most settlements are attractive and well-kept with gardens and
flowers. Some almost have a suburban American appearance.
Others, it is clear, are struggling. Some of the settlements are
bedroom communities for nearby cities, like Ma'ale Adumim,
located just east of Jerusalem with a population of one thousand
families (Israel tabulates settlement populations according to the
number of families). Others are tiny, eking out an existence.
Carmel, with twenty-three families, is located about ten miles
southeast of Hebron deep in the West Bank. Many are not eco-
nomically self-sufficient.

Many take biblical names, like the most famous settlement,

Kiryat Arba, population four thousand, overlooking Hebron from the east. It was an alternative name for Hebron in the Bible (see Genesis 23:2). Another took the name of Tekoa, the prophet Amos's hometown. Shiloh, population 435, is north of Jerusalem near the site of ancient Shiloh where Israel worshiped (1 Samuel 1:3). In Kiryat Arba, 22 percent of the vote went to Rabbi Meir Kahane in the 1984 national elections. About half the adults in Kiryat Arba commute to Jerusalem to work; the others do stone and marble work locally.

Lawlessness and Zealousness

As Jewish settlers have poured by the thousands into the West Bank, tensions have been heightened and acts of terrorism on both sides have proliferated. The biggest, and most serious, domestic story during my three years in Israel was the Jewish underground reign of terror against the Arabs. One Shabbat in April 1984, it came to light.

After an almost year-long trial, a band of settlers was found guilty of maiming two Palestinian mayors on the West Bank by planting bombs in their cars in 1980, plotting to blow up the Dome of the Rock on Temple Mount on grounds the Moslems had desecrated it, spraying the campus of Islamic University in Hebron with gunfire in July 1983, killing three Arab students and wounding thirty-three others, and finally—the incident that led to the cracking of the ring—planting bombs on five Arab buses in April 1984. The consequences of some of those acts would have been shocking: Blowing up the Dome of the Rock, the third most holy spot in Islam, might well have led to holy war. Had the bombs on those five buses actually gone off, the toll could have been 250 lives.

During their trial, the accused were permitted to mix and mingle freely with their families. On one occasion, while on a trip, the guards stopped so the defendants could go swimming and have a picnic lunch. Yitzhak Shamir, who was prime minister when they were charged, said they were "basically good boys who erred."

It must be said in fairness to Israeli justice, however, that the settlers were put on trial, found guilty, and sentenced. It would be hard to imagine the reverse—an Arab nation putting an Arab on trial for acts of terrorism against a Jew. Three settlers got mandatory life sentences for the killing of the college students in Hebron, but the others received light terms of from four months to seven years. The only seven-year sentence went to Yehuda Etzion, mastermind of the plot to blow up the Dome of the Rock, located on a site holy to three faiths.

Yet it was the pedigree of these convicted killers and terrorists that cast their activities into stark perspective. These young men were not your common thugs. They were described by Daniella Weiss as "some of the (movement's) most prominent . . . to some extent, the symbols" of the Gush Emunim.

"How come people of such pure interests, integrity—religious people who live by the Torah, the Bible—did what they did?" she asked. Answering her own question, she said the Jewish underground grew out of two things—failure of the government to provide adequate security for the settlers, and the defendants' belief they had to act or abandon the settlements.

Zvi Katsover, who runs a cafeteria and souvenir shop in overwhelmingly Arab Hebron not far from the burial place of Abraham, Isaac, and Jacob, said bluntly after the trial that Arabs live by "retribution" and "the law of the desert." The raid on Islamic College, he said, was effective because it had cut down on attacks on the Jewish community.

Zev Chafets, who was Begin's director of the Government Press Office—an American-born and educated Jew—said: "What arouses the most sympathy, and the most alarm, is the fact that the terrorists acted out of fear and frustration—emotions that few Israelis are not subject to from time to time. There is nothing surprising about this; generations of war and unremitting Arab hostility have left people here increasingly vulnerable to such outbursts. The fact that the perpetrators were among the best Israelis, and not simply deranged misfits, causes all of us to ponder the limits of our self-restraint and how we might react to similar stress."[13]

There is no indication whatsoever that most or even many Palestinians participate in guerrilla actions against the Jews, a fact

---

13. Reported in *The Los Angeles Times*, July 12, 1985.

acknowledged by the Israeli army occupying the West Bank and Gaza Strip. A ranking IDF officer put it this way when asked if many are involved in terrorist acts. "No." I pressed: "Are a few involved in terrorist acts?" "Yes," he said. "Our feeling is that most of the people are sick and tired of terrorism. They don't think it is helpful."

Hebron and Miriam Levinger

Miriam Levinger recalls being raised in The Bronx as a spoiled "JAP" (Jewish American Princess). She was the youngest of six children. Several of her brothers and sisters went into show business and they took her along as a teen-ager to the night clubs where they were performing. The experience changed her life in an unexpected way.

"I saw people in night clubs around tables, really bored," she says. "I wanted a larger life than that." She also remembered the anti-Semitism she experienced growing up and says she determined then and there her life would be different. So she went to Israel, became a nurse, and married Moshe Levinger, whose family had come to Israel from the threatening storm clouds in Germany in the 1930s. Rabbi Levinger became the spiritual leader of the Jewish settlement movement.

Jewish settlers established a settlement, Kiryat Arba, overlooking Hebron from the east. But this did not satisfy Rabbi Levinger's yearnings. In 1968, one year after the Six-Day War during which Israel had captured the West Bank, including Hebron, Levinger and his wife led a small band of Jews to form a settlement in the heart of Hebron. No Jew had lived in Hebron since 1929 when sixty-three Jews were killed in Arab rioting and the remaining seven hundred families fled. Since 1968, Jews have used old property deeds which date prior to 1929 to prove their legal basis for owning some of the land in Hebron. In 1972 the settlement of Kiryat Arba was established on a hilltop overlooking Hebron from the east.

Unlike most Jewish settlers elsewhere in the West Bank, the Levingers, their eleven children, and two hundred other Jews live in the very center of town. They are near the Casbah (market) and literally rub shoulders with Arabs every day. The Jews—even teenagers—carry weapons; Israeli soldiers help protect them.

The settlers have rebuilt the sixteenth-century Abraham Avinu synagogue in Hebron as a symbol of their determination to restore their roots. About ten families, unable to get official permission to build houses, live in mobile homes in the old Jewish Quarter. When I was there, six families—one with eleven children—were living in mobile homes on Tel Rumeida, an area approximately five acres in size on a sheer hillside overlooking the market. Facilities have been added for another eleven families in Beit Hadassah, the old clinic situated on the main street leading into the center of Hebron.

Blood flows frequently there. One provocative act follows another. In 1980, six Jews returning from prayers at the Patriarchs' Tomb were gunned down by Arabs in front of Beit Hadassah. Some of the settlers retaliated with the assassination attempts that maimed two West Bank mayors, and Israelis tore down several houses and shops across the street from Beit Hadassah. In July 1983, an American émigré, Aharon Gross, nineteen, a yeshiva student, was stabbed near the market. After his funeral that night, Jewish settlers set fires in the market. The next day, the Israeli army ousted Mayor Mustafe Natshe, the second Hebron mayor to suffer that fate. Two weeks later, Jewish settlers crawled up the western stone wall at Hebron University and sprayed the campus with gunfire. Three students died and thirty-three were wounded. The blood has not stopped flowing since.

Meanwhile, the Arabs are building a new mosque of Mamaluke design on the edge of Kiryat Arba. The Jews say it is financed by Saudi Arabia.

Miriam Levinger talked passionately about her life one day while chain-smoking and hanging up her laundry on their rooftop. "How do I regard violence?" she asked. "I grew up in the East Bronx. The Puerto Ricans and the Negroes moved in. As a child growing up, I suffered a lot at their hands. What did the Jews do? They took off," a pattern she said persecuted Jews have always followed. "I am not going to do what the Jews have done throughout the centuries. If there is violence, then I will do my best to defend myself. I am not running away from here."

When pressed as to whether she believed Arabs are worse in their treatment of Jews than the Soviets and others, she replied tersely: "No." "Does God love the Arabs?" I asked. "Of course. It is required that the Jews should be the example of ethics and everyone in the world should see that example of ethics." But asked to justify the actions of Jewish settlers, she replied: "You have to be you. . . . I'm not going to speak for God."

Her views and the actions of her son-in-law are not held in isolation among Jews in Hebron. Jonah Chaiken, who arrived recently from Springfield, Massachusetts, is a hi-tech computer specialist who is developing software for marketing in the United States. "It was a hollow existence in Boston. It was the end of the American dream. It was easy to make a lot of money. No pressure," he says. "I've come here to fight. . . . I would force all Arabs to leave the land of Israel. . . . Rabbi Kahane is the only person who has the most elementary common sense about security." Chaiken, a small, intense man, said no, he had never asked an Arab to coffee. And he said he had no non-Jewish friends in America.

The words of Miriam Levinger, Chaiken, and others illustrate that even being raised in America—presumably amid the expression of democratic ideals—does not make one immune to zealotry invested in a cause. As with all patriots, the tension of the life Miriam Levinger has chosen has taken its toll, her zeal pretty much quenching the puckish sense of humor she had as a child, and which occasionally surfaces now.

Nablus and Roman Alduby

The strategy to establish a Jewish settlement in Nablus, or, as the Jews refer to it, Shechem (*Shem* in the modern Hebrew pronunciation) has been different from that of Hebron. In Hebron the plan has been to reestablish the Jewish Quarter. In Nablus, the scheme is to sprinkle Jewish settlers throughout the ancient city.

Shechem already was a thriving place when Abraham stopped there some four thousand years ago on his trip to the Promised Land. Several hundred years later, Moses told the Israelites after they had fled Egypt that they should build an altar of stones on

119

Mount Ebal in the Promised Land and offer burnt sacrifices there (Deuteronomy 27:4-5); Joshua did just that (Joshua 8:30-35). Archeologist Adam Zertal has unearthed at the ruins of ancient Shechem what may well have been the altar that Joshua built (see page 221 for more discussion of this).

On Mount Gerizim, near ancient Shechem, some of the 550 surviving Samaritans still gather every year to observe Passover meticulously and strictly according to Exodus 12. They consider themselves to be descendants of the tribes of Levi, Ephraim, and Manasseh, having broken off from Judaism about 500 B.C. Nowadays, some fifty men and their sons in white robes and red tarbooshes bring their finest year-old male lambs, and, at the appointed moment, amid chants and praises, slit the animals' throats. Then they put a dab of blood on their foreheads, marking the time when the Lord "passed over" all slave Israelite houses in Egypt where blood had been smeared on the doorposts. Quickly the Samaritans scald the lambs they have killed, pluck off the wool, and carve out the entrails for burning. Then they skewer the carcasses and roast them for an evening feast.

On the south edge of Shechem itself are Joseph's tomb (Joshua 24:32) and Jacob's Well, where Jesus had a candid conversation with the much-married Samaritan woman (John 4).

Today, Nablus has a population of more than one hundred thousand. It has been only slightly freer of Arab-Jewish violence than its twin city of Hebron to the south. The city's deposed Mayor Bassam Shakaa had his legs blown off in 1980 by Jewish terrorists, and an eleven-year-old Arab girl was shot and killed by a Jewish settler in a bakery in 1983.

For the last few years, under the leadership of Roman Alduby, a sabra in his early twenties, approximately fifteen Jewish students have commuted to Nablus daily to study at a yeshiva, or Jewish seminary, that functions in a makeshift tent alongside Joseph's tomb. The Israeli army, which maintains a guard at the tomb, enforces regulations prohibiting them from staying overnight.

With Alduby acting as master strategist, about twenty-five Jewish families have been meeting regularly to make plans to purchase pieces of property scattered throughout Nablus. Alduby says that the Jews in Nablus are generally much poorer than those in

Hebron and own no property. Therefore they must start from scratch. Since an Arab can be sentenced to death for selling property to a Jew, any purchases must be done through absentee landlords and a complicated series of middlemen. The Arab owner does not know that the property eventually will wind up in the hands of a Jew. Because each middleman gets a cut, the price of the property generally runs 20 to 25 percent higher than the average market price. Alduby raises money in the United States.

Law of the Land

The West Bank Data Base Project, headed by former Jerusalem Deputy Mayor Meron Benvenisti, has concluded that 36 percent of the West Bank area is now under exclusive Israeli control.[14] Benvenisti says the Israelis have used several methods to gain this control: (1) expropriation of absentee-owned lands whose Arab landlords left before 1967; (2) seizure of land for military purposes; (3) designating certain real estate for such "public purposes" as roads; (4) designating land a natural reserve, which imposes severe restrictions on how it may be used; and (5) imposing restrictions on crop use.[15]

This legal process of "declaration of state lands" has slowed considerably, says Benvenisti, in the wake of the 1986 disclosure of a land scam.[16] An Israeli state comptroller's report found that 12,500 of 17,500 acres had been obtained by the Israelis irregularly. The report was revealed by Knesset member Yossi Sarid, then a member of the Labor Party. "All this high-flown talk of 'redeeming the land, Zionism, and pioneering' serves as a cover for corruption and cheating," Sarid said. "Most of the land deals in the area are rooted in forgery, deceit pressures, and threats."

About the same time, a special Cabinet committee overruled Israeli state archivist Avraham Alsberg and kept classified a secret document on Israel's expulsion of Arabs and the expropriation of

---

14. See the West Bank Data Base Project report, published by *The Jerusalem Post*, p. 37. The Project is funded by the Rockefeller and Ford Foundations and is administered by the Brookings Institute in Washington, D.C.

15. Ibid.

16. Ibid.

Arab property during the 1948 War. "The material may not make pleasant reading," Alsberg says, "but after looking at the material, I did not agree with the decision (not to declassify)."

Punishment and Fear

A shocking study in contrast can be made of the light sentences given Jewish settlers on the West Bank and the harsh punishment meted out to Arab offenders there. A Palestinian boy who throws stones is likely to be sentenced by an Israeli military court to six months in jail. Membership in the PLO will get him a two-year jail sentence.

"There is certainly a double standard. In the West Bank, Arabs can receive punishment twenty times as severe," says Israel Shahak, a professor at the Hebrew University and chairman of the Israel's League of Human Rights. Shahak has catalogued the status of law in the occupied territories since 1968.

The Israeli army would not respond to my staff's queries about the unevenness in crime and punishment on the West Bank. The Israeli government suppressed for more than one year a report showing that Israeli police were lax in investigating Arab complaints against Jewish settlers on the West Bank. Compiled by Assistant Attorney General Judith Karp, the 33-page report reviewed more than 70 cases of violence or threats. Only fifteen had been brought to some sort of trial; the other investigations ended inconclusively.

Gaza Strip

Gaza, with a population of 525,000, is one of the most densely populated areas in the world. More than half of the people are Palestinian refugees. It is not a pretty place. A six-mile by 25-mile rectangular strip of land between Egypt and Israel, Gaza takes its name from one of the five cities of the ancient, seafaring Philistines. This region was also a crossroads for north-south traffic between Egypt and Mesopotamia, and east-west traffic on the Nabatean trail. Ironically, Gaza City is located a mere half-mile from the shore of the Mediterranean, yet port facilities do not now exist.

Gaza long has suffered a lack of identity. Anan Safadi, an Israeli Arab journalist, has said that Gaza "always was the loose protectorate of somebody, an area no authority wanted to involve itself with, and always it was the gateway for forbidden trade in drugs, foreign currency, etc." Gaza was part of Palestine under the British mandate. The 1947 U.N. partition plan specified that Gaza should become part of the Arab state in Palestine. Egyptian troops entered Gaza during the 1948 War and occupied it afterwards. Israel conquered Gaza in the 1967 War and has occupied it ever since. Neither Arafat nor Hussein nor Mubarak talk much about Gaza. No one wants it.

The city of Rafah dominates the southern border of Gaza, its population divided by a barbed-wire fence that separates Israeli-occupied territory from Egypt. Rafah has been a divided city since Israel returned the Sinai to Egypt under terms of their 1979 peace treaty. Every day a dozen or more Palestinians—mothers with children, elderly men, teenagers—yell family news to their relatives stranded in Camp Canada on the Egyptian side one hundred yards away. Camp Canada, so named because of Canada's contribution to the U.N. emergency force which patrolled the area before the 1967 War, was a housing project built by Israel in 1972.

In the Gaza Strip, children by the hordes play in the streets. Their tin-hut dwellings can barely be called homes. The United Nations Relief and Works Agency provides an elementary education. Raw sewage runs in the dirt streets. The military government handles the health needs; the stench of despair is everywhere. During one visit, the Israeli van carrying several of us foreign correspondents got stuck in the sand along a coastal road. Every one of six or seven Arab drivers went by without stopping—refusing to stop and help, betraying the omnipresent hostility.

There is no unemployment in Gaza. The Israeli army contends that the standard of living there has shown great improvement. Paradoxically, the most improvement has taken place among the refugees. One officer admitted, "There is improvement in Gaza, not in feeling but in electricity and TV sets."

There are eight refugee camps in Gaza; the largest, Jabalia, has forty-five thousand occupants. Jewish settlements have been planted there also—fourteen in all, with a population of two

123

thousand seven hundred. Here, too, the settlements have a life unto themselves. In Elei Sinai ("toward Sinai"), located in northern Gaza a half-mile from the sea, ten families live in mobile homes. The adults commute 100 to 120 kilometers a day to work in Tel Aviv, Beersheba, or Ashkelon. Most of the settlements are in the southern part of Gaza, where tomatoes, strawberries, and other vegetables and fruit are raised for export to the United States and Europe. In Ganei-Tal ("dew of heaven," Genesis 27:28, the settlers' translation), the settlers raise tomatoes without soil in a greenhouse by drip-feeding them with nutrients.

In Kfar Darom, Reuben Rosenblat, president of the settlers' regional council, expresses a desire to live in peace with the Arabs—but again, he is adamant. "I don't want to throw the Arab out. But he must agree he lives within an Israeli country," he says. Rosenblat is a Polish-born Jew who survived Hitler's camps to migrate to Israel in 1949. "If my children go to Gaza [City] at night, they will be killed. An Arab can go to Tel Aviv and no one will do anything to him."

Justice and Peace

Israel must ask itself difficult questions about the West Bank and Gaza. Assuming the validity of the ancient Promise of the Land and acknowledging Israel's security needs, are these enough to justify taking land that has been occupied by the Arabs for hundreds of years, or taking land that was 100 percent Arab in population? Do those factors justify flouting the principles of justice and mercy? The Arabs have a few questions to answer as well. When, ever, is the taking of innocent lives in acts of terrorism justified? When have Arab countries ever put on trial Arabs for crimes against Jews? And what is the responsibility of the other Arabs toward the Palestinians in the West Bank and Gaza, a responsibility by and large ignored in the past forty years? There seems to be enough guilt to shame both sides.

5

The Villainy of the West

"For behold, in those days and at that time, when I restore the fortunes of Judah and Jerusalem, I will gather all the nations and bring them down to the valley of Jehoshaphat, and I will enter into judgment with them there, on account of my people and my heritage Israel, because they have scattered them among the nations, and have divided up my land, and have cast lots for my people, and have given a boy for a harlot, and have sold a girl for wine, and have drunk it."

—Joel 3:1-3

The nineteenth-century imperialism of the West is nowhere more illustrated than in the architecture of Jerusalem. The West engaged in a competition of construction in the late 1800s and early 1900s in a way that forever changed the skyline of the Eternal City. It was almost as if there were a contest to see who could build the highest, biggest structures.

The first settlement outside the Old City was started in about 1860 on the western slopes close to Jaffa Gate. That settlement was called Yemin Moshe, and its great benefactor was Sir Moses Montefiore, a British Jew. The race had begun. At approximately the same time, the Russians acquired the land now called the Russian Compound. Where an angel of the Lord slew 185,000 invading Assyrian soldiers to preserve the reign of good King Hezekiah (2 Kings 19) two thousand five hundred years ago, there is now the Jerusalem police station and jail. On this spot also the Russians built the green-domed Russian Cathedral and to match it, on the Mount of Olives, the Church of Mary Magdalene. This latter structure has seven onion-shaped domes, typically Russian, and a Russian church and monastery.

In 1885, the French laid the first stone for the massive Notre Dame of Jerusalem, now a lovely guest house, on the crest of the hill at the northwest corner of the Old City. To note Kaiser Wilhelm's visit in 1898, the Germans built Dormition Abbey on Mount Zion, a soaring structure far out of proportion to the importance of the site it commemorates (it is one of the traditional sites of the death of the Virgin Mary). In the Old City, the Germans built the Church of the Redeemer, a large structure near the Church of the Holy Sepulchre; and on the Mount of Olives, they erected the Augusta-Victoria Hospital with its high tower. In 1934, the British countered with the squat, graham-cracker box-shaped King David Hotel, looming over Yemin Moshe. After the 1967 War, Yemin Moshe was restored and now is one of Jerusalem's most elegant residential districts. Montefiore's windmill still presides over the neighborhood.

Now a super-power competition of a different, more bloody sort is going on. From 1981 to 1985, the United States and the Soviet Union poured $33.5 billion worth of arms into the Middle East; the Soviets supplied $18.4 billion and the United States supplied arms valued at $15.1 billion.[1] "The Big Powers have greatly contributed to the prolongation of the conflict for nearly four decades by supplying arms," says Nadav Safran.

The amount spent in the Middle East for weapons of death—largely provided by the Americans and Russians—is shocking. Here are categories and how Israel and selected Arab nations rank among *all* the nations of the world:

- Military expenditures—7. Saudi Arabia, 16. Israel, 20. Egypt.
- Size of the armed forces—7. Iraq, 15. Egypt, 19. Syria, 31. Israel.
- Arms imports—5. Egypt, 6. Syria, 15. Israel.
- Arms exports—22. Israel, 25. Egypt.[2]

---

1. *World Military Expenditures and Arms Transfers*, p. 11.

2. Ibid., 16, 17 (It must be noted, however, that these statistics do not tell the full story. To whom and from whom were arms bought and sold? What kind of arms?) An Israeli Foreign Ministry spokesman, replying to my question, said Israel never comments on its arms sales. There is speculation that Israel sells to South Africa, Iran, and even China.

- Military expenditures as a percentage of gross national product—3. Israel, 5. Syria, 6. Saudi Arabia, 7. Jordan.
- Military expenditures as a percentage of the government's budget—10. Syria, 13. Jordan, 19. Saudi Arabia, 26. Israel.
- Military expenditures per capita—4. Israel, 8. Iraq, 15. Syria.
- Armed forces per population—1. Iraq, 2. Israel, 4. Syria, 6. Jordan.

The Jews had an ancient claim. And, in the wake of the pogroms and the Holocaust, where in the world could they have found a homeland that would not have dislodged someone? The Arabs also had a claim, based on continuous residency for more than a thousand years. The real villains in the Middle East are not the Jews nor the Arabs. No, the real villains are the West, particularly the British and the French.

Deceit of the British and the French

A stone memorial bearing the names of some eighty Jews stands mute at the hairpin curve in Jerusalem's northern Sheikh Jarrah neighborhood on the road to Nablus. During the waning days of the British mandate, as tensions grew between Arabs and Jews, the British stood idly by at the American Colony Hotel as Arabs picked off a convoy of Jewish civilians, mostly physicians and nurses, en route from central Jerusalem to Hadassah-Mount Scopus Hospital. The British refused to intervene despite repeated appeals.

The Ottoman Empire had controlled the Middle East for four hundred years until early in this century. The British, French, and Russians all looked covetously at the Middle East. They wanted that land for themselves, regardless of Western principles of democracy and self-determination. The Arabs knew and feared these "European designs."[3]

---

3. George Antonius, *The Arab Awakening*, written in 1938 and reprinted in 1969 (Beirut: Librairie du Liban), 153. Antonius, a Lebanese Christian, has written what has been called the classic treatment of Arab nationalism. Edward Said, the Palestinian scholar, says it is "the finest Arab study of the struggle for independence" (Said, p. 20). Antonius's book, however, must be evaluated in the

One of the most significant results of World War I was the way it shaped—tragically in a negative way—the destiny of the Middle East for the next half-century. As the war broke out, the Arabs were torn. Should they support the Turks on the basis of their shared faith in Islam? Or should they support the Allies in the hope that they would help them gain their freedom after the war?

The Sultan of Turkey, in his capacity as caliph of the Moslems, was aware of the dilemma facing the Arabs. Hoping to enlist the Arabs in the war as brother Moslems, the Shaikh al-Islam, the highest theological official in the Ottoman Empire, declared a *jihad* against Britain, France, and Russia on November 7, 1914. On the other hand, Britain wanted to woo the Arabs into the war on its side, with France and Russia, against Germany, Austro-Hungary, and Turkey.

Sir Henry McMahon, the British High Commissioner in Egypt, exchanged a series of letters with Sharif Hussein in 1915 and 1916 in which Britain promised the Arab people their freedom after the war. Reading these letters is an instruction in duplicity.

McMahon's note of December 13, 1915, assured Hussein: "You may rest confident that Great Britain does not intend to conclude any peace treaty whatsoever, of which the freedom of the Arab peoples and their liberation from German and Turkish domination do not form an essential condition." Palestine was not mentioned per se.

On the strength of the British promise, Hussein ignited the Arab Revolt in Mecca on June 5, 1916, and the Arabs joined with the British in the war against the Turks and Germans. As Antonius writes: "The Allied cause had become identical with the cause of Arab independence. . . . the triumph of Allied arms would bring freedom to the Arab peoples."[4]

---

context of newly revealed documents and information. See Albert Hourani, *The Emergence of the Modern Middle East* (Berkeley and Los Angeles: University of California Press, 1981), and his chapter "The Arab Awakening Forty Years After."

4. Antonius, 225. Hourani agrees with the thrust of many of Antonius's conclusions. "There seems no doubt that in the letters sent by McMahon, expressions were used which Husayn (sic) could legitimately regard as constituting pledges" (Hourani, p. 209).

But almost at that very moment, in May 1916, Britain and France signed the Sykes-Picot Agreement, named after the negotiators, in which they carved up the Middle East into postwar colonies. France would get the northern coastal region, now the coast of Lebanon and Turkey, and Britain would have Iraq. Palestine would have a special international administration of some kind, with Britain receiving the main port of Haifa. The vast desert in the middle would be an independent Arab state.[5]

Meanwhile, the Arabs fought their brother Moslems. Jemal Pasha, the Turkish governor in Syria, raged against the Arabs. According to Antonius, famine and disease killed 300,000, and the Arabs killed, captured or contained an estimated 35,000 Turkish troops. One of the British officers who appeared in the Arabian peninsula was T. E. Lawrence, and the movie, *Lawrence of Arabia*, taking literary license, portrayed him as the leader of the Arabian capture of Aqaba and the march to Damascus. The movie itself speaks of the Arab expectation that this would lead to Arab independence. Sharif Hussein was proclaimed King of the Arab Countries on November 2, 1916.

From the standpoint of the Allies, the Arab intervention on their side helped keep the Red Sea and the Persian Gulf safe for them and barred any Turko-German southward movement. As Hussein's sons Faisal and Abdullah moved up the Arabian peninsula, the British, under Sir Edmund Allenby, moved from Egypt into Palestine and took Jerusalem on December 9, 1917, a month after the Balfour Declaration was issued guaranteeing the Jews "a national home." By what authority and why had Britain issued that declaration? Safran has speculated that the British issued the declaration as an incentive to Russian Jews involved in the Russian Revolution, to help keep Russia in the world war, as a prod to American Jews who had an antipathy toward the war because of the Jew-baiting Czarist Russians, and to forestall an expected

---

5. Hourani says it is less certain that the British pledges given to the Arabs were incompatible with those given the French. But he says, "When talking to Husayn or the Syrian nationalists, there seems no doubt that British officials did all they could to persuade them that their government accepted the Arab interpretation" (Hourani, pp. 209–210).

German declaration in favor of the Jews.[6] Some Israelis also say Britain issued the Balfour Declaration to help build its case for keeping control of Palestine after the war.

The Russian Revolution exposed the British duplicity. The Bolsheviks had seized power in Russia two months previous to the Balfour Declaration and quickly published the secret text of the Sykes-Picot Agreement. The Turks lost no time in calling this to the attention of King Hussein a few days before Allenby took Jerusalem. Hussein was gravely perturbed and asked the British for an explanation, but he sent the Turks a curt rejection of any peace overtures.

The British continued their double dealing. Sir Reginald Wingate, now the British High Commissioner in Egypt, sent Hussein a telegram saying the Turks, "whether from ignorance or from malice," had distorted the original purpose of Sykes-Picot and had overlooked its stipulations. In June 1918 the British in a "Declaration to the Seven" (key Arabs), again asserted "the principle of consent of the governed" in Arab lands liberated from Turkish rule by the Allies. In November, after the armistice with Turkey, the Anglo-French Joint Declaration called for "the complete and final liberation of the peoples who for so long have been oppressed by the Turks." But it also confirmed the Sykes-Picot Agreement by dividing the Arab regions of the Ottoman Empire between Britain and France.

On November 11, 1918, the war was won. As Antonius put it, "the Arab national movement stood abreast of its destiny."[7]

But that grand design already had been dashed, despite all the grand promises of the British and French. Faisal, son of King Hussein, as head of the Arab delegation, went to the Peace Conference, where cruel reality hit the young man. In his middle thirties with no experience in the seamy side of European diplomacy, he was told by the French that they could not regard him in an official capacity. The British used Lawrence to try to pressure Faisal into giving formal recognition to Zionist aspirations in Palestine.

---

6. Safran, 25.
7. Antonius, 276.

At the Peace Conference, on January 29, 1919, Faisal asked that the Arabs be recognized as "independent sovereign peoples, under the guarantee of the League of Nations." Faisal returned to Damascus in May to find restlessness and anxiety. In July, the General Syrian Congress met and, besides asserting a desire for independence, said that if foreign assistance came "for a limited period," preference should be given to American assistance. Relations between the French and the British were becoming greatly strained, and the British decided the only way to placate the French was to give them what the Sykes-Picot Agreement had defined for them, what is now Syria and Lebanon. Faisal took strong exception in a note to the British on October 11, 1919. Faisal did agree with the French for French occupation of Lebanon and coastal Syria. In March 1920, the General Syrian Congress proclaimed independence with Faisal as king. Iraqi leaders passed a similar resolution and chose Faisal's brother Abdullah as king. The French and British, declaring the proceedings in Damascus invalid, convened the Allied Supreme Council in San Remo, Italy, in April 1920; it gave the British and the French the mandates they wanted. Syria was broken up into Palestine, Lebanon, and Syria. France was given a single mandate over Syria and Lebanon; Britain was given mandates over Iraq and Palestine. This was in violation of the Covenant of the League of Nations, which declared that the wishes of the population concerned were to be a principal consideration in the selection of the mandates.

Within weeks, a French army landed in Lebanon and marched on Damascus. They occupied Damascus on July 25 and Faisal was sent into exile three days later. As Sir John Glubb put it so succinctly: "The Arab state ceased to exist."[8] In 1922 the Council of the League of Nations confirmed the mandates, expressly providing for a Jewish national home in Palestine and incorporating almost verbatim the language of the Balfour Declaration.

The Arabs began to resist, with serious outbreaks in Jerusalem and throughout Syria and Iraq. At the Cairo Conference in March 1921, with Winston Churchill in the position of Colonial Secretary, the British decided to proclaim Faisal king of Iraq.

---

8. Glubb, 277.

Churchill went on to Jerusalem to meet with Abdullah. Abdullah's recommendation for a single Arab state of Palestine and Transjordan was rejected by Churchill on grounds it conflicted with British promises to the Zionists. It was agreed provisionally, finally, that Abdullah should remain in Transjordan where he eventually became king.

The British mandate over Iraq lasted for twelve years. Faisal, as king, lived just long enough to see Iraq win emancipation and become a member of the League of Nations. The other mandates split Syria into three parts—Syria and Lebanon making up the French mandate, and Palestine, the British mandate. Antonius contends the boundary between Palestine and Lebanon "violated almost every known law of human and physical demarcation."[9] This remains the troublesome boundary between Israel and Lebanon.

The last mandate to pass away in the Middle East was that of the British in Palestine. The Peel Commission in 1937, claiming it had investigated contradictory British actions in the past decades, wound up calling for a partition of Palestine. An Arab state and a Jewish state consisting of a narrow coastal strip from Tel Aviv to Haifa and the Galilee would both be recognized as sovereign, independent national entities. A British white paper in 1939 proposed the creation of an independent, predominantly Arab Palestinian state and a limit of seventy-five thousand Jewish immigrants during the next five years. After that there would be a total halt to immigration. The Arabs rejected both proposals.

In World War II, both Arabs and Jews again fought on the side of the Allies. But the British and French still had their mandates in the Middle East. The French still occupied Syria and Lebanon when France fell to the Germans. In June 1941, the British and Free French invaded Syria and the Free French promised independence to Syria. After the war, as the French again showed no inclination to leave, demonstrations broke out. Finally, French and British armies were withdrawn in 1946 and, thirty years after the McMahon letters, Syria and Lebanon gained their independence.

The British tried to stop Jewish refugees from reaching Palestine after World War II. They abstained when the U.N.

---

9. Antonius, 357.

General Assembly approved a partition plan for Palestine on November 29, 1947, a vote that led to the establishment of a Jewish state six months later. The British did not abandon their mandate until May 14, 1948—thirty-three years after McMahon's promises to Hussein. *Within hours the Jews declared the modern state of Israel.*

(The traditional British bias may have been changed a bit by Prime Minister Margaret Thatcher in 1986 when she visited Israel and wept at the Yad Vashem, the memorial to victims of the Holocaust. At her news conference at the King David Hotel, blown up by Jewish guerrillas in 1946 with great loss of life to the British, a Palestinian reporter asked her about the Palestinian right to a homeland. She repeated twice what a powerful impact it made simply to view that memorial.)

History is generally the story of nations pursuing their self-interests, as Britain and France did after World War I. But I have often wondered what would have happened had the British and French said openly and candidly to the Arabs, "We will keep our promise to give you your freedom. For reasons you are familiar with, there is one small area where we will have to renege—Palestine—but all the rest of your territory—Lebanon, Syria, Iraq, Trans-Jordan—we return to you." That is, the British would have offered the Arabs their independence in exchange for their acceptance of the Balfour Declaration. Harvard's Safran says it is questionable whether this would have made a difference in the long term, but, he adds, "At the very least, you would have had a different start." This could well have defused much of the appropriate Arab anger. Instead, the Arabs got almost nothing for years and their fury was unleashed at the Jews.

Gun-slinging of the United States and Soviet Union

I remember it as though it were yesterday. It was my birthday in 1948. I went with my brother Paul to radio station KSMN where he was a staff member. The station was located on the site where our father had attended a one-room country school. There I walked over to what always fascinated me—the wire service printer—and coming across the wire that day was a dispatch about a remarkable announcement. The new State of Israel had been proclaimed at a seaside building in Tel Aviv, and within minutes, President Harry S. Truman had recognized it on behalf of the United States.

His two-sentence announcement said: "This government has been informed that a new Jewish state has been proclaimed in Palestine, and recognition has been requested by the provisional government thereof. The United States recognizes the provisional government as the de facto authority of the new State of Israel."

The Israeli-Soviet relationship is complicated. Despite the Soviet hostility of recent years, many Israelis have their roots in Russia and, indeed, many Israeli songs carry wafts of old Russian tunes. (See the section on Soviet Jewry in the next chapter.)

The Soviet Union voted in the General Assembly in 1947 for the partition of Palestine, providing for the establishment of a Jewish state. The Soviets were the first to recognize Israel formally in 1948, edging the United States. But the Soviets were unhappy when Israel pursued Western-style democracy, not communism. In 1967, after the Six-Day War, the Soviet Union broke off diplomatic relations with Israel. For the next twenty years contacts were rare, almost nonexistent. Yet sometimes, when a rare contact took place, perhaps at the United Nations, the human dimension broke through. Prime Minister Yitzhak Shamir says that on one occasion he was speaking to Foreign Secretary Andrei Gromyko and the Soviet official turned to him and said, "Do you see this hand? It is the one I lifted in the United Nations in 1947 that helped establish the Jewish state."

Despite the Soviets' hostility toward Israel and their arming of Egypt and Syria, Menachem Begin never forgot what the Soviet Union had done for Israel and the Jews. "Thanks to the Soviet Union hundreds of thousands of Jews were saved from Nazi hands," he wrote. "When the Soviet Union concluded, if only temporarily, that our striving for Jewish independence in Palestine was not a comedy dictated by British imperialists, but a purpose as serious as death . . . it helped us to achieve the first stage of our independence."[10] As is clear from his remark, whatever charity Begin felt toward the Russians, he

---

10. Menachem Begin, *The Revolt* (Jerusalem: Steimatzky, 1977), 13.

felt none whatsoever toward the despised British. Israel's first minister to the Soviet Union was Golda Meir, who was born in Kiev. In 1948, on Rosh Hashanah, the Jewish New Year, while she was on diplomatic duty in the U.S.S.R., she went to Moscow's Great Synagogue. On coming out, to her astonishment, a crowd of close to fifty thousand awaited her, calling "Nasha Golda" (our Golda), "shalom," and crying.[11] But the Soviets did not take kindly to her plea for Soviet Jews to emigrate to Israel. In 1984, the Soviets arrested and interrogated former Israel president Ephraim Katzir during his visit. President Herzog called it a "despicable act . . . an impardonable insult."

The United States supported the Arab cause at the critical moments after World War I, just as it quickly recognized Israel in 1948. President Woodrow Wilson approved Faisal's request that the Arabs be recognized as "independent sovereign peoples," and suggested a four-power commission of inquiry go to Syria to negotiate. Only the United States went ahead with the Allies' commission of inquiry; the other three powers backing out. The American commissioners, Henry King and Charles Crane, favored a mandatory system for Syria-Palestine and Iraq for a limited period aimed at bringing them to independence as quickly as possible.

The United States and Israel have been like lovers who quarrel occasionally but whose bond is never in doubt. (I am indebted to *Israel: The Embattled Ally,* by Nadav Safran, for much of the following discussion.) Safran speaks repeatedly of the United States' "moral interest" in Israel.

As we have suggested earlier, the American commitment to Israel is based on the Judeo-Christian tradition—a highly influential and articulate Jewish community in the United States and the 50 million to 60 million fundamentalist and evangelical Christian Americans, many of whom believe that modern Israel is the fulfillment of biblical prophecy. This broad popular support is best expressed politically through Congress, which always has been supportive of Israel. The chinks in this support generally have taken place in the State Department; professional diplomats are

---

11. Golda Meir, *My Life* (New York: Dell, 1975), 240.

more sensitive to the Middle East as a whole and thus more likely to be responsive to Arab sensitivities. Truman flouted the recommendations of the State Department in his recognition of Israel in 1948.

Every president from Truman to Reagan has supported Israel, especially at election time. But secretaries of state—notably Republicans John Foster Dulles during the Eisenhower administration, William Rogers during the Nixon administration, and Henry Kissinger in the Nixon and Ford administrations—have sought to court and woo the Arabs countries as well.

U.S.-Israeli relations may be summarized in the following manner.

Exodus

Initially, most Americans took a romantic view toward the renewed state of Israel as dramatized in Leon Uris's novel, *Exodus*. This was especially true of American Jews, and fundamentalist and evangelical Christians who saw God's "chosen people" giving fresh life to the Land of the Bible. Americans in general saw Israel as the well-deserved home for the Jewish people in the wake of the Holocaust. They also saw Israel as a youthful, lean, dynamic nation capable of miracles comparable to what the biblical Israelites had experienced. Probably few Americans stopped to consider that solving the Jewish problem might aggravate an Arab problem.

America and the Baghdad Pact

In the "cold war" following World War II, Eisenhower's secretary of state, John Foster Dulles, tried to organize the northern tier of the Middle East as a key part of a "massive retaliation" against encroaching communism. Thus, the 1955 Baghdad Pact was conceived. This was an alliance of Turkey, Iran, and Pakistan, the Arab country of Iraq and one Western country, Britain. The Soviet Union, Israel, and southern Arab nations observed this development with alarm, each for its own reasons. In 1958, the pro-American government in Iraq was overthrown; the new government proclaimed its support for Arab solidarity and closer ties with the Soviet Union.

136

Partly as a consequence of the Baghdad Pact, the Soviet Union agreed in 1955 to sell Egypt $100 million worth of arms, giving the Russians a significant, long-sought inroad in the Middle East. This time the United States was alarmed. To placate Egypt's Nasser, Dulles offered to help Egypt build a new Aswan Dam while spurning Israel's plea for arms. But then Dulles withdrew the offer and encouraged the French to supply Israel with arms. A few days later, on July 26, 1956, Nasser retaliated by nationalizing the French-and British-owned Suez Canal Company—eighty-seven long years after the Suez had been opened. Nasser also defied the U.N. Security Council and closed the Suez to Israeli shipping. Three months later, Israel, Britain, and France went to war against Egypt. In the United Nations, the United States and the Soviet Union joined in calling for a quick end to the fighting and an immediate withdrawal of foreign troops from Egypt.

Safran points out that the outcome of these events greatly enhanced Nasser's stature as a leader of Arab nationalism and the position of the Soviets as his proven friends. (I first visited Egypt in 1964. At the Aswan dam site, Russian equipment and one thousand eight hundred Russians were much in evidence among the thirty thousand workers, dumping granite rock and dune sand into the Nile to create the embankment. Russian cars sped along the blacktop between the dam and the town of Aswan. Three months later, Soviet leader Nikita Khrushchev paid a triumphant visit for the formal closure of the dam. When I returned to Aswan fourteen years later in the press entourage with President Jimmy Carter, how things had changed! The Egyptians had replaced the Soviets with the Americans. Carter held a brief meeting with Egyptian President Anwar Sadat, a conversation that was one of the developments leading to the 1979 Egyptian-Israeli peace treaty.)

The Rogers Plan

The one-thousand-day Kennedy administration sought to promote a rift between Egypt and the Soviet Union by associating the United States with Nasser's Arab socialism. "The new thesis prevailing in Washington was that the United States should be on the side of those forces in the Third World that would have a decisive voice in politics in the future," one analyst said.[12] "With reference to the Arab world it meant that the United States should range itself on the side of the 'progressive' forces such as Egypt's Nasser and his followers throughout the Arab world." The Kennedy administration also sent defensive Hawk missiles to Israel; this was the first time the United States had supplied arms.

The Johnson administration sought to maintain a balance of power between Israel and the Arab countries, and thus sent large quantities of "offensive" tanks and fifty *Phantom* fighter-bombers to the Jewish state.

With the election of Richard Nixon in 1968, the United States pursued aggressive diplomacy. His first secretary of state, William P. Rogers, quickly proposed a cease-fire in the dispiriting War of Attrition; and in what came to be known as the Rogers Plan, he proposed a binding Israeli-Egyptian peace treaty. This treaty would be based on an Israeli withdrawal from lands conquered in the 1967 War, free navigation, settlement of the Palestinian refugee problem—itself based on repatriation or compensation—and the uniting of Jerusalem by Jordan and Israel in an agreement reflecting the interests of the three dominant faiths.

When the War of Attrition heated up in its final stages, Nasser went to Moscow to ask for more arms, but was rebuffed. So he returned to Cairo and accepted Roger's proposal for a cease-fire in August 1970. The Egyptian move away from the Soviets and toward the Americans took on momentum.

The 1973 War and the Egyptian Tilt toward the U.S.

With Richard Nixon deeply enmeshed in the unraveling of the Watergate cover-up and Vice-President Spiro T. Agnew resigning, Secretary of State Henry Kissinger was free to dictate U.S. policy during the 1973 Yom Kippur War. He used pressure to persuade the Israelis to permit supplies to reach the trapped Egyp-

---

12. George Lenczowski, *The Middle East in World Affairs*, 4th ed. (Ithaca: Cornell), 803.

tian army at the war's end. This act helped persuade Sadat that it was the United States, not the Soviet Union, that could influence Israel and thus help shape events in the Middle East. Thus, the long process that would climax with the 1979 Egyptian-Israeli peace treaty was set in motion.

Kissinger's subsequent "shuttle diplomacy" kept up the momentum. His jetting back and forth between Mideast capitals resulted in Sinai I, disengagement agreements between Israel and Egypt in January 1974, and Israel and Syria in May 1974; and in Sinai II, an agreement between Israel and Egypt in September 1975.

Jimmy Carter and the 1979 Camp David Accords

On November 20, 1977, in the most dramatic development so far in the long Israeli-Arab struggle for peace, Anwar Sadat flew to Jerusalem. In Washington, President Jimmy Carter went to the First Baptist Church and offered a public prayer for peace.

Less than a year later, Carter summoned Israel's Menachem Begin and Egypt's Anwar Sadat to rustic Camp David atop the Catoctin Mountains; there they stayed for nearly two weeks. It was an unusual triumvirate. Sadat was a Moslem and Begin a hard-liner member of the Likud bloc in Israel. Carter was a devout Christian who had taken office eighteen months earlier with no experience in foreign affairs. His interest in the Middle East probably was born in what he once called "a childhood steeped in the Bible." Several times during his first year in office he had spoken of "a Palestinian homeland," something no previous American president had ever done.

"They and we as Christians worship the same God," Carter said. "I think they understand the prophecy in Isaiah (19:23-24), as applying to both peoples, that peace between Egypt and Israel is foreordained by God and that they play a role in carrying out God's purposes." Ironically, it was during this period that the Palestinians mounted their worst guerrilla attacks against the Israelis (see chapter 2).

When Carter, Sadat, and Begin descended from the summit, they had agreed on a framework for a peace treaty. And the following March, in a ceremony on the White House north lawn, the three men signed the Egyptian-Israeli Peace Treaty.

Reagan, Pollard and Irangate

President Ronald Reagan proposed a plan in 1982 for a Palestinian homeland "in association" with Jordan, a proposal that acknowledged the large number of Palestinians in Jordan but did not recognize the PLO as their spokesman. Reagan's secretary of state, George P. Shultz, was considered by many to be one of the strongest supporters Israel had had in that post.

Numerous incidents proved an embarrassment to both Israel and the United States in the eighties. Jonathan Pollard, an American Jew, did the unthinkable—he spied for Israel against its closest ally, the United States, giving Israel secret information on the U.S. Navy. Dan Fisher of the *Los Angeles Times* reported that Pollard made contact with Rafael Eytan, the head of Israel Defense Ministry's Bureau of Scientific Affairs. Israel apologized for the incident and Eytan was removed from his post.[13] After being arrested in November 1985, Pollard was sentenced to life in prison. His wife, Anne Henderson-Pollard, pleaded guilty to lesser charges and went to prison. Israel insisted that despite rumors to the contrary, it carried on no other espionage activities against the United States.

The following year, Israel acted as a middleman between the United States and Iran by selling arms to the despised Khomeini regime. The sale caused a political crisis for President Reagan, but Israel defended itself with "clean hands."

"We were asked to help the U.S. on limited terms," Shimon Peres, who was prime minister at the time, said later, to help win release of the American hostages and to find out if contact might be made with possible successors to Ayatollah Ruhollah Khomeini. "In that end, Israel helped bone fide on a limited

---

13. See p. 49.
14. From a public address; see n. 2, chap. 1.

operation. We don't feel we have to apologize for it.[14] He said Israel also acted out of concern for Iranian Jews.

Almost $1,000 in U.S. Aid for Every Israeli

The Americans' largesse for Israel has been sizable and steadily increasing. The United States appropriated $3 billion in foreign assistance for 1988—$1.2 billion in economic support, and $1.8 billion in foreign military sales credit. It figures out to almost $1,000 for every Jewish man, woman, and child in Israel. This does not include the massive donations by American Jews and Christians, or the purchase of bonds, or tourism.

PART II
THE SONS OF ABRAHAM

6

Isaac's Children

On that day the Lord made a covenant with Abram and said, "To your descendants I give this land, from the river of Egypt to the great river, the river Euphrates. . . ."
—Gen. 15:18, repeated in Deuteronomy 11:24, Joshua 1:4

The Jews of Israel

Noonday traffic in Jerusalem on Fridays is the worst imaginable. If it were your misfortune to have to attend a special briefing at the Foreign Ministry at 11 A.M., and then drive back through the markets in the Mahane Yehuda neighborhood to Beit Agron—a distance of only 1.5 miles—you would face the maddening ordeal of barely crawling, bumper-to-bumper traffic. But then by 1 or 1:30 P.M., almost abruptly, the streets would empty and become silent. Shabbat was coming to Jerusalem, and the city would remain quiet, almost inert, until dusk Saturday. Then, on Saturday night the city would turn lively once again.

The Ultra-Orthodox

Jerusalem is a "holy city," but the Shabbat is not the only sign. An ever-increasing number of ultra-Orthodox Jews live in Jerusalem. They are the "blacks," easily identified by the black hats, suits, and shoes worn by the men; the long-sleeved dresses of the women; and the large number of children frequently in their tow.

Jerusalem's uniqueness spills over into official public life, often in shocking ways. A train hit a school bus in June 1985, killing

145

twenty-one children from Petah Tikva, near Tel-Aviv. Interior Minister Yitzhak Peretz of the Sephardi Tora Guardians (Shas), an ultra-Orthodox party, declared the tragedy was "divine retribution" over the opening of a cinema in Petah Tikva on Friday nights.

A year earlier, one of Peretz's colleagues in the Shas party, Rabbi Shimon Ben-Shlomo, blamed Israel's many casualties in Lebanon on the promiscuity of female Israeli soldiers.

During the summer of 1985, Arabs accosted and killed three Israeli couples in out of the way places. In each case, as it turned out, the couples were not married to each other. Partly in jest, this writer called the Interior Ministry to ask if Peretz felt God was using the slayings to punish adulterous relationships. Instead of hanging up in disgust at the query, a spokesman said, "I'll check." A few moments later, the spokesman called back and said, "I asked the Interior minister and he said no, he doesn't think so."

"God is punishing Israel through its current economic crisis for having gone wrong," the chief rabbis told this writer.

Two Israeli soldiers, seriously burned in a bombing near the Lebanese border, were taken to Hadassah Hospital in Jerusalem in desperate need of skin grafts. But a few years earlier, the Orthodox community had pushed through the Knesset the Pathology Law prohibiting the storage of human organs for transplantation. Hence, Hadassah had no skin bank and when the wounded soldiers arrived, no donors were immediately available. Because of the ultra-Orthodox, no skin was available for the soldiers who had risked their lives in war for Israel.

Unbelievable? Consider this: The Neturei Kartho ("Guardians of the Holy City") Organization of Orthodox Jewry in Jerusalem congratulated Yasser Arafat and expressed a desire to become "loyal subjects" of the PLO in a Palestinian nonsectarian state. Rabbi Moshe Hirsch and the Neturei Kartho reject Zionism and the modern state of Israel. Looking forward to the coming of the Messiah as the one who will create the real Israel, they told Arafat: "until that time, we are bound by divine oaths to take no concerted or forcible action to regain the Land on our own."

Many orthodox men wear *kippas,* or skull caps, the only outward sign of their devotion. The ultra-Orthodox Jews are much more obvious. They wear the black suits, long jackets, hats, and earlocks in every season. One wonders how they survive in the summer heat. The attire actually is patterned after that worn by the eastern European gentry and nobility, their persecutors. They have appropriated it for themselves now. Although they are often called "the blacks," the more formal name for them is the Hassidim.

In *The Witness*, an American movie about the Amish people, a little Amish boy goes to the railroad station in Philadelphia for the first time in his life. He is awestruck by it all. Then he sees what he thinks is an Amish man, dressed in a black hat, a long black coat—a reassuring figure to the lad. The man has a *Jerusalem Post* tucked under his arm; he is a Hassidic Jew and bewildered by the boy's familiarity. It's a touching scene, although to be really pure about it, an ultra-Orthodox Jew would not be reading *The Jerusalem Post!*

The ultra-Orthodox, like many zealots, have a tendency to be ugly. They are utterly oblivious to the existence of anyone else—that is, unless one of their laws is broken. In Mea Shearim, their neighborhood in Jerusalem, many, many signs are posted warning against any travel in the neighborhood by auto, and warning women against appearing with bare arms or other "indecent" apparel. But they object as well to driving anywhere in Jerusalem. I was once driving in West Jerusalem on a Friday night and an ultra-Orthodox man shouted at me, "Shabbat! Shabbat!" I couldn't resist rolling down my window and shouting back, "*Hesed! Hesed!*" *Hesed* is the Hebrew word for "mercy." They once beat up Mayor Teddy Kollek for making an appearance there on a Shabbat. If one drives on a holy day or on the Shabbat, one can be stoned, if he or she encounters "the blacks." Or if a woman strolls in Mea Shearim with uncovered arms, she can expect the same treatment. It is difficult to make an arrest because all the ultra-Orthodox look alike; and they will gang up on anyone, including police, who tries to restrain them.

On an airliner, they can be seen reading their Hebrew Bibles and dipping their heads rapidly in prayer, or eating their own food—as if they were the only persons on the plane. They spend much of their time locked in study and vigorous discussion on some minor point. I once walked by a group of them on Mount Zion and heard them debating how Aaron's wife Elizabeth died. (The Bible doesn't say.) They are committed to Israel as a spiritual or messianic concept, and they therefore have little to do with the State of Israel. Many of them resist and actively oppose the government of Israel.

The last story I covered on assignment in Israel was the widespread burning and vandalizing of Jerusalem's attractive bus shelters by ultra-Orthodox Jews who were offended by the shelter advertisements showing bare limbs. "They want to impose standards on the streets by their laws," said the mayor's spokesman, Rafi Davara. "They start [attacking] bare limbs and will end [attacking] any photo of a girl. Next year it will be any photo of a boy."

My colleague James Dorsey went to the police station about 2 A.M. one night when he found his car had been broken into. At that same time, police dragged in a Hassidic boy, his earlocks flying and carrying a bucket of paint. "What have you been doing?" the policeman demanded of him. "Studying with my rabbi!" the terrified boy said creatively.

Hasidism grew in eastern Europe in the eighteenth century in response to the climate of the times. Jewish learning and scholarship had reached a zenith in the sixteenth century but declined in the next century because of the virulent anti-Semitism. Israel Ben Eliezer, the founder of Hasidism, felt that the Judaism of his day had lost important principles. Also known as the Baal Shem Tov, he saw in the Judaism of Eastern Europe a tendency to rote, hair-splitting observance of the Law, an imbalanced emphasis on learning, and a lack of fervor and joy. This general depression, or *atsvoot*, was the No. 1 enemy of man, in the Baal Shem Tov's view. In the beginning, the Hassidim emphasize faith over learning, service over power. These "Hassidim" would have as their goal to be absolutely aflame with prayer and spirituality. They would sing and dance freely, and this they did; one account even tells of someone somersaulting during prayer in his excitement.

This seems a far cry from the deadly somber Hassidic of the current day. Patricia Behre, who studied at Hebrew University, has made a fascinating comparison of Jesus and the Baal Shem

Tov. Both were pitted against the religious establishment of their day, she says, both worked miracles and taught through parables, and both emphasized faith rather than rote observance of the Law. "It should be noted, however, that the Baal Shem remains a human figure with a slight trace—though not much—of human frailty, while Jesus, particularly as portrayed in the Gospel of John, is identified as clearly divine," Behre wrote in an unpublished paper.

For the journalist, especially the foreign correspondent, the ultra-Orthodox are the least covered group in Israel. Abraham Rabinovich, a native New Yorker who was assigned to them for *The Jerusalem Post* for five years, told me it is very hard to cover them. They have no spokesmen, no sources, and they won't talk.

The ultra-Orthodox are increasing in numbers—they have very large families—and in influence. As we have noted, the Labor and the Likud have had to strike deals with the religious parties in order to gain power, agreeing to the demands of the religious parties in exchange for their support. Safran has pointed out that other parties have broad-based platforms regarding domestic and foreign policies; and deals with Labor or the Likud have been difficult to make. The religious parties, however, have been willing to let Labor or the Likud have its way on all other issues provided they got their way on religious matters.[1]

One key issue in which the religious parties have not prevailed in the Knesset thus far, despite annual attempts, is the "Who is a Jew?" legislation. That bill, technically, is an amendment to the Law of Return, which makes all Jews eligible for Israeli citizenship if they claim it. It would restrict the definition of a Jew to those born of a Jewish mother or converted by Orthodox rabbis. This would rule out Jews converted through Reform or Conservative Jewry—the major and liberal branches of Judaism in the United States. At most, only about a dozen new immigrants a year would be affected were this legislation to pass. Knesset member Avner Sciaky of the National Religious Party vows, "We will bring it back again and again, until we are successful with the help of God."

Many Jews and Gentiles say the rising numbers and influence of

---

1. Safran, 207.

the ultra-Orthodox have become the most serious problem facing Israel. Mayor Teddy Kollek has said that the population of the religious Jews in Jerusalem is increasing by five hundred families a year, while that of secular Jews grows by two hundred families. All other conflict, including that of Arab and Jew, pales into insignificance beside this. It is a battle of zealots vs. secularists, not dissimilar from battles being waged in Islam and Christianity. "Israel is fighting a holy war," it has been said partly in jest, "and the problem is that God is winning."

About 14 percent of all Israeli Jews observe religious tradition strictly, 20 percent do so to a large extent, 41 percent do so to a small extent, and 25 percent do not at all. More than half of them read the Tanach (the Old Testament) seldom or never, and only one in five reads the Scripture very often. These findings were based on a July 1983 sampling. The Bible Society commissioned the Israeli Institute of Applied Social Research, in collaboration with Hebrew University's Communications Institute, to measure public attitudes toward the Bible and religious institutions. Curiously, the Ashkenazi Jew was more likely to own a New Testament, the Sephardic Jew more likely to read it.

The kosher laws make exchanges of entertaining difficult. When my wife and I entertained, we always had to be very careful with our menu. Observant Jews simply cannot eat food prepared in a Gentile's kitchen, although Gentiles obviously have no problem eating in a Jewish home. My wife and the widow of an orthodox rabbi downstairs got around the difficulty, whenever she was our guest, in this way; the lady would bring her own food and eating utensils. Becky served from the kitchen and none of the other guests was the wiser.

One holiday we had two guests for dinner; one, a government official, and the other, an Israeli journalist. They both came about a half-hour late, which is the Middle-Eastern custom. "Well! You both arrived at the same time," I greeted them, somewhat stating the obvious. "Oh, no," said the official, who was Orthodox, but not especially strict. "I've been downstairs waiting for someone to open the door or ring the buzzer." Because it was a holy day, to have rung the buzzer or opened the door would have constituted work, and that would have been a sin.

About dusk, while the guests were still there, the telephone rang. It was the official's son. "I can't talk to him because I haven't read my prayer book yet for the end of the Shabbat," the official told my wife. "He wants to use your car" Becky told him. "Tell him that he will have to bring over my prayer book first," the official said. Soon, the son arrived. The official gave the prayer book a fast scan and then said, "OK, you can have the car!"

Many hotels have elevators that stop automatically on every floor on the Shabbat and holy days, so that guests won't have to push the button. Our next-door neighbors, the Samuelses, despite their advanced age, worked on behalf of others in Katamon, the poor neighborhood of Jerusalem. But from Friday evening until Saturday evening every week not a sound would be heard from their apartment, nor would we see a light, for they observed the day strictly.

The Temple

The temple was built on Mount Moriah by Solomon (1 Kings 6–7; 2 Chronicles 2–4) in 950 B.C. The site was Mount Moriah, where Abraham had prepared to offer his son Isaac as a sacrifice to God (Genesis 22) centuries earlier. Actually, Mount Moriah is less than a half mile from the city of the Jebusites which had been inhabited at an even earlier date, and it is altogether possible they observed what Abraham was about to do.

Solomon's temple was destroyed by Nebuchadnezzer in 587 B.C. (2 Kings 25:9; 2 Chronicles 36:19) and Herod's rebuilt temple was destroyed by the Romans under Titus in A.D. 70. On that site the Dome of the Rock was built in the seventh century to mark the place where, according to Islamic tradition, the prophet Mohammed began his nighttime journey to heaven. Now the Dome of the Rock is the third most holy site to Moslems. All that remains of the Jewish temple is the western part of the foundation—the Western or Wailing Wall, as it frequently is called—the most holy site in Judaism. To many Jews, the most significant aspect of the 1967 Six-Day War was Israel's capture of the Old City, thus enabling the Jews to return to the Wailing Wall for the first time in twenty years. Since the destruction of the Second Temple, Jews have been prohibited from going on Temple Mount lest they walk unwittingly on holy places.

Many Jews and Christians believe the temple must be rebuilt as a precursor to the coming of the Messiah (for the Jews, the first time, and for Christians, the second!). They base this on Daniel 9:25–27, which speaks of restoring Jerusalem before the coming of "the anointed one." This was why some ultra-Orthodox Jews have plotted to blow up the Dome of the Rock and thus "cleanse" Temple Mount. Some Christian fundamentalists in the United States have raised money to support a project to rebuild the temple. This is the central purpose of a group called "The Jerusalem Temple Foundation," which is incorporated in the United States. Its theme is "Build Thy Temple Speedily."

Any such act probably would lead to a holy war between Moslems and Jews, with much bloodshed. It is well to remember that God would not let David build the first temple because his reign had been so bloody (1 Chronicles 22:8 and 28:3). (See also pp. 191, 192.)

Secular Jews

An Israeli journalist of my acquaintance has an unusual personal life. Raven-haired, striking in her appearance, and verbal, she is a war widow who now lives with another man. Both have children from previous marriages and they have had one child together. The relationship she had with her late husband, the fallen soldier, she says nonchalantly, was the least satisfactory. After her husband was killed in the war, she and a new boyfriend—"a conceptual artist," she told me—went to the Dead Sea, scooped up a jar of water, and flew to South Africa. There, at the confluence of the Atlantic and Indian oceans, they poured out the water from the Dead Sea.

She frequently asked an American woman journalist why she didn't find "a bronzed young Israeli soldier and leap into bed." Her casual attitude toward sex, and life, is typical of many Israelis. Premarital sex, for instance, is accepted as a way of life among many. If two people are dating, it is assumed they are sleeping together.

This journalist was also a member of Peace Now, an Israeli anti-war group that believes in complete equality for Arabs. One day she and I traveled to Bir Zeit University near Ramallah to cover a student demonstration that had erupted into bloodshed when Israeli soldiers fired and killed one student. On the way, she told me how much she resisted the "don'ts" of Judaism, especially in eating and holy-day practices. She asked me whether the Christian faith has such prohibitions. I replied, not really, but yes, there are some things that Christians don't do—not so much because they are intrinsically wrong, but because they are not edifying. I told her about the centrality of Jesus Christ and added that the Christian is more committed to justice and mercy than to prohibitions against certain things. "Oh!" she interrupted cheerily, "I may be more of a Christian than a Jew."

Estimates vary as to the number of secular Jews in Israel. Safran estimates that about half of the Israelis are secular and a third of the people are "determined secularizers." My own opinion is that belief and devoutness take on a bell-shaped curve—about 20 percent of the people are Orthodox, about 20 percent are secular, and the balance are somewhere in between.

The Jaffe Center for Strategic Studies at Tel Aviv University asked 1,172 Israelis to identify the "guardian" in the verse, "The guardian of Israel slumbers not, nor sleeps" (Psalm 121:4, Jaffe translation). According to the poll, 57 percent said the "guardian" is "the army," 17 percent said "God," 13 percent said "the State of Israel," and 10 percent said "the United States."

The chief rabbis dispute the contention that Israel is secular. Eliyahu told me that the eating of kosher food, even though this practice is more expensive, and the observance of the Jewish holidays show that Israelis as a whole are not secular. "I do not ignore the fact that, here and there, there are some people who have opinions against (religion) but those are very few," he said. "Most of the nation is comprised of people who love tradition, keep it, love the Torah, and try as much as they can to fulfill the laws and rules of the people of Israel."

Many secular Jews are returning to orthodoxy. We personally knew of one Jew, a handsome, swarthy, former El Al steward. He lived a profligate life, but then turned to orthodoxy and began to live a disciplined life. In this new devotion, he rarely looked at women, let alone talk with or touch one. He knew he had to make a total break with his past. And he changed from modish attire to ultra-Orthodox garb. His friends would not recognize him when they bumped into him.

Ashkenazi and Sephardic

My wife was in Hadassah Hospital in Jerusalem for three weeks while she was carrying Elizabeth. The first week or so, she was in a small room with five Jews, all Sephardics; and for two more weeks she shared a room with Ashkenazi Jews. This was near the time of the 1984 national elections. She found that all of the Sephardics were conservative and would vote for the Likud and Shamir. They spoke only Hebrew. They were hostile toward Arabs, but had respect for the religious Jews. It was just the opposite in the other room. Several of the Ashkenazis were members of Peace Now, the peace movement that grew to large proportions during the invasion of Lebanon, and all of them spoke English. They were sympathetic with Arabs; all were college graduates.

Israel suffers from a sort of cultural schizophrenia. Ashkenazi is a Hebrew word meaning German, and Ashkenazi Jews came from Europe, especially Eastern Europe. The Ashkenazi Jews were the dominant Jews to come to Israel in the early years of Zionism. They got acclimated, went into the professions, and assumed the leadership positions in the new state. The Labor Party's name may suggest that is is composed of the working class, but in actual fact, it has been the party of the professional as well. It was the leading political force in Israel for the first thirty years and it actually became the "establishment" party. David Ben-Gurion and Golda Meir were Ashkenazi Jews, as are Menachem Begin, Yitzhak Shamir and Shimon Peres. Because the Ashkenazis were Europeans, Israel took on a Western hue from the beginning and, indeed, has been considered a Western nation. Much of the early success of Israel was considered due to the industriousness and ingenuity of the European Jews. And, as often is the case, the establishment and the *nouveau riche* succumbed to the temptation of becoming arrogant and insensitive.

Now, however, the Ashkenazis are outnumbered by the Sephardics. Of Israel's 82 percent-Jewish population, Sephardics comprise 42 percent and Ashkenazi 40 percent.

The name *Sephardic* (see Obadiah 20) means Spanish, and refers to the Jews who were expelled from Spain during the Inquisition in 1492, the year Columbus discovered America for Ferdinand and Isabella. Nowadays, Sephardic is taken to mean the Oriental Jew, but this, too, is misleading. The simplest way to define Sephardic Jews is to say they come from Arab countries. Centuries ago they were the elite among the Jews, but now they are poorer and less educated than the Ashkenazis. The presence of the Sephardim has made Israel, in effect, a typical Middle Eastern country. Their pace is much slower, there is more intrigue, compared with the Ashkenazim.

Modern Israel, in short, is a western-styled nation that acts in an eastern manner, and the result is often chaotic.

Actually, the 25,000 to 50,000 Jews in Palestine in 1882 at the start of the *aliyot* (the Hebrew word for "going up" that has come to refer to the return to the Promised Land) were mostly Sephardim. Yemenite Jews and the descendants of the Jews who had been expelled from Spain arrived before the influx of European Jews.

The majority of immigrants who swarmed to Israel in the first three years after statehood were Ashkenazim. From then on, however, the majority have been Sephardim. In 1949, the entire Yemenite Jewish community of thirty five thousand arrived. About one hundred thousand came from Iraq in 1951, following in the path of another Iraqi, the patriarch Abraham. From 1952 to 1968, between 30 and 40 percent of the immigrants came from Morocco, among them David Levy, about whom we will have more to say.[2]

Even though Menachem Begin is an Ashkenazi Jew, he knew how to touch a responsive chord with the flood of Sephardic Jews in the country and was able to convert this to a Likud

---

2. Friedlander and Goldscheider, 13, 21.

victory in 1977. This demonstrates how critical a proper sensitivity or perceived sensitivity is in politics. In 1984, the Likud bloc was burdened with an unpopular war in Lebanon and inflation was raging at a rate of 400 percent a year—a sure-fire formula for losing an election. Yet, the Likud managed to break even in the election and go on to help form a coalition government. The shrewd Kahane, who is not a Sephardic, freely admits he believes his route to electoral success will be through courting the Sephardim.

One of the families that arrived from Spain in the 1500s was that of Yitzhak Navon, the former president of Israel and now perhaps the state's most beloved politician. His family is one of the three oldest in Jerusalem. His mother, who was born in Morocco, learned to read and write at age sixty-five so she could write him while he was a diplomat assigned to Argentina. The affable Navon, a member of the Labor party, speaks several languages and is a playwright as well. (I saw the sixty-seven-year-old Navon one day at a reception, accompanied by his son, and I overheard a well-dressed, unctuous woman say to him, "Oh, President Navon, how proud you must be of your grandson!" He smiled graciously and said, "My son." She evaporated.)

David Levy was born in Morocco and was among the thousands of Sephardic Jews who emigrated to Israel in 1957. He was nineteen. He toiled as a construction worker in Beit Shean, got involved in the Histadrut labor federation, and wound up in the Knesset as a member of the Likud. Today, he is deputy prime minister and housing minister, and considered the most likely of the new generation in Israel to become prime minister. He is well-coiffed and dapper—and does not speak English. Nadav Safran, sixty-two, the Harvard scholar, was born in Cairo and fought for the Israelis in the War of Independence. Victor Smadja, fifty-three, whose father was a wool trader in Tunisia, came to Israel about the same time as Levy. Now Smadja operates a major commercial printing press in Jerusalem and is the leader of the Messianic Jewish community in Israel.

Ashkenazi arrogance through the years was only partially balanced by the fact that the Sephardim had not endured the Holocaust and the other persecutions in Europe. While the Ashkenazim were in control of the government, they did not use Sephardic spokesmen—as well they might have very effectively—to make the point in world opinion that the number of Jewish refugees from Arab countries was about equal to the number of Palestinian refugees in Israeli-conquered territories.

Whatever polarization might exist between Ashkenazi and Sephardic, Navon feels, is being solved by intermarriage. A decade ago, 11 percent of all marriages were mixed; in 1984, the percentage had risen to 23 percent. The educational gap is narrowing. In years past, less than half of the Sephardic Jews finished elementary school; now 95 percent finish.

The Ashkenazim and the Sephardim each have a chief rabbi in Israel, who, together, form the Chief Rabbinate. This office was formed in 1921 during the British mandate to oversee religious law, which includes regulations dealing with diet, the Shabbat, marriage, and divorce. The chief rabbis are elected for five-year terms by a council of rabbis and laymen. Avraham Shapira, 67, is the Ashkenazi chief rabbi, and Mordechai Eliyahu, 56, the Sephardic chief rabbi. But we are leaping far ahead of our story which actually began around four thousand years ago.

The Promised Land

Abraham was a wealthy cattleman living in what is now Iraq when the Lord's call came: "Pull up stakes, and leave." Abraham had already moved his belongings into Canaan when the promise came. That piece of land, from the river of Egypt (probably not the Nile but the Wadi el'Arish in the middle of the Sinai) to the Euphrates River, including Lebanon, would belong to Abraham and his descendants. The Lord also promised to make him "a great nation" (Gen. 12:2). (As a matter of fact, the descendants of Abraham almost never have occupied that much real estate. David's (1 Chronicles 18:3) and Solomon's (1 Kings 4:21 and 2 Chronicles 9:26) drives in the tenth century B.C. were about the only times. Israel is the most powerful state in the region today, but it in no way compares to its relative strength and size in Solomon's day. Ariel Sharon, who was architect of Israel's 1982 invasion of Lebanon, has talked about taking the east bank of the

Jordan, but no reasonable person has proposed another drive to the Euphrates.)

Moshe Dayan describes what this change of land meant to Abraham:

> In his northern birthplace, Ur of the Chaldees in Mesopotamia, springs gush forth in abundance, rains pour from the heavens, green pastures and golden cornfields flourish, and the land is alive with sheep and cattle, with men, women and children. In the south, whither Abraham turned his face, all was desert. In the Negev, in Beer-sheba, and beyond Mount Hermon, rainfall is slight, pastureland is poor, springs are meager and the population is sparse.[3]

But Abraham went without hesitation.

The same promise was repeated to Isaac and Jacob (Genesis 26:3 and 35:12) as well as to Joshua (Josh. 1:3, 4). Some Jews—and Canadians—joke that Moses misunderstood God when he led the Israelites out of Egypt. Moses, who couldn't speak clearly himself, thought God had said Canaan when the divine order actually was to go to Canada!

From the beginning, the land, specifically *this* land, has been vital to the Jews. In Hebrew, they call it *Eretz Israel*, the Land of Israel, or, *Ha'aretz*, simply, the Land. The most respected newspaper in modern Israel is called *Ha-aretz*.

William D. Davies, whose books *The Gospel and the Land* and *Jewish Territorial Doctrine*[4] are classic treatments of the Jewish belief in the land, has said, "The implication is that Jewish sanctity, holiness, is only fully possible in The Land of Israel, and outside The Land only strictly personal laws can be fulfilled, that is, the moral law, sexual law, Shabbat law, circumcision, dietary laws, etc. . . . . The exiled life is, necessarily, an emaciated, broken, incomplete life."

Davies has said there is a sort of "umbilical cord" between the Land and Israel (Evangelical Round Table: Christianity and the Arab-Israeli Conflict, 1985, St. Davids, Penn.). "Alongside the

---

3. Moshe Dayan, *Living with the Bible* (New York: William Morrow, 1978), 15.

4. Published by the University of California Press (Berkeley and Los Angeles), 1974.

belief in the promise, the conviction prevailed that this promised land belonged peculiarly to Yahweh. . . . it was his peculiar possession to give to his own peculiar people: the election of the people was bound up with his promise to give his own land to them. . . . there emerged what has to be regarded as an essential belief of religious Jews . . . an indissoluble, eternal connection between these three: land, people and God." One-third of the Mishna, or Pharisaic legal code, and all the agricultural laws in the Old Testament are concerned with "the Land of Israel only."

Not all Christians accept the interpretation that the promise to Abraham was intended to translate into real estate for modern Israel. Colin Chapman, an evangelical Christian who has worked with university students in the Middle East since 1968, believes most prophetic passages dealing with the Land and Israel are intended to be fulfilled post-New Testament in a *spiritual* way.

Once the New Testament writers had seen the significance of the land and the nation in the context of the kingdom of God which had come into being in Jesus of Nazareth, they ceased to look forward to a literal fulfillment of Old Testament prophecies of a return to the land and a restored Jewish state. The one and only fulfillment of all the promises and prophecies was already there before their eyes in the person of Jesus.[5]

During the Diaspora the Jews never could erase the memory of the Land from their consciousness. While they were in exile in Babylon during the sixth century B.C., they cried, "How shall we sing the Lord's song in a foreign land? If I forget you, O Jerusalem, let my right hand wither!" (Psalm 137:4, 5). But their return from Babylon was only temporary. The Romans destroyed the temple in Jerusalem in about A.D. 70, and by the third century, the Jews were scattered throughout the world; only a few thousand remained in Palestine.

For long centuries Jews were scattered—discriminated against, segregated, and persecuted. As Nadav Safran has pointed out, it was unthinkable to the Jews to believe that God had reneged on

5. *Whose Promised Land?* (Herts, England: Lion Publishing, 1983), 153.

his promise. "Their suffering was only an episode and would have a sequel in their redemption and return to the land, Palestine." And the Jews' yearning cry at every celebration of the Passover was: "next year in Jerusalem!" Next year, in the Land of Israel, they would celebrate.

Over the centuries a mystique grew up around the notion of the Land. Although Jews gained a worldwide reputation as savvy merchants and traders, when Zionism emerged their inextricable devotion to the Land once again was demonstrated.

Modern Israelis say very little about God's promise of the Land to Abraham. Amos Elon, one of the two or three most prominent contemporary Israeli writers, wrote a book called *The Israelis: Founders and Sons* on the origins of modern Israel.[6] In it he talks at length about the ferment of ideas and the persecution of the Jews in eastern Europe in the late 1800s that led to the Jews' *aliyot*. But Elon makes not one mention of the promise to Abraham.

But the land is always present in Jewish consciousness, perhaps subliminally. David Ben-Gurion, the father of modern Israel, told a British commission in 1937, "I say on behalf of the Jews that the Bible is our Mandate, the Bible which was written by us, in our own language, in Hebrew in this very country. That is our Mandate."

As Conor Cruise O'Brien points out:

> Not only were their imaginations saturated in the Bible, but their burning faith in the restoration of the Chosen People to the Promised Land—even if they chose not to put it that way—made them, if not religious leaders, at least men fitted to lead those who saw their movement as essentially religious, and secular only in outward form.[7]

By and large, the ancient promise to Abraham and "the Land" have had a profound effect on modern Israel. The Jews *did* flock by the millions back to the land that God promised Abraham. They did not go to Uganda in East Africa, which was proposed as a possible homeland, or any other alternative spot. They went to

---

6. Published in Jerusalem by Adam in 1981.
7. Conor Cruise O'Brien, *The Siege: The Saga of Israel and Zionism* (New York: Simon and Schuster, 1986), 50.

Israel. Ben-Gurion said this of the return of the Jews to the Promised Land: "to become laborers, to work with our hands, was one of the basic purposes in our coming to the country—to build the land ourselves, rather than to leave the physical labor to the Arabs, and to create a Jewish working population rather than a class of overseers."[8]

I have seen Jews in Israel, even professional persons, turn to the land in a way that can't be fully explained in rational terms. Dr. Nissan has developed magnificent orchards and gardens in his homes at Migdal overlooking the Sea of Galilee and in Moza Ilit on the western slopes of Jerusalem, grafting limbs from one tree on another with surgical precision. He has planted a cedar of Lebanon and a date palm—a horticultural contradiction because cedars of Lebanon come from snowy mountains and date palms are a desert plant—side by side in his backyard just as the psalmist described (92:12, 13). The Jews' love for the land can't fully be explained.

Zionism

No more than thirty thousand Jews remained in Palestine at the time of Mohammed; the start of the Arabic immigration began in the seventh century. There were few Arabs in Palestine, if any, at that time. By 1882, when the Zionist return began, approximately 50,000 Jews and 500,000 Arabs were in Palestine.

Zionism, which is derived from the poetic name for Jerusalem, is the movement of the return of the Jews to the Promised Land.[9] It is the result of three things: (1) the intellectual ferment in Europe in the nineteenth century, the Enlightenment, a time of liberalism and the origins of nationalism, which spilled over and moved the Jews, (2) something that seemed a blatant contradiction of that liberalism, surging anti-Semitism, especially in eastern Europe and Russia, and (3) the biblical promise of the Land, although this was not spoken very much by the secular-minded Zionists.

---

8. Terrence Prittie, *Israel: Miracle in the Desert* (Baltimore: Penguin, 1967), 16.

9. The author is indebted for this discussion to Elon's *The Israelis: Founders and Sons*, 33–147, and Safran's *Israel: The Embattled Ally*, 14–32.

Zionism was a secular, nationalistic movement conceived in that ancient promise to Abraham, shaped in the womb of the ideas and ideals of the nineteenth-century Age of Enlightenment and Rationalism, and born in the persecution of anti-Semitism and the Russian pogroms.

Nationalism was flourishing in Europe in the early nineteenth century. The American and French revolutions had fed the flames of freedom. In the middle 1800s my own great-grandfather on my father's side left Germany for the United States; and a few years later, my maternal grandfather came to America from Norway. With France providing the model, the 1.5 million Jews in western Europe gained freedom and equality. But in Czarist Russia and Romania, things slid the other way; the assassination of the liberal Alexander II in Russia in 1881 ignited the worst pogroms or organized attacks against the Jews since the Middle Ages against the 6 million Jews in the *shtetls*, or communities, of eastern Europe. In the mass migration that followed, about 2.5 million Jews left, most of them for the United States; and a comparative handful went to Palestine. The Return had started.

The musical *Fiddler on the Roof* portrays sympathetically the ordeal that Russian Jews faced. In 1887 they were barred from attending universities and high schools in Russia so some of them started attending school in Germany and Switzerland, where they were exposed to revolutionary thought. Between 1891 and 1903 pogroms swept Russia, as Elon says, "partly government-inspired and partly government-ignored.[10] Havoc spread; Jews were killed, maimed, raped, robbed, and made homeless. It was the period of the great Russian literature. But Tolstoy remained silent and Dostoyevsky was anti-Semitic. There had been persecution of the Jews in Poland and the Ukraine in the seventeenth century, but this was the worst violence against the Jews since the Crusades nearly a millennium earlier.

Zionism in the nineteenth century had its prophets—and practitioners—too. Moses Hess wrote a Zionist tract, *Rome and Jerusalem*, in 1862, urging peaceful establishment of a socialist Jewish community in Palestine. A group of Hungarian Jews founded

---

10. Elon, 53.

Palestine's first new settlement, Petah Tikva ("Gate of Hope"), in 1878. Dr. Leo Pinsker, a Russian physician, wrote a pamphlet, *Auto-Emancipation*, in 1882, condemning anti-Semitism as an incurable disease and naming it as the main cause of the homelessness of the modern Jew. Moses Lilienblum, a former teacher at an orthodox seminary, became the first prominent ideologist of Jewish nationalism in Russia and inspired the first Jews who left Russia in 1882 to settle in Palestine.

A Lithuanian Jew named Eliezer Perlman arrived in Jerusalem in 1882, changed his name to Ben Yehuda, and set about to restore to life a language dead for centuries, Hebrew. His determination was awesome, if ignoble. Ben Yehuda told his wife on board ship they would speak nothing but Hebrew. Even though she was sickly, they did not obtain a maid lest she speak a language other than Hebrew in the presence of their son. His wife died in 1891 of tuberculosis contracted from her husband. When his aged mother, who did not know Hebrew, came to visit him, he refused to speak to her in anything but Hebrew. But Ben Yehuda's perseverance paid off; today, Israelis speak Hebrew. Ultra-Orthodox Jews, who oppose the use of Hebrew as an everyday language, continually rip a memorial plaque off Ben Yehuda's home across from the Ethiopian church in Jerusalem.

Theodor Herzl

The father of Zionism was Theodor Herzl, a Vienna reporter assigned to Paris. He covered the 1894 court martial that found a French army officer, Captain Alfred Dreyfus, a Jew, guilty of treason. Dreyfus was stripped of his rank and discharged amid cries, "Death to the Jews!" The conviction was based on perjured testimony, which was exposed four years later. Herzl was upset by the entire proceeding. He went on to initiate the First Zionist Congress in Basel, Switzerland, in 1897, which called specifically for a Jewish state in Palestine.

It will be helpful to take a closer look at what was happening concomitantly in Palestine and in Europe among the Jews. For nearly four hundred years Palestine had been under the control of the Turkish Ottoman Empire. The end of the empire came in

World War I and the division of the Middle East by the French and the British may well have been one of the most significant long-range results of that war (see chapter 5).

In November 1917, British Foreign Minister Arthur Balfour wrote a one-sentence letter to Lord Rothschild as representative of the Zionists. It said:

> His Majesty's Government view with favor the establishment in Palestine of a national home for the Jewish people, and will use their best endeavors to facilitate the achievements of this object, it being clearly understood that nothing shall be done which may prejudice the civil and religious rights of existing non-Jewish communities in Palestine, or the rights and political status enjoyed by Jews in any other country.

It became known as the Balfour Declaration and later was endorsed by the League of Nations. The Declaration was ambiguous, stating "national home" not "national homeland," and seeming not to deprive the Arabs of their personal rights. It was typical of the British at that time for simultaneously, Britain was wooing the Arabs into the war against the Ottoman Empire by promising them their independence, and collaborating with the French to divide up the Arab world after the war was over. The next month after Balfour, General Allenby walked through the Jaffa Gate into Jerusalem's walled Old City to claim Palestine for the British Empire.

Nearly seventy years later, Prime Minister Shimon Peres compared the Balfour Declaration to the declaration of Cyrus, king of Persia (Ezra 1:2–4). "Like Cyrus some 2,500 years ago, so the Balfour Declaration in 1917 heralded the end of Jewish exile and a return to our homeland," he said.

The British have been viewed as sympathetic to the Palestinian cause for many years, a sympathy that often has expressed itself in hostility toward Israel if not blatant partiality during the 1948 War of Independence. O'Brien makes note of these British views and points out that even so, the British stuck to their support of the Balfour Declaration during the early years when it counted. Then he writes: "If a Zionist, of the pious sort, were to tell me that the true explanation of this phenomenon was that God had decided that it was time for His people to come home, I should no doubt express polite skepticism. But if the same pious Zionist were then to ask me whether I can discern any explanation, in terms of Britain's material interests, for the British Government's reinforcement of the Balfour Declaration, in the circumstances of the early twenties, I should have to say that I can't find any such explanation."[11] Yet, Britain was acting through the Balfour Declaration to strengthen its own claim on Palestine and, a decade later, took action that nearly nullified the declaration.

The Peel Commission, named for Lord Peel, visited Palestine in 1936 charged with the responsibility to look into "the roots of the problem." Haj Amin el Husseini, the pro-Nazi Grand Mufti, told the commission, "The Jews' ultimate aim is the reconstruction of the Temple of King Solomon on the ruins of the Haram ash-Sharif, the El-Aksa Mosque and the Holy Dome of the Rock."[12]

The commission, noting an "irrepressible conflict" between a million Arabs and 400,000 Jews, proposed a small Jewish state made up of a coastal strip from south of Tel Aviv to north of Haifa, and the Galilee to the Syrian border. Amos Elon said this was little more than "a tiny free-city-of-Danzig-type."[13] Yet it was important because it recommended establishment of a Jewish state. The Arabs turned down the proposal. The 1939 British white paper set a limit of 75,000 Jewish immigrants, in effect canceling the Balfour Declaration; it strictly regulated land sales and looked toward establishment of a Palestinian state within ten years.

But just ahead loomed World War II, the Nazis, and the Holocaust. Six million Jews died in the gas chambers, one out of every three Jews on the face of the earth, but even that was not enough to persuade the world to establish a Jewish state. The British refused to let the ship *Exodus*, carrying 4,500 concentration-camp survivors, dock in Palestine in 1947; it had to turn back to France. Menachem Begin's Irgun turned to terrorism, among other things, blowing up the King David Hotel in Jerusalem in 1946.

---

11. O'Brien, 152.
12. O'Brien, 226.
13. Elon, 27.

Finally, on November 29, 1947, the U.N. General Assembly voted 33–13—with both the United States and the Soviet Union in the affirmative—in favor of partitioning the holy land into Jewish and Arab states. Ben-Gurion declared the modern State of Israel on May 14, 1948, and Britain ended its mandate, fully expecting the Arabs to defeat the Jews in the subsequent war. Eleven minutes after the end of the mandate, Harry S. Truman defied the State Department and recognized the new State of Israel. The Soviet Union also recognized Israel. For the first time since before the time of Christ, a Jewish state existed.

The *Aliyah* and Immigration

As we have noted, at the time of the first *aliyah* in 1882 some fifty thousand Jews were in Palestine. Two-thirds of them lived in the holy city of Jerusalem. They were devout, holy people, not nationalistically motivated.

Compared to the mass migration later, only a few Jews went at first to Palestine. In the first *aliyah*, 1882–1903, twenty-five thousand Jews emigrated mainly from Russia. In the second *aliyah*, 1904–14, forty to fifty-five thousand emigrated, also mainly from Russia.[14] Their move instigated by the 1903 pogroms, these people developed the origins of much of the structure of modern Israel, including the kibbutz and the Histadrut labor federation. David Ben-Gurion, who was to become the father of modern Israel, arrived from Plonsk, Poland, in 1906 as a young man of twenty. Moshe Dayan was born at Kibbutz Deganiah at the end of this period of immigrant parents. The city of Tel Aviv ("hill of spring") was founded in the sand dunes just north of Jaffa in 1909, and has become one of the world's largest new cities of the twentieth century.

The next three *aliyoth* and their statistics are:

- Third *aliyah*, 1919–23—thirty-five thousand Jews mainly from Russia and Poland, following the Balfour Declaration. Golda

---

14. Statistics from Friedlander and Goldscheider, 6.

Meir, who was born in Russia, arrived from the United States in 1921 and settled on Kibbutz Merhavia in the Plain of Jezreel.

- Fourth *aliyah*, 1924–28—sixty-seven thousand Jews, half of them middle-class, urban Poles. They tended to settle in the cities of Jerusalem, Tel Aviv, and Haifa.
- Fifth *aliyah*, 1929–39—two hundred fifty thousand Jews, a quarter of them refugees from Nazi Germany, including many professional people.

Although these numbers may seem large, they are comparatively small when it is recognized that during the same period, 1880–1930, almost 3 million Jewish immigrants came to the United States.

Nazi Germany's Holocaust, in which six million Jews were gassed in the ovens, was an indescribable horror. "Nothing can be found to bind our open wound," Prime Minister Shimon Peres said in Berlin four decades after the war. "The survivors of the Holocaust, who reached the shores of their homeland, may have lost their possessions but have carried with them their human pride, their resolve for a new life. They brought to the newborn state their memories, their talents, their dedication, their pain and their strength."

In the three years between the end of World War II and the War of Independence, seventy-five thousand more Jews arrived, most of them illegally. When statehood was declared in 1948, there were 806,000 people in Israel, including 650,000 Jews. Jews comprised 81 percent of Israel's population—the same percentage as now.

In the three years after independence was proclaimed, 690,000 Jews arrived from Europe, Asia, and North Africa. In 1950, the Knesset passed the Law of Return which gave all Jews the right to immigrate to Israel. By 1951, the Jewish population had doubled to 1.4 million.[15] The mass immigration helped mute the huge cultural differences among the Jews, thus helping solidify the young state quickly.

---

15. Friedlander and Goldscheider, 21.

From the establishment of the state in 1948 until 1984, some 1,750,000 Jews moved to Israel, indicating a sharp decline after the first few years. According to *Ha'aretz*, about 10 percent of those who immigrated to Israel later left the country. *Ha'aretz* said that figure is actually quite low compared to other countries that allow immigration, such as the United States, Australia, and Argentina. It is estimated, however, that one in three Jews from Western countries who emigrate to Israel return to their countries of origin within three years.[16]

Today, 27 percent of the world's 13 million Jews live in Israel. New York City has the largest Jewish population in the world, not Jerusalem or Tel Aviv.

One of the livelier spirits in Jerusalem is Fred Weisgal, former U.S. Justice Department lawyer and director of the American Law section in Israel's Justice Ministry. He is as well an art dealer and plays the piano at the American Colony Hotel. "I've been in Israel so long I forget I'm Jewish," he says.

The Jews did not arrive in Israel in a vacuum, despite Golda Meir's remark that Palestinians did not exist when they began arriving.[17] They returned to Palestine to find a half million Arabs there. The conflict started quickly, as we shall discuss in the next chapter.

Soviet Jews

Men wept as Anatoly Shcharansky, freed from the Soviet gulag, was reunited in Israel with his wife Avital, with whom he had spent only the first night of their twelve-year marriage. When he stepped off the small plane at Ben-Gurion in the night air, ten thousand Israelis sang and wept their welcome, their laughter mixed with their tears. Shcharansky, even before he went home with Avital, paid a triumphant visit to the Wailing Wall.

His was one of the most dramatic returns in the long, long history of the Return. The short, bald mathematician, now forty, was imprisoned in the Soviet Union from 1978 to 1986 for his human rights activities. Avital had flown on to Israel the day after

---

16. Friedlander and Goldscheider, 12.
17. Hirst, 264, quoting London *Sunday Times*, June 15, 1969.

their wedding and had taken her crusade for his release to America time and again. In prison, Shcharansky said, he protested by going on hunger strikes. His captors retaliated by putting him in solitary confinement. He read Socrates and other classics in the KGB library in Moscow, unusually well-stocked with volumes looted in the 1930s from other libraries. He kept a sharp sense of humor. "I used this weapon of mine to defend myself every day from this dirty reality," he said, continuing to make small jokes as soon as he stepped from the plane in Israel. Although he was not allowed to speak the languages in prison, he is articulate in English and Hebrew. Admittedly not an Orthodox Jew, he carried in prison a Hebrew Book of the Psalms, a gift from Avital. His favorite was from Psalm 27: "The Lord is my light and my salvation; whom shall I fear?"

Between 1968 and 1987, 272,181 Soviet Jews left the Soviet Union, but only some 164,000 of them went to Israel.[18] This reflects a persistent problem—that Jews leaving the Soviet Union prefer to go not to Israel, but to the United States. In recent years, the emigration of Jews from the Soviet Union has risen as high as 51,320 in 1979, and dipped to 896 in 1984. The number rose to 8,155 in 1987, short of speculation that the figure might reach 11,000. There are now 2.1 million Jews in the Soviet Union. An estimated twenty thousand "refuseniks" have been denied permission to leave, and more than 350,000 have begun the visa application process. Prime Minister Yitzhak Shamir estimates that close to 440,000 Soviet Jews have indicated their desire to leave. There appears to be some loosening of the reins under Soviet leader Mikhail Gorbachev's *glasnost* policies (openness) although he contends there is no discrimination against the Jews in the Soviet Union.

The Falashas

The last major influx of Jews to Israel was the secret airlift of seven thousand five hundred Ethiopian Jews in late 1984 and

---

18. Figures are from the Coalition to Free Soviet Jews, 8 West 40th Street, Suite 1510, New York, NY 10018.

1985 in what was appropriately called "Operation Moses." As the Ethiopian Jews struggled to live in the squalor and starvation of the African famine, their ranks dwindled to twenty-five thousand. Finally, the Israeli government made arrangements to spirit them to Israel. There the story broke in early January 1985. Their arrival immediately confronted Israel with serious questions about racial attitudes and religious dogma.

The "Falashas," as they are sometimes called, appear African in coloring and clothing and they are believed to be descended from King Solomon and the Queen of Sheba, who according to some interpretations, is probably the black woman of whom Solomon sang (Song of Solomon 1:5). In 1975, Israel's chief rabbis ruled that the Falashas were the descendants of the tribe of Dan. They practice a form of Judaism that uses only the Pentateuch.

In Israel, the Falashas, like their predecessors entering Israel, went to absorption centers. There they were given baths and new clothes. Some of them arrived literally with only the clothing they were wearing. Many were illiterate. They became an unusual sight in the streets of Jerusalem—tall, slender Africans wearing *kippas.*

The chief rabbis ruled that the Falashas must undergo a ritual conversion rite—a baptism—in order to marry, because of the possibility that their ancestors might have intermarried over the years. The Falashas replied that to undergo the ceremony would be humiliating—"it's as if we aren't Jews," Tuvia Semani, their spokesman, said. Hundreds of them went on strike for a month, camping across the street from Jerusalem's Great Synagogue. Finally, the Falashas and the chief rabbis agreed to set up a special rabbinical court that would deal with marriage and divorce; and an unwritten understanding provided that the court would be composed of rabbis who were known to be willing to classify the entire community as Jews, and not require that each individual Falashas prove his or her Jewishness.

The remaining ten thousand Jews in Ethiopia are no longer free to leave. Ethiopian Jews are not the only blacks with whom Israel has had problems. A group of several hundred American blacks, calling themselves "Black Hebrews," moved to Israel from the United States in the late 1960s and early 1970s. Most of them were from inner-city areas of American metropolises. About three thousand now live in Dimona, in southern Israel. The state has never accepted them, has denied them residence visas, and has sought to deport them ever since their arrival.

Jews in Arab Lands

The Jews of Egypt have celebrated one wedding and one birth in the last generation, and those may be the last such celebrations in Egypt—ever. The number of Israelites in Egypt reached about six hundred thousand men, plus women and children (Exodus 12:37) during the years in slavery more than three thousand five hundred years ago. That number has dropped from 120,000 in 1948—during another great exodus—to a mere two hundred now. Most of Egypt's Jews are aged.

The plight of the Egyptian Jews is similar to that of Jews in other Arab countries—vastly dwindled numbers, and lives torn between a basic loyalty to the Jewish faith and a lifelong immersion in a Moslem culture antithetical to that faith.

In Cairo, only three Jewish families remain. In 1984, the daughter of David Salim, a textile engineer living in suburban Naser City, married a son of one of the other families, Benoit Fabienne Rousseau. The families had to bring in a rabbi from Jerusalem to conduct the ceremony, just as the community must do for Passover and for Yom Kippur holy days. About five hundred Jews, Christians, and Moslems went to the wedding at "Gates of Heaven" Synagogue in Cairo. A year later the new couple gave birth to their first child, a daughter; it was the first birth in the community in twenty-five years.

The Jews of Egypt profess to have no problems. They say they are doing just fine, thanks.

Carmen Weinstein is a stationer on a busy street in central Cairo. The divided loyalties in her life are apparent on her office wall where hang pictures of Anwar Sadat and Hosni Mubarak, Egyptian presidents, alongside an Israeli calendar of eighteenth-century Jewish art. She politely serves coffee with typical Arab graciousness, but is reluctant to speak about her Jewish roots. How are things going? she is asked. "Perfectly," she replies

171

tersely. With a cynicism typical of an Israeli, she adds: "The youth left Egypt to date and marry other Jews. So they go to the European nations—and marry Gentiles. I have three cousins. Two married Gentiles and one married another Jew—and got divorced."

Eventually the community will die out completely. Elsewhere in Cairo, on the eighteenth floor of an office building, in a neighborhood near the Pyramids, the Israeli Embassy is located, well-secured. At least twice within a few months, members of the small embassy staff have been shot en route to the embassy.

The World Organization of Jews from Arab Countries (WO-JAC) lists, in descending order, the number of Jews in Arab or Moslem countries in 1948 when Israel was established, and the number now:

Iran—25,000 now.
Turkey—12,000 now.
Morocco—285,000 in 1948; 10–12,000 now.
Syria—18,000 in 1948; 4,000 now.
Tunisia—110,000 in 1948; 3,500 now.
Yemen—55,000 in 1948; 1,200 now.
Iraq—140,000 in 1948; 300 now.
Egypt—75,000 in 1948; 200 now.
Lebanon—2,000 in 1948; 200 now.
Libya—38,000 in 1948; only 3 or 4 now.
Jordan and Sudan—none.

When Israel became a state in 1948, there were approximately 856,000 Jews living in Arab countries.[19] In the two decades that followed, nearly 90 percent of them left. But they did not always leave because of persecution.

"We have to be fair to the Arab countries," says WOJAC Chairman Mordechai Ben-Porat, a former Israeli Cabinet minister. "We didn't experience [in the Arab lands] what the Jews in Europe did in the Holocaust. The killings and arrests and pogroms in Arab countries didn't reach the stage that Europe's did."

---

19. Maurice M. Roumani, *The Case of the Jews from Arab Countries: A Neglected Issue* (Tel Aviv: World Organization of Jews from Arab Countries), 2.

Ben-Porat was the eldest of thirteen children born to a Jewish building material storekeeper in Baghdad. He went to Palestine in 1945 and fought in the 1948 War. He returned to Iraq in 1949 and 1950 to organize the gigantic "Operation Ezra and Nehemiah" that brought almost the entire population of Iraq's 120,000 destitute Jews to Israel. Even though he spoke Arabic impeccably, four times he was arrested. He attempted the same mission in Iran in 1979 after Ayatollah Ruhollah Khomeini took power.

Here are thumbnail sketches, based on information from Ben-Porat and Egyptian-born and raised Yitshak Noriel, now back in Cairo as an attaché at the Israeli embassy:

Morocco—The Jews have the best treatment of any Jews in the Arab world. They are free to come and go, and to engage in business. Ben-Porat warns that their fortunes might change if anything happens to King Hassan II, who sponsored a ceremony marking the 950th birthday of the Jewish philosopher-physician Maimonides.

Syria—The Jews suffer the worst treatment of any in the Arab world. In 1985, their situation had improved, with heads of families returning to business; once again they were able to get telephones and enroll in universities. But in 1986, new restrictions were imposed, such as a ban on any travel west.

Lebanon—Four Jews were kidnapped in 1985 by "the Organization for the Oppressed on Earth" and three others are missing. About one hundred Jews left for the United States in 1985.

Libya—Only three Jews, an aged woman and her two sons, remain in Tripoli, according to Giorgio Raccah, a Jewish reporter in Israel for the Italian News Agency ANSA. Raccah was born and raised in Libya. His father, an agent for several international companies, left all his property behind when he and most other Jews left Libya after the 1967 War. Most went to Italy.

Tunisia—The plight of the Jews has steadily declined since they flourished during the 1881–1942 French protectorate. After the 1967 War, Jewish shops were plundered and Jews were subjected to discrimination. Two synagogues have been burned and two Jews were killed in 1985 while praying.

Yemen—The Jews may not emigrate and the officials "count them like cattle," Ben-Porat says.

173

Iraq—The Jews "are worthless from the point of view of the regime," Ben-Porat says.

Ben-Porat claims that between 1948 and 1967, there were more Jewish refugees from Arab lands than Palestinian refugees. The difference, he said, is that Israel accepted the Jewish refugees while Arab countries did little to assimilate the Palestinian refugees. Ben-Porat puts the number at 600,000 Jewish refugees and 590,000 Palestinian refugees. The United Nations Relief and Works Agency estimates that in 1984 there were 760,000 Palestinian refugees in the Israeli-Occupied West Bank and Gaza, and 1.3 million elsewhere in the Arab world.

Elie Eliachar, a member of a long-time Jerusalem family and a formar deputy mayor, expressed[20] the belief that the number of Jews displaced from Arab countries at the time of the 1948 War of Independence was about the same as the number of Palestinian refugees, but Israel failed to make that point effectively in the United Nations or world fora. In part, this was the result of internal Israeli discrimination. The Sephardic Jews knew intimately the condition of Jews in Arab countries, but Ashkenazi Jews held the positions of leadership and did not use the Sephardim to state the case.

---

20. Philip Gillon, *Israelis & Palestinians: Coexistence Or . . .* (London: Collins, 1978), 103, 106.

7

Ishmael's Children

Fear not; for God has heard the voice of the lad where he is. Arise, lift up the lad, and hold him fast with your hand; for I will make him a great nation.
—God reassuring Hagar about her son Ishmael in Genesis 21:17, 18

God loves the Jew. He also loves the Arab. Isaiah points out that "in that day," a term often used in apocalyptic literature to refer to the last days, there will be "a sign and witness to the Lord of hosts in the land of Egypt. . . . And the Lord will make himself known to the Egyptians; and the Egyptians will know the Lord in that day . . ." (19:20, 21). Likewise, Isaiah says, "Blessed be Egypt my people, and Assyria the work of my hands, and Israel my heritage" (19:25).

Jesus said that Tyre and Sidon, the southern port cities in Lebanon, would have repented long before the cities of Bethsaida and Corazin, located in what is now Israel, and that "it shall be more tolerable on the day of judgment for Tyre and Sidon than for you" (Matt. 11:22). Tyre and Sidon are Arab cities.

The Palestinians

The name *Palestinian* comes from the Philistines of Old Testament days. They were seafaring people who lived in the fertile area south of what is now Tel Aviv, and their main cities were Ashdod, Ashkelon, Gath, Gaza, and Ekron. They were quite unlike today's Palestinians, who are mainly farmers and villagers living in the hills of what is central Israel and the occupied territories. The name, but not the Philistine people, has survived. Nowadays, and in

Scripture, the Philistines are portrayed as crude, Goliath-like people. Actually, as Israeli archeologist Trude Dothan's work has enlightened us, the Philistines were artistic and materially accomplished.[1]

I often have shocked audiences—of either Israeli or Palestinian sympathizers; it doesn't matter—by proposing my own somewhat jocular solution to the Middle East controversy. We must pay attention to ancient claims, I say. Thus, the West Bank, because it contains so many Jewish holy sites—Hebron, Nablus, and even Bethlehem—clearly goes to Israel, the Jewish state. This satisfies many Israeli sympathizers. The territory of the five ancient Philistine cities and the rich farmland and coastal plain south of Tel Aviv, go to the Palestinians. This outrages the Israeli sympathizers!

The name "Palestine" goes back to Roman times.

Edward W. Said, a leading Palestinian intellectual and a professor of literature at Columbia University, says that from the eighth century A.D. on, Arab geographers, historians, philosophers, and poets made reference to Palestine; and there were innumerable references to Palestine in European literature from the Middle Ages to the present. He says that Palestine became predominantly Arab and Islamic by the end of the seventh century.[2] The Palestinians felt themselves to be a part of the great Arab awakening in the late nineteenth century that led to the drive for Arab nationalism.

It is true that in decades past, the British and even the Jews called themselves *Palestinians*. But in recent years it has taken on a political significance; now it refers to Arabs whose origins were in what was known as Palestine.

The Palestinians on the West Bank constitute not quite half of the four million Palestinians in the world, but they constitute a larger percentage of that total population than do the Jews in Israel of the total world population of Jews. Of the Palestinians living under Israeli occupation, some 813,000 of them live on the West

---

1. Trude Dothan, "What We Know About the Philistines," *Biblical Archaeology Review*, VIII:4, (July/August, 1982), 20–44.

2. Edward W. Said, *The Question of Palestine* (New York: Times, 1979), 10.

Bank; 525,000 live on the Gaza Strip. About half of the 700,000 Arabs in Israel proper live in the Galilee, while the rest reside either in Jerusalem or in all-Arab villages. Another 2.2 million Palestinians live elsewhere in the world.

The Palestinians are the most highly educated people in the Arab world. In the most recent study, there were twenty university students among every one thousand Palestinian people contrasted to four students among every one thousand throughout the Arab world, including the West Bank and Gaza.[3] And the number of students is rising. Unfortunately, few of these educated Palestinians work in the West Bank and the Gaza Strip. Some seventy thousand Palestinians are university graduates, but only 10 percent of them work in Israeli-occupied territories.[4] The implications of an educated Palestinian populace are as serious for Israel as they are hopeful for the Palestinians. It means that in the future Israel must deal with a highly educated, sophisticated people who are demanding their freedom.

The Arabs

It was the most unusual wedding I ever have attended—in Cana of Galilee (modern Kafr Kanna), where Jesus worked his first miracle, turning water into wine (John 2:1-11). The ceremony was held in a small Greek Orthodox church said to be on the very site where Jesus' miracle took place, some ten miles northeast of his hometown of Nazareth. What also made this wedding unusual was that the bridegroom, Kamal Ibrahim Copty, was one of the 1,150 convicted Arab terrorists who had been exchanged six months earlier for three Israeli prisoners of war held in Lebanon.

In the 1970s Copty had been sentenced to two life terms for putting bombs in a movie theater in Haifa. There were no casualties. His brother, whom I know, and who claimed Kamal was a model prisoner, had asked me to help get him released. I had, with

3. Muhammad Hallaj, "The Mission of Palestinian Higher Education," *Journal of Palestine Studies*, IX:4, (Summer, 1980), 77. (1976-77 figures most recent available.)

4. Ibid., 79.

what I thought was little effect, talked to a key official about it, but on the strength of my meager effort, the family invited my wife and me to the wedding. We were treated royally. The Copty family invited us to their home after the ceremony to join the bridal couple and the family members. We were even invited to ride in the same car with the newlyweds en route to the reception. And at the home, we joined the other guests—the women seated along one wall in the spacious living room, the men on the other side—for a dinner that continued for hours to the accompaniment of very loud music. This was a typical form of Arab courtesy shown a guest, even if the guest was not especially well-acquainted with the host.

Courtesy and Candor

I had been in Israel several weeks when I went to a service in St. George's Cathedral in Jerusalem. I inadvertently had gone to the first service of the day, the Arab service. And I remember being surprised that this was the best-dressed audience I had seen in Israel; the men wore suits and white shirts, the women were in dresses and heels. It was a remarkable contrast to the dress-down of the Israelis.

It was an adventure to shop in Arab East Jerusalem, to duck in and out of the uncounted little shops on Saladin Street, and the shops on the streets and alleys leading off Saladin Street. Almost always I could find what I needed, and always I was treated with more courtesy than in West Jerusalem. The two men who operate City Grocery in East Jerusalem invariably were nattily dressed in jacket and tie, and had as much savoir-faire as anybody I had met in Israel.

The Arabs are courteous and dignified, and exhibit such hospitality that places them among the world's most charming people. Sir John Glubb, a Britisher who spent much of his adult life among the Arabs, said of them: "It is not possible, as a result, for persons living far from the Arab countries to form any idea of these people. Only those who have lived among them can know their irresistible charm, their warm-hearted kindness, their

178

tender pity for the weak, their fantastic hospitality or their extravagant generosity."[5]

There are other traits about the Palestinians that Westerners would do well to emulate. Sexual purity among Arab young women—a certain male chauvinism is at work here, admittedly—is revered and often enforced by male members of their families. Another trait is the *sulha*, or reconciliation, which often balances the practice of retaliation.

In September 1984, nine Druze militiamen belonging to the South Lebanon Army (SLA) entered the Shiite village of Sohmor in search of a terrorist gang of six to eight members. According to the account provided by the Israeli army, which occupied southern Lebanon at the time, "terrorist villagers" opened fire, killing four militiamen. Approximately five hundred men and boys of the village were rounded up for questioning. Nine hours after the shooting, fifteen other SLA Druze militiamen, wearing the red headband symbolic of revenge, stormed into the village and opened fire on the groups that had been rounded up, killing thirteen civilians and wounding twenty-eight. As I and other reporters looked on later, young villagers in their grief picked aimlessly through shoes and bloodied shirts and jackets left by the victims. Three weeks later, Druze and Shiite leaders participated in a *sulha* at the home of SLA Commander Antoine Lahad. Lahad said afterward that he would not yield to Israeli army demands to punish the fifteen Druze militiamen severely. "You do not understand our customs or way of life," he told Israel Radio. "Heavy punishment of the guilty will solve nothing."

Principle almost always prevails over pragmatics among the Arabs. In practice, this can become a certain intransigence, an unwillingness to compromise merely for the sake of a solution. The Arabs turned down the 1937 Peel Commission recommendation for a small Jewish state made up of a coastal strip between Tel Aviv and Haifa, and the Galilee to the Syrian border. The Arabs turned down the 1947 U.N. Partition Plan that would have given the Jews a state but restricted the area to little more

_____

5. Glubb, 286.

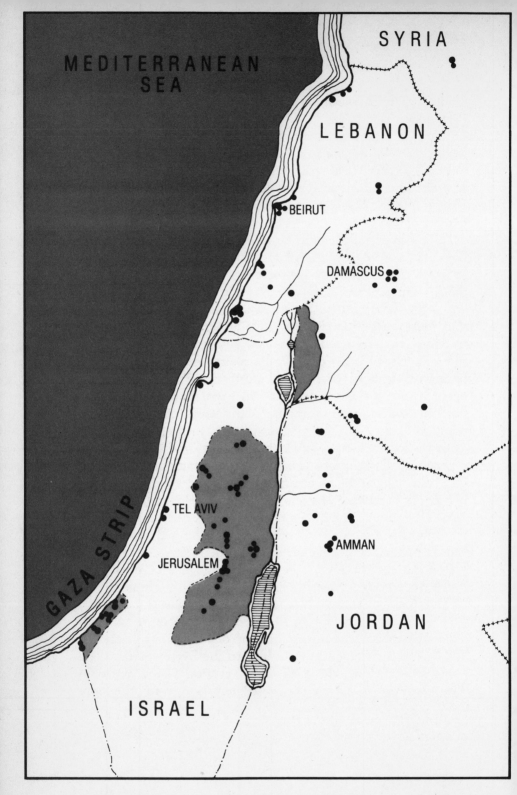

United Nations Palestine Refugee Camps and Cities

than the Negev. The following year, the British mandate having ended, Zionists declared the state of Israel and the Israelis defeated the Arabs in a war that left the Jewish state with the boundaries that have prevailed since. According to former Israeli Prime Minister Shimon Peres, Jordan turned down then Prime Minister Levi Eshkol's plea to stay out of the 1967 Six-Day War. Except for Egypt, the Arabs have avoided making peace with the Israelis.

What has been the result? After the 1967 Six-Day War, Israel controlled eighteen times as much area as would have been allocated under the Peel partition thirty years earlier. Now Egypt, the only Arab country to make peace, has regained all of its land but Gaza (which was never an integral part of Egypt). Jordan entered the 1967 War and lost Jerusalem and the West Bank. Jordan and Syria, who refuse to negotiate, have not regained the West Bank and the Golan. The Arab commitment to principle—intransigence—has been costly.

Fratricide and Truth

Often, a person's gift can become a curse; one's skills, a burden. This is true in the case of the Arab.

Sometimes, candor is sacrificed for charm. Someone has said that with an Israeli, the behavior may be abrasive but what you see is what you get; with an Arab, you are treated with consummate courtesy but you don't know what he is thinking. The cultural gap can become a chasm. You may think you are dealing with a charming, handsome person in Western dress, but it may be more realistic to see that person in your mind as wearing a *kafiyah* (Arab headdress).

The Arabs' desire to be courteous becomes a desire to say what they think the listener wants to hear; and in the process, candor and accuracy may be sacrificed. The Arabs' great sensitivity is caught up in the desire to communicate deep feeling when speaking; and this becomes soaring rhetoric and gross exaggeration. Again, accuracy and candor are sacrificed. The Arab emphasizes family honor, and this has led even to the "blood revenge" slaying of daughters or sisters who have brought dishonor on the family.

181

The Arabs are devout, but their devotion can become zealotry that is used to justify terrorism and suicide missions.

A certain tribalism has thwarted both Arab nationalism and pan-nationalism, a tribalism of the desert that has hurt Arab influence in a modern, increasingly urban world. The American success in large part grew out of the ability of the thirteen original colonies to knit together tightly. (If the black nations of Africa and the Arab states of the Middle East had been able to join together as those thirteen colonies did, the Damascus-Cairo-Nairobi axis would rule the world. But pan-Africa and pan-Arabism remain mere dreams.)

One of my colleagues, not known for his love of Israel, maintains that the Israeli army isn't so strong; it's merely been lucky in its choice of enemies. No matter how grievous the wars between Israel and the Arabs, the internecine wars among the Arabs—"the brothers," as they call themselves—have been worse. No matter what occurred in the Israeli invasion of southern Lebanon, a decade of bloodletting among the Lebanese themselves has been much more grotesque. There is little evidence that most other Arabs care one whit about the fate of the Palestinians on the West Bank. The Palestinians themselves are deeply, bloodily divided among Yasser Arafat's Fatah and other factions. The fighting among the Arab "brothers" is an abomination to the Palestinian cause. It is an enmity they cannot lay at the feet of the Israelis.

The problem of the Arab handling of truth is equally complex. Let me illustrate. (Our UPI bureaus in Israel cover Israel and the occupied territories, and our Beirut bureau covers Lebanon. But it was always uncertain whose responsibility it was to cover southern Lebanon during the three-year occupation. Often our coverage overlapped and we could compare how our different offices covered the same story.)

After Israel announced in January 1985 its intention to withdraw from southern Lebanon, bitter resistance erupted on the part of the Shiite Moslems in southwestern Lebanon. Shiite suicide bombings led to the Israeli "iron fist." On the night of Tuesday, February 5, the Israeli army spokesman, whose office was only a few steps from my bureau, announced in a typically terse statement that ten Israeli soldiers had been wounded, none seriously, when an explosion had gone off as a convoy passed through the Borj al-Chemali refugee camp area east of Tyre. The next morning, the state-owned Beirut Radio said twenty-five Lebanese children and students had been "killed or wounded" at the Jabal Amal school (in the same area east of Tyre) by Israeli helicopter gunships and troop carriers which destroyed a wing of the school. A short time later, in a story we slugged "urgent," Beirut Radio reported that 100 Israeli soldiers had been "killed or wounded" by a suicide bomber. I dashed to the army to get a reaction. The acting spokesman, reservist Zev Chafets, called it "a lie." I messaged this to our Beirut bureau, but the great bulk of the stories coming out of Beirut continued to treat the killing or wounding of the 25 Lebanese students and 100 Israeli soldiers as fact.

Had 125 been killed or wounded, as the Lebanese reported? Or was it a lie, as Israel maintained?

Not until the next day was I able to sort things out through an independent source. The UNIFIL spokesman, Timor Goksel, gave this chronology: On Tuesday evening, a roadside bomb went off near Borj al-Chemali refugee camp southeast of Tyre. No one was injured, but in the confusion a white Mercedes, carrying a bomb, sneaked into the convoy between the second and third cars. It blew up and injured several Israeli soldiers. (This probably was the basis of the Israeli army report that night.) On Wednesday morning, Israeli soldiers launched a search operation at nursing and vocational schools in the area, firing as they went, breaking windows in the school. Goksel said that as a result of the suicide bombing of the convoy and the firing at the school, there were no deaths but thirty Lebanese were hurt; of these, eleven needed hospitalization, primarily because of flying glass, and four were in serious condition from gunshot wounds.

Later that year, on April 9, the Lebanese National Resistance Front reported that a sixteen-year-old suicide bomber had driven a booby-trapped car into a group of Israeli soldiers near Jezzine in southern Lebanon, causing an estimated fifty Israeli casualties. A few minutes later, Israeli military sources reported the same incident, saying two soldiers had been killed and two slightly injured. It immediately became clear who was telling the truth, for it would be impossible to hide fifty casualties in Israel. When I asked our Beirut bureau chief, who was Lebanese, about the exaggerated reports, he messaged back simply, "This is the Middle East."

It seems to me that among Arabs there is a tendency to revere the word so much that ultimately they do harm to the cause of truth. It is almost as if not to say something means it didn't happen, or conversely, to say something happened makes it so. There is a mixing of fact and fantasy. The use of hyperbole and telling the hearer what he or she wants to hear is a Mediterranean trait. Contrast how preposterous the Greek myths appear when matched to the stark realism of the Hebrew Bible. The Arab word for "express" is *balagh*; the word for "exaggerate" is almost identical— *bolagh*. The subtle suggestion seems to be that only a thin line differentiates fact from fiction.

Arabs also use exaggeration to try to convey deep feelings, as if by exaggerating they deepen the sense of pain. We understand this when we realize this is the technique of drama—to overstate to make a point. There *is* a measure of truth in this, for playwright Harold Pinter's fiction goes infinitely further in communicating reality than do the bare-bone statistics of the bureaucrats.

I also recognize that the mere recitation of accurate detail does not necessarily assure the communication of truth; or conversely, I recognize that great truth often can be communicated effectively through myth and impressions. In *The Third Way*, Raja Shehadeh writes: "As a lawyer I have to rely, almost always, on frightened, confusing and often conflicting memories as my sole evidence against the meticulously documented version of the Israeli authorities. I know very well how much goodwill and patience are needed to piece together and believe the accounts I rely upon. . . . I know very well the psychological mechanism that makes people believe the concise, documented account as opposed to the confused, incoherent, verbal one. I know this all so well that I sometimes feel that it is ludicrous, irrational, to expect anyone to believe the story of the weak."[6]

Nonetheless, I found that regrettably I could not trust what I

------

6. Shehadeh, 69; see p. 101.

heard from many Arab sources without further checking; neither could my colleagues, many of whom are anti-Israeli and pro-Palestinian in their personal points of view. The Arabs' handling of facts has done irreparable damage in communicating their cause.

Arab History

Mayor Elias Freij of Bethlehem once told me, "My family has lived here five hundred years." Walid Fahoum, a lawyer in Nazareth, made the same remark to me. Actually, Arabs came to Palestine in the seventh century, more than a thousand years ago. Those are rather substantial squatters' rights.[7]

The name *Arab* is not mentioned in Genesis in the Bible. But both the Arab and the Hebrew (Eber in Genesis 10:24) are believed to be the descendants of Noah's son Shem; hence, both the Arab and the Jew are Semitic people.

Arabs and Islam are closely linked, but it must be emphasized that they are not synonymous. Although all Arab countries are predominantly Moslem, not all Arabs are Moslems. In Israel, for instance, about one Arab in seven is a Christian, which we will discuss in greater detail in chapter 8. Not all Moslem countries are Arab—Turkey, Iran, and Indonesia, particularly, fit that description.

Originally, the word *Arab* meant a member of the nomadic tribes that roamed the Arabian peninsula. Gradually it came to mean a citizen of the extensive Arab world. In the seventh century, the prophet Mohammed was born in Mecca, in the peninsula of Arabia. His religion became known as Islam. The process of islamization and of arabization set in motion forces that reached out to millions in the Middle East and northern Africa. Every country that became arabized also became islamized, although the converse is not true. The process of arabization involved making Arabic the spoken language and Arabic the dominant culture.

In some ways, the Arab Empire was western-like. The Arabs inaugurated a welfare state with free medical care, a free university

---

7. I am indebted for much of the following discussion to *The Arab Awakening* by George Antonius, and *The Question of Palestine* by Edward W. Said. See n.3, p. 127. These have the merit of being books about Arabs written by Arabs.

education, and some degree of liberation of females. Tenth-century writers in Baghdad spoke of women who became lawyers, physicians, professors, and officials.

The Arabs were warriors, romantics, and poets; they were passionate devotees of poetry. The Arab Moslems entered Palestine as conquerors, but they made no attempt to convert the Christians and Jews to Islam.

The Christian Crusaders and the Mamelukes, slave-soldiers mostly of Turkish descent, shared the next four hundred years, until approximately 1500. The main street in Arab East Jerusalem is Saladin, named for the Kurd who conquered the Crusaders in the Battle of Hittim in 1187.

Next came the Ottoman Empire, which ruled the Middle East for four hundred years exactly, 1517-1917. The Ottomans were a mixed race, composed partly of Turks but including also Islamic converts—Greeks, Serbs, Albanians, and Bulgarians by racial origin. Their empire stretched from Hungary to the Persian Gulf and northern Africa; their capital was Constantinople, one of the great cities of the world. Salim was the sultan of the Ottomans who conquered Palestine. Upon his death in 1520, he was succeeded by his son, Sulaiman the Magnificent, who deserved his name because of the remarkable things he did, including the last reconstruction of the wall around the Old City in Jerusalem.

Arab Nationalism and Christianity

The Christian faith helped arouse Arab nationalism in much the same way that biblical claims helped ignite Zionism.

Missionaries often are condemned for transporting Western culture along with the gospel. Yet, traditionally they have helped acquaint local peoples, like the African and the Arab, with Western ideas and techniques, especially through mission schools.

George Antonius, an Arab Christian, attributes the start of Arab nationalism to Christian missions. He points out that the missionaries emphasized not only English, but also the mass printing and distribution of books in Arabic. He credits missionaries with the rediscovery of education, with the foundations in Beirut and Jerusalem. To the missionary, the word was important, and the word became all powerful to the Arab.

The first Jesuit missionaries arrived in Lebanon in 1625. They opened the first modern school in any Arab country in 1734. American Presbyterian missionaries landed in Beirut in 1820 and opened what is now the American University of Beirut in 1866.

"A competition began between Catholic and Presbyterian, which attaining at times to the asperity of a duel, caused them to vie with each other for influence and supremacy," says Antonius. ". . . in so striving, to set in train a revival of the Arabic language and, with it, a movement of ideas which, in a short lifetime, was to leap from literature to politics."[8] But Western education also had its negative side; it emphasized sectarian divisions and encouraged clergy to go into politics.

Antonius also pinpoints the first organized effort in Arab nationalism, which he says began with the secret meeting of five Christian young men in 1875. This and other secret societies distributed literature calling for the granting of independence to Syria in union with Lebanon, the recognition of Arabic as the official language, and freedom of expression. Thus, Antonius says, nationalism "had come into being, thanks to a cultural and social awakening of which the mainsprings were the literary revival and the revulsion of feeling caused by the massacres of 1860 [the killing of Christians in Lebanon and Damascus]. The forces that had set it in motion were not only of a moral order, unaffected by economic needs or political theories; but they were also forces of spontaneous origin, generated by emotions from within."[9]

Moshe Maoz says there were parallel Muslim and Christian nationalistic movements among the Arabs in Palestine, both based, in part, on Jerusalem as the social and cultural center of the land.[10] These combined into one intellectual and patriotic Palestinian trend as a reaction to the Jewish-Zionist immigration. By 1911, however, the initiative for Arab nationalism had passed

---

8. Antonius, 37.
9. Antonius, 85.
10. Maoz, 1.

into the hands of the Moslems.[11] Meanwhile, Zionism was under way in earnest, and already the second *aliyah* was bringing Jews to Palestine.

Resistance to Zionism

I remarked to a Jordanian diplomat on one occasion that the ancient claim of the Promised Land is what complicates the dispute between Jews and Arabs, for differences over religion always tend to make conflict.

"Yes," he said with a tolerant smile, "we just want Ishmael's share."

The Arabs say that as the eldest son of Abraham, Ishmael was entitled to the inheritance. (According to Hebrews 11:9, the promise to Abraham extended through Isaac, the son of Sarah, not through Ishmael, his half-brother and the son of the slave woman, Hagar.) As always, resistance takes more than one form. Edward Said says the Jews who reclaimed Abraham's promise used two methods to fight the Palestinians: (1) to deny their existence in Palestine, and (2) if they did exist, to state that they were disreputable people who did not deserve the land. The first was the more subtle, the second the more overt.

Said also says there was "a systematic denial"[12] of a substantial native Arab presence in Palestine. Herzl's colleague Israel Zwangwill wrote in 1901 that Palestine was "a land without a people, waiting for a people without a land."[13] But of course the fact is that the Palestinians have lived in Palestine for hundreds of years. In Said's view, the unbroken existence of the Arabs in Palestine "had and still has an incomparably greater moral authority" than what he calls the European imperialism of Zionism.[14] Said's position does not take into consideration the Jews' own unbroken existence in Palestine and their desperate need for a homeland because of persecution.

---

11. Antonius, 111.
12. Said, 20, 21.
13. Hirst, 19.
14. Said, 22.

The second thing that Zionists did, in Said's view, was to portray Arabs as clever but deceitful, treacherous, and unattractive. There is a nagging persistence of that stereotype to this day in the West. Palestinians are identified as being in opposition to Zionism, as being the "heart" of the Middle East problem—or worse. To many, a Palestinian is a terrorist is a Palestinian. The typical picture that leaps into many people's minds in the West is that of an Arab in a *kafiyah*, or headdress, with a gasoline pump in one hand and a grenade in the other.

As Said says:

The dehumanization of the Arab, which began with the view that Palestinians were either not there or were savages or both, saturates everything in Israeli society.[15]

"There was no more fundamental and obvious test by which the Zionists should be judged than the way they treated their Palestinian neighbors," Hirst says.[16] As Said has said: "It has been the Palestinian who has born the brunt of Zionism's extraordinary human cost."[17]

By 1918, the Jewish immigrants had acquired 2 percent of the land of Palestine; of all land acquired by 1929, the Jews had gotten 90 percent of it from absentee Arab landlords. The Arabs often hurt their own cause; Hirst says these absentee land sellers "typified the Palestinians' response to Zionism at its most self-destructive."[18]

As early as 1891, the merchants and craftsmen of Jerusalem protested Jewish immigration. Nine years later, Turkish troops broke up a confrontation between Arab peasants and real-estate agents staking out land purchased by the Jews. In 1920, Arabs attacked the Jewish Quarter in the walled Old City of Jerusalem; forty-eight Arabs and forty-seven Jews were killed. It was even worse in 1929. Violence erupted in several parts of the land, leaving 133 Jews and 110 Arabs dead. Then, after several years of

15. Said, 90.
16. Hirst, 23.
17. Said, 54.
18. Hirst, 79.

relative calm, a dual revolt broke out. The 1936–39 Arab revolt spread throughout the country in the form of rioting and general strikes, leaving hundreds dead, often with other Arabs the victims of Arab violence. To quell the revolt, the British sent twenty thousand troops into the country. Hitler's Nazi anti-Semitism triggered a Jewish protest against the 1939 British white paper limiting Jewish immigration to seventy-five thousand during the next five years. World War II and the Holocaust lay just ahead.

As O'Brien says, "the Arabs loved their country as much as the Jews did. Instinctively they understood Zionist aspirations very well, and their decision to resist them was only natural."[19] Hirst quotes an American reporter on the scene, "I was bitterly indignant with the Zionists for having brought on this disaster; I was shocked into hysteria by the ferocity of the Arab anger; and I was aghast at the inadequacy of the British government."[20]

Islam

Five times a day the muezzin calls the faithful to prayer. One of the few sounds to break the night silence in Jerusalem is the 4 A.M. call. As a Christian I found the muezzin's wail to have a haunting appeal, and I was only slightly disillusioned to find that almost all of them nowadays are tape-recorded.

Islam, along with Judaism and Christianity, is one of the great monotheistic religions in the world. There is a certain kinship among the three in that all look to Abraham as father. It was this kinship that Jimmy Carter sought to employ when bringing together Menachem Begin and Anwar Sadat at Camp David in 1978. It was not that the three men believed the same thing, but rather, each found roots in Abraham and took belief seriously.

About one person in five in the world is a Moslem—there are in all nations more than 800 million. Islam is divided into two

---

19. O'Brien, 175.
20. Hirst, 71.

main factions—the more numerous Sunnis and the downtrodden Shiites, whom we shall discuss in some detail.

Mohammed, founder of Islam, was born in Mecca in the Arabian peninsula in approximately A.D. 575. An orphan who became a merchant, he led caravans, was married, and had a vision that affected the world.

There are six theological "Pillars of Islam"—(1) the Creed, "There is no God but Allah and Mohammed is his prophet"; (2) prayer five times a day while facing toward Mecca; (3) the giving of alms; (4) the fast during the month of Ramadan; (5) the Pilgrimage to Mecca at least once in a lifetime; and (6) the *jihad,* or striving, or, as it is sometimes translated, "holy war."

Temple Mount—Jewish, Christian, and Moslem Aspirations

Mecca, Medina (where Mohammed is buried), and Jerusalem— *al Quds* in Arabic, or "the holy"—are the three holiest cities in Islam. Jerusalem is so designated because it was from a rock on Mount Moriah, according to Islamic tradition, that Mohammed began his nighttime celestial journey. The golden Dome of the Rock, a Moslem holy site—the most photographed spot in Jerusalem—was built on this place. This is also the site where Abraham prepared to sacrifice his son, Isaac, and where Solomon built the temple.

For hundreds of years, except for the brief period of the Crusades, Palestine has remained under Moslem control. The Israelis failed to conquer the walled Old City in the 1948 War and the Dome of the Rock continued under Moslem control. After the 1967 War, when Israel succeeded in conquering East Jerusalem, Israel gave full control and autonomy over the thirty-six acre Temple Mount—the site of the Dome of the Rock—to the Waqf, a department of the Supreme Moslem Council. Israel extends similar autonomy to Christian sites.

Recently, a squat, stone marker memorializing the 1982 Palestinian massacre at the Sabra and Shatilla refugee camps in Beirut was laid among the pine, olive, and cypress trees on a

191

Moslem prayer platform between the Golden Gate and the Dome of the Rock. When, in retaliation, Chief Rabbi Mordechai Eliyahu proposed building a synagogue on Temple Mount, *Ha'aretz* newspaper reported the Supreme Moslem Council as saying whoever tried to do so would have to do so over the bodies of ten thousand Moslems.

Several Jewish terrorists convicted in 1985 were charged with trying to blow up Temple Mount; they said they had purposed to do it because the Moslems had contaminated it. Any attempt to rebuild the temple would surely result in a bloodbath. If the Israelis had wanted to take full control of that holy site, they should have done so during the Six-Day War, on the assumption that anything goes in war. By not doing so, they effectively forfeited any way of reclaiming Temple Mount.

There is a fusion between religion and politics in Islam which is extremely important. If a politician believes he is acting on behalf of God, how does one reach a compromise or even negotiate with such a man? Implicit in democracy is the possibility that a people's leaders can err, and that therefore the people can replace them. But if the leaders claim to be God's representatives, how can they be replaced? This is why Carter, himself a devout Christian, found it utterly impossible to negotiate with Khomeini. And it also explains why Khomeini, and other Moslems as well, use theological language or "God talk."

"Allah Akbar! Allah Akbar!" they chant, meaning "God the greatest! God the greatest!" This is true, of course, but the tenets of Islam that lead the faithful Moslems to chant this also leads them to call the United States "the great Satan."

The fusion between religion and politics affects not only the leadership, but the common people as well.

In 1985, seventeen-year-old Mayilla Soufangi and two brothers-in-arms were sent on a mission with a mule carrying 150 kilograms of explosives. She was a young Moslem woman from a poor family living near the village of Kama Delouz who had decided to join the resistance. As she and her two companions approached a unit of the pro-Israel South Lebanon Army, the militiamen, alert to what was going on, opened fire. The mule exploded, killing the two brothers and wounding Mayilla. When they searched her, she was carrying a small red note that she had found in a case of hand grenades sent by Khomeini. On the note was a verse from the Koran which read, "Those who die in the holy war will enter Paradise." Syrian TV reported her dead. She told a reporter in the hospital in Marjayoun in southern Lebanon, "Tell my parents that I love them and that I would like to be back home."

Shiites

The Shiites, for centuries the downtrodden of the Moslem world, make up 20 percent of the world's 800 million Moslems. There are no Shiites in Israel, but the Shiites have deeply affected Israel's recent history.

The Shiites split away from the Sunni mainstream Moslems after the prophet Mohammed died in 632. It was the greatest schism in Islamic history. The dispute began as a simple one—many Moslems believed that Ali, Mohammed's son-in-law, should have succeeded him. Ali was assassinated and his son Hussein was tortured and beheaded. Their martyrdom provided fertile ground for their successors, the Shiites. The Shiites resented that they were oppressed and downtrodden. Almost always through the centuries, the Shiites were outnumbered by the better-educated, better-off Sunnis.

"This was the soil everything was planted in," says Clinton Bailey, the Israeli specialist on Shiites. "For the most part, the Shiites have had to live under Sunni dominance, Sunni governments." As a result, he says, "What there is in Shia is a feistiness, a sense of persecution. They are resentful."

Because of the Shiites' long-term persecution and resentment, they adopted tactics of terrorism in the mid-1980s that had their origins in the deserts of the Middle East. This terrorism is bolstered by their belief that martyrdom is religiously important. That all martyrs go straight to heaven is a tenet held by all Moslems, but Shiites hold to it with a particular fervor.

"Shiite terrorism is a phenomenon that has developed over the years and it has been nourished by the Iranians and Syrians," says Aharon Yariv, head of the Jaffe Center and a former military intelligence officer. "Shiite terrorism looks more terrifying and aggressive than Palestinian terror," adds Ze'ev Schiff, military analyst for *Ha'aretz*. "This is because of its inherent religious mysticism, fanaticism and readiness to commit suicide in the course of an action."

Bailey says the Shiites have traditionally been residing in very remote and impoverished areas and have been controlled by their own Shiite landlords, who were given power by the French in the 1920s. The Israeli newspaper *Ma'ariv* said with reference to their recent past, "most Shiites were employed as tenant farmers, mainly growing tobacco, and a handful worked at menial service jobs, living in pitiful villages in the poor neighborhoods of the suburbs of large cities." The 1943 national pact in Lebanon that gave the presidency to the Maronite Christians and the prime ministry to the Sunnis gave only the post of speaker of the house to the Shiites.

With high birth rates and declining death rates, the Shiites grew in numbers; they now make up 40 percent of Lebanon's 3 million people. They also have begun to stir. In 1969, through the efforts of a Shiite clergyman, Imam Moussa Sadr, they split off from the Sunni-dominated Supreme Moslem Council and set up their own council to choose their own judges and clerk.

The charismatic Sadr was a powerful speaker who inflamed the Shiites. His slogan was, "A weapon is a man's jewelry." In 1975, he founded Amal, an Arabic acronym for "Battalions of Lebanese Resistance." Sadr's confidant, Nabih Berri, was the organizer.

Amal is essentially a secular movement. Its members believe that an Islamic state would drive out the Christians and the Druze, and that it would be the end of Lebanon, to which they feel allegiance. Sixty to 70 percent of the Shiites in Lebanon belong to Amal.

The PLO, expelled from Jordan in 1970, moved into southern Lebanon and took over—at the expense of the Shiites. "The PLO was running their lives and they didn't like it," says Bailey, "The PLO was running the south, and lorded it over the Shiites, the most depressed part of the population and the lowest rung on the social ladder. The Amal became a discernible factor in fighting the PLO in 1978."

That same year, Sadr disappeared during a flight from Libya to Rome and Berri eventually succeeded him. Berri, now in his forties, would become justice minister in the Lebanese government in 1984 and hold the portfolio for southern Lebanon. His former wife and children live in Detroit, Michigan.

In the view of Othman Hallak, a Palestinian industrialist and political moderate in East Jerusalem, the Shiites responded to the rhetoric and mystical dreams articulated by Ayatollah Ruhollah Khomeini and the clergy in Iran in the late 1970s. As Khomeini called the United States "the great Satan," his followers held 52 Americans hostage in Iran for 444 days starting in 1979, almost immobilizing U.S. President Jimmy Carter.

Khomeini became the Shiites' hero during America's long hostage nightmare that stretched into 1981. "He put the Shiites on the map. He's spoken out, he's acted, he can't be ignored," Bailey says. "He's put the fear of God into everybody. He's shown by being militant that they can get their place in the sun."

Inspired by their "hero," the Shiites had burst into the world's consciousness to stay. They had come from such obscurity that even in his memoirs, Carter did not use the term "Shiites" once in describing the ordeal. According to Israeli Prime Minister Shimon Peres, Shiite militants had been responsible for the hijacking of seven airliners before the seizure of the TWA jet. The Jaffe Center for Strategic Studies in Tel Aviv says 394 people were killed around the world in 1984 in 412 incidents of terrorism, with the Shiites blamed for about 50 of them, more than any other single group.

During the initial Palestinian occupation of southern Lebanon, two hundred thousand Shiites had fled to the poverty-wracked suburbs of Beirut. There they were further radicalized. When Israel invaded southern Lebanon in 1982, it appeared to have a confluence of interests with the Shiites—both wanted the destruction of the PLO. With the coming of the Israelis, many of the Shiites went back to their villages. But whatever goodwill there might have been was lost during the prolonged Israeli occupation of heavily Shiite southern Lebanon. The Israelis also sowed enmity by taking the twelve hundred Shiite prisoners to Israel.

In February 1985, Daoud Daoud, a bearded political leader of the Amal Shiites—a moderate secular group to which 60 to 70 percent of the Shiites in Lebanon belong—sat sipping tea in his village in the predominantly Shiite area east of the port of Tyre. The Israeli withdrawal from southern Lebanon was underway. Despite the withdrawal, or perhaps because of it, Daoud was talking tough. The resistance always seems to talk tougher when the opposing army is in retreat.

"Every rock, every tree, every woman, every man will fight you," the former teacher said, as if he were addressing Israelis. He was speaking to Curtis Wilkie of *The Boston Globe*, Ian Black of *The Guardian*, and me. "We are stronger. We believe we are stronger in our will to resist."

In the neighboring village of Maaraka, Daoud's talk was echoed by Khalil Jradi, the twenty-five-year-old local resistance leader. Using revolutionary rhetoric, he told us "forty-five martyrs" were willing to die for the Shiite cause. Less than one month after our visit, Jradi, Mohammed Saad (believed to be the mastermind of numerous guerrilla attacks), and several colleagues were dead—victims of a bomb that had been planted in the bare, Islamic Religious Center where Jradi had his second-floor office.

Often a light remark is required to ease the tension after a brush with death. Wilkie provided it: "I hope they don't think we planted the bomb."

"The Israeli incursion . . . eliminated a main factor inside Lebanon—the Palestinian one," said an Israeli intelligence officer during the final stages of Israel's withdrawal in 1985. "The Israeli withdrawal from Lebanon brought up another, the Shiite factor. This is the main outcome of the war of 1982," the officer said. Bailey and Yariv believe the Shiites would have become more assertive anyway.

According to Israeli intelligence, two thousand members of the Iranian Revolutionary Guards moved into Baalbek in northern Lebanon in the eighties, although experts say only four hundred to five hundred now remain. The ancient city, covered with posters of Khomeini, took on the appearance of an Iranian city.

More extreme Shiite groups, perhaps as many as fifteen, have begun to challenge the Amal. The largest is the Hizbollah ("The Party of God"). Says Bailey: "Shiites can be very reasonable and practical. But after a long history of persecution, they are very sensitive to what they view as injustice and contempt—and can go as far as martyrdom in order to deal with it."

8

The Christians

So [Jesus'] fame spread throughout all Syria . . . and a great multitude
of people from all Judea and Jerusalem and the seacoast of Tyre and
Sidon . . . came to hear him and to be healed of their diseases. . . .
—Matt. 4:24; Luke 6:17

From my office on the fourth floor of Beit Agron in Jerusalem,
I could sit at my desk and see the southwest corner of the walled
Old City. Just to the right of it was Mount Zion. The dominant
structure on Mount Zion since 1906 has been the Dormition
Abbey, constructed by the Germans on one of the places where
Mary the mother of Jesus is supposed to have died. But my
favorite place on Mount Zion is the traditional location of
David's Tomb (1 Kings 2:10) and, in the same building, the Upper Room, accessible from the other side. On this location, tradition has it, Jesus ate his last supper (Matthew 26:20–29, Mark
14:17–25, and Luke 22:14–23) and the Holy Spirit came on Pentecost (Acts 2:1–4).

I love Jerusalem and never tired of it. I must hold some sort
of record for tours—I took between twenty and thirty tours of
Jerusalem, either those provided free on Saturday morning by
Mayor Teddy Kollek's office, or solo tours with the help of a
guidebook. My office was only a ten-minute walk from the
Church of the Holy Sepulchre in the Old City, and sometimes I
went there, climbed the narrow steps just inside the door and sat
and prayed for a few moments in front of the altar on the site of
Calvary.

Many Christian pilgrims come to Israel in search of a spiritual
experience only to be disillusioned. They are put off by the frenzied

198

atmosphere so typical of the Middle East, by the dark and dank air of the Church of the Holy Sepulchre or the Church of the Nativity, or by the aggressive, ubiquitous postcard and film vendors. Would it have been much different in Jesus' day? Today, some are bothered because Bethlehem's Manger Square is crowded and carnival-like on Christmas Eve. (The Israeli army runs everyone who wants to visit Manger Square on Christmas Eve through a security check, and it has cracked down on beer drinkers.) But we ought not forget that so many people jammed Bethlehem on the first Christmas that there was no room at the inn (Luke 2:7). And why shouldn't Christmas be festive?

The astute shopper can bargain to rock-bottom prices for just about anything in Jerusalem's Old City. We had our kitchen knives sharpened at a shop two doors from the Church of the Holy Sepulchre. Moneychangers in the Old City offer Israeli shekels at a much higher rate than at banks. If this strikes a chord of response, remember that it was no different in Jesus' day. On his first full day in Jerusalem during his last week on earth, he threw the moneychangers out of the temple (Matthew 21:12, 13; Mark 11:15-19; and Luke 19:45-48). If the Church of the Holy Sepulchre seems depressing, one ought to recall Jesus' last words and his agony (Matthew 27:46 and Mark 15:34) as he hung on the cross, probably at that same spot.

And we should not be surprised at the plethora of churches, synagogues, and mosques. It is only natural that the faithful through the ages have sought to preserve the places where something special happened spiritually. This is why, for instance, one can find in the Mount of Olives the beautiful Church of the Pater Noster, which marks the place (Luke 11:1-4) where Jesus taught his disciples to pray. The Lord's Prayer is written in many languages along the arcade. Nearby, in a small, empty, dome-capped chapel, is the traditional place of Jesus' ascension into heaven (Luke 24:50, 51). We are aided in pinpointing these two locations because both events took place near Bethany, immediately southeast of the Mount of Olives. Walking down the Mount of Olives toward the Old City, on probably the same path that Jesus took on Palm Sunday (Matthew 21, Mark 11 and Luke 19), one finds, side by side, the tombs of the prophets Haggai, Malachi, and

Christians Disagree On Tomb Location

By Wesley G. Pippert
United Press International

JERUSALEM—Scholars and the faithful still disagree on the sites of Jesus Christ's Crucifixion and Resurrection, the most important events in the Christian religion. The two locations are far apart.

The Garden Tomb, just north of the Old City's Damascus Gate, is a sylvan plot of Aleppo pine, cyprus, fig, orange, lemon and almond trees. A limestone hill in the likeness of a skull looms nearby. Emblazoned across the modern wooden door at the entrance to the rock-hewn tomb are the words: "He is not here, He is risen."

A half mile south, among the narrow alleys and Arab shops inside the Old City, is the labyrinthine Church of the Holy Sepulchre. It is dark and musty and smells of incense. People in religious attire scurry about.

Both places will be jammed with pilgrims this Holy Week—some 45,000, the Israeli Tourism Ministry estimates.

Observance of the Crucifixion and Resurrection varies. Evangelical Protestants favor the Garden Tomb. Latin Catholics will celebrate Easter Sunday April 7 in the Church of the Holy Sepulchre. Syrian and Coptic Christians will celebrate in the church on April 14 because of the difference in the Gregorian and Julian calendars.

Jewish and Christian scholars point to evidence that as early as 200 A.D. Christians believed their savior was resurrected on the site of the ancient Christian church. "I'm very much convinced that Jesus was buried here," says Dan Bahat, Israel's chief Jerusalem district archeologist.

According to the Bible, Jesus was taken outside the city to Golgotha, meaning "the place of a skull," near a highway and then buried in a tomb hewn from rock in a nearby garden.

Evangelical Protestants believe the Garden Tomb, which is outside the walled Old City and is close to the roads leading to Nablus, Damascus, Jericho and Jaffa (now Tel Aviv), fits that description. The "Skull Hill," or Golgotha, overlooks the teeming central Arab bus station.

The Rev. Bill White, an Anglican rector from England and general secretary of the small interdenominational English society that owns the Garden Tomb, believes Jesus was crucified where the depot is located. He says the body was carried to the Garden Tomb.

White is more concerned about the spiritual message than the archeological argument surrounding the Garden Tomb. "Its simplicity and naturalness provide the finest visual aid of the Easter story. Never under any circumstances will a church building be erected here—thank God."

The origins of the Church of the Holy Sepulchre date back to 327 A.D. Emperor Constantine had converted to Christianity. His mother, Helena, identified the sites of the Crucifixion and the Resurrection in the Holy Land. The church was built on the remains of first-century Jewish tombs.

But the controversy is not a major issue, religious leaders say. "The tomb is not important," says White. "The Lord is risen. This is the emphasis we try to make."

Zechariah, and the common grave of those who were killed when the Jewish Quarter of the Old City fell in the 1948 War of Independence.

Some of the sites are based on legend. At the base of the hill where sits the Israeli Knesset is the sprawling, sixth-century Monastery of the Cross, where a fifteenth-century legend says grew the tree—part cedar, pine, and cypress—from which the cross of Calvary was carved. I once visited a church in Beit Sahour on the site of the pool of water where, according to legend, Mary, Joseph, and the baby Jesus stopped for a drink of water en route to Egypt. Three months before our visit, hundreds of people reportedly had seen a vision of Mary in the pool.

One of my favorite sites in Israel was the Sea of Galilee, surrounded by the rolling countryside. The countryside, the lake, and the violet hue hanging over it clearly are little changed from the way they appeared in Jesus' time. I now understand why Jesus, who surely appreciated the aesthetic, abandoned dreary Nazareth and chose to headquarter in Capernaum (Luke 4:31) on the north shore with its breathtaking view. The Germans excavated Capernaum and Simon's house; one day I saw West German Chancellor Helmut Kohl visiting there. Another day, Becky and I were visiting the church on the Mount of the Beatitudes, where Jesus preached his most famous sermon, and Hal Lindsey of *The Late Great Planet Earth* fame was leading a communion service in the serene surroundings.

The Locals

Arab Christians

The overwhelming majority of Israel's Christians are Arabs. In fact, one in every seven Arabs there is identified as a Christian, according to available statistics. Like other educated minorities elsewhere, their influence is disproportionately large.

Most Arab Christians were members of the earliest Eastern church. Today they are members of the Greek Orthodox Church. Daoud Kuttab, managing editor of the English edition of *Al-Fajr* newspaper, lists Palestinian Christians who hold positions of authority: Bethlehem Mayor Elias Freij; Dr. George Habash, head of the Popular Front for the Liberation of Palestine; Nayef Hawatmeh, head of the Democratic Front for the Liberation of Palestine—both leftist factions in the PLO; Hanna Siniora, publisher of *Al-Fajr*, others.

Christian missionaries helped spark Arab nationalism. In the nineteenth century, Western Christians opened schools that provided a vehicle to political and social prominence across Arab life. Kuttab tells of one small way in which this occurred. Children who attended government schools didn't start learning English until the sixth year while children in mission schools began learning it in the first grade. Thus, graduates of mission schools were more proficient in the English language and Western ways than their counterparts.

"Most of the Christian Arabs are quite well-educated," Kuttab told me while sitting in his East Jerusalem office of *Al-Fajr*. He credits his own managerial position to foreign missionaries, who established schools as one way of spreading the gospel. The invisible benefit to him was a better preparation for leadership. His father, George Kuttab, pastors a Church of the Nazarene congregation of five or six families in the Old City. Daoud attended St. George's Anglican School in Jerusalem and a Mennonite high school in Bethlehem. In the 1960s, his father took the family of four brothers and three sisters to the United States. Daoud and his brother, Jonathan, a prominent West Bank lawyer, received scholarships to attend the evangelical Messiah College near Harrisburg, Pennsylvania.

"Now many of these [Christian] schools are top private schools and have an even higher percentage of Moslems," Kuttab said.

Most of the schools are concentrated in the Jerusalem-Bethlehem-Ramallah area. One of the West Bank's largest colleges, Bethlehem University, is run by the Vatican. Bir Zeit University's exiled president, Hanna Nasser, and its acting president, Gabriel Baramki, are Christians.

Christian Arabs seem to be no less given to violent resistance than Moslem Arabs. It was, after all, the Christian Falange in

Roman Catholic monks in a candlelight procession as they descend to the Grotto of the Nativity, traditional birthplace of Jesus Christ, inside the Church of the Nativity. *Photo by Jim Hollander.*

The author and Bethlehem Mayor Elias Freij at a party at the Cremisan Monastery (above). *Photo by Zeev Ackerman.* Below, a nun and an Arab Christian watch the Christmas procession in Bethlehem's Manger Square, December 1986. *Photo by Jim Hollander.*

REUTERS BETTMANN

REUTERS BETTMANN

Filipino Alves, a Roman Catholic priest from Brazil, recites prayers on the banks of the Jordan River in October 1985 as an Israeli soldier peers toward Jordanian territory. Some two hundred Catholic pilgrims held a mass that day at the site where, according to Christian tradition, Jesus was baptized. *Photo by Jim Hollander.*

REUTERS BETTMANN

Above, the coffin of Rabbi Moshe Feinstein is covered with a prayer shawl as a crowd of 200,000 ultra-Orthodox Jews take part in his funeral procession in March 1986. The rabbi, a leading authority on Jewish religious law, died at age 91 in New York City. *Photo by Jim Hollander.* Below, the body of Zafer Al-Masri, mayor of Nablus who was assassinated by another Palestinian in March 1986, is carried covered in a Palestinian flag as the funeral procession makes its way through the streets. *Photo by Havakuk Levison.*

REUTERS BETTMANN

Many believe "Warren's Shaft," excavated by Yigal Shiloh and opened to the public in 1985, is the tunnel through which Joab climbed to surprise the Jebusites and allow David to claim the city (2 Samuel 5; 1 Chronicles 11). *Photo by R. Milon.*

The "archeological garden" at the City of David (above) which was excavated by Yigal Shiloh. He found the remains of a house dating back 2,000 years before David. The City of David is the most ancient part of Jerusalem and is located just southeast of the Old City. *Photo by R. Milon.* Below, an ancient Israelite well in Ramon Park in the Negev.

The Visitors' Center at Ramon Park, Israel's "Grand Canyon" in the Negev. The Ramon Crater is twenty-four miles long, five miles wide, and twelve hundred feet deep, making it the largest crater in the world.

REUTERS BETTMANN

A swimming pool at Kibbutz Shefayim, just north of Tel Aviv along the Mediterranean. Israel's once austere kibbutzim appear affluent and have increasingly turned their swimming pools into tourist attractions, with fancy slides, to boost their economy. *Photo by Havakuk Levison.*

Pilgrims carry a large wooden cross during the Good Friday procession along the Via Dolorosa in Jerusalem's Old City. The pilgrims, some gripping Bibles and fingering rosaries, followed the route Christ took to his crucifixion. *Photo by Havakuk Levison.*

REUTERS BETTMANN

Lebanon who fired away with abandon in the Sabra and Shatilla Palestinian refugee camps in 1982. Bishop Elias Khoury, the leader of the Anglican Church in Jordan and occupant of the "Christian seat" on the PLO's Executive Committee, is a Palestinian Christian who has mixed faith, politics—and violence. Khoury was expelled by Israel in 1969 after allegations he helped smuggle explosives used in the bombing of the Supersol (the supermarket where Becky and I regularly shopped) in Jerusalem that left two shoppers dead and eight wounded. British Prime Minister Margaret Thatcher invited him and former Halhoul Mayor Mohammed Milhelm to talks in September 1985 but withdrew the invitation the next month in accusing them of reneging on a promise to renounce terrorism.

"To resist injustice is a virtue," Khoury told *The New York Times* later. "Look how you in the West still glorify the resistance movements in the Second World War."

Messianic Jews

Victor Smadja, leader of the Messianic Jews in Israel, firmly rejects the term "Christians" or "Hebrew Christians," when referring to his spiritual flock; and he does not refer to them as "converts." To him, they are "Messianic Jews." One thing is beyond dispute: Messianic Jews believe in Jesus.

"We believe faith in Jesus is a Jewish faith," Smadja says.

The number of Messianic Jews, especially among Israeli youth, is "growing slowly but steadfastly," he says, despite abuse by ultra-Orthodox Jews. "More young people come to the Lord than middle-aged or older people." And of the children of Messianic Jews, "a great majority are following the Lord."

The two thousand Messianic Jews are organized in twenty-six to twenty-eight congregations throughout Israel. Some meet in homes; others assemble in undisclosed places. All are subject to persecution by the ultra-Orthodox.

Smadja, 53, is a Sephardic Jew who came to Israel from Tunisia in 1956. He runs a commercial printing press in Jerusalem and is head elder in the Messianic Assembly. The worship service there is marked by hymns set to a typical Israeli beat and Smadja's hour-long sermons.

While Smadja was broadcasting evangelistic programs several years ago, he was harassed by telephone calls "day and night" and a bomb was placed on his doorstep. He shrugged it off. "It's all in the family," he said.

The Messianic Assembly he leads, the largest of the congregations, with 50 to 60 members and an overflow crow of 100 to 120 people every Saturday, was set afire in 1984. Arsonists poured kerosene on the piano, organ, and a bench stacked with Bibles.

That same year, the Peniel Fellowship in Tiberias, a group of approximately eighty, equally divided between Gentiles and persons who consider themselves Jews, was harassed weekly. Ultra-Orthodox Jews burst into their meeting place in an old hotel one Saturday, snapped photographs of the worshipers, and posted them around town in order to ridicule them. The next Saturday, they returned to shout, throw stones, and break windows. During a communion service, a rock grazed the head of Mrs. Ken Crowell, wife of one of the leaders of the fellowship. The worship leader calmly laid the rock on the communion table and the service continued. On Christmas Day, ultra-Orthodox stormed inside the meeting place, broke furniture, and set fire to it.

The fellowship began meeting at the Tiberias Y.M.C.A. on the shores of the Sea of Galilee until the board, to the astonishment of the group, refused them permission to continue. Finally, to avoid harassment, the fellowship began meeting outdoors in unannounced places. In 1986, in a leap of faith, the group purchased a ground-floor apartment in Tiberias. Child psychologist Wendell Stearnes, a leader of the fellowship and a Christian who is married to a Jew, said the abuse and harassment harmed the children emotionally.

In Rehovot, southeast of Tel Aviv, is the Grace and Truth Christian Assembly, a congregation of some twenty-five—mostly Israeli adults. It was organized and licensed in 1978, and in 1984 moved to a building the group had rented and renovated. Pastor Baruch Maoz, a Boston native who has lived in Israel since 1953, said that one week after the relocation the town's chief rabbi led a demonstration into the building, taking Bibles and hymnals into the street and trampling them. They shoved Maoz, who is crippled, up against an auto.

Police confirmed the bulk of Maoz's account. A spokesman for the municipality explained that the new meeting place was in an observant Orthodox Jewish neighborhood, and the move was a provocation. The spokesman said he was sure the assembly picked the site "because there are so many school boys around they can try to convert." For weeks, picketing continued at Maoz's apartment. The assembly finally decided in 1985 to return temporarily to its previous location.

The Pilgrims

Converts and Missionaries

Baptist pastor Robert Lindsey estimates that throughout Israel forty to fifty Jews express belief in Jesus each year and take the crucial step of identifying with other Christians. A much smaller number of Moslems convert. This compares with only four or five Jews annually a few years ago. But four hundred to five hundred persons convert to Judaism in Israel every year.

Some Christians contend that it is easier for a secular Jew to become a Christian than it is for an ultra-Orthodox person. They reason that the secular Jew carries less theological "baggage" that would hinder his or her believing in Jesus as the Messiah. Lindsey agrees. But he added: "When an ultra-Orthodox does become a Christian, he or she becomes a powerful one because of being so well-grounded in the Scriptures."

In Israel, the law prohibits activity by Christian missionaries. Specifically, it prohibits the offer of any material inducement for evangelistic purposes. Thus, even giving out a tract, being a thing of value, is against the law. The law has never been invoked. A certain Rabbi Shmuel Golding, who claims he was once an evangelical Christian, has been active in advertising and conducting seminars to help families who have been affected by Christian missionaries. The irony is that, as we have noted, far more Christians become Jews every year than Jews become Christians.

Some Christians in Israel, such as those affiliated with the International Christian Embassy, do not believe in witnessing to the Jews on the basis of Romans 11:25–27, that "all Israel will be saved," and, therefore, there is no need to witness individually. It would seem that Rabbi Golding has a better understanding of Christian belief than these do. "Any Christian worth his salt," he says, "if he is an evangelical, fundamentalist Christian, then he is trying to do his little bit to spread the word."[1]

The chief rabbis express strong anti-Christian feelings. "We are adamantly opposed that Christians conduct missionary activities here," Shapira told me. "The Holocaust was created by Christians and Christians stood by. True, we don't bear a grudge. But for them to come here to the remnant of Jews and conduct a campaign among them for Christianity, this is unbearable to us." A Bible Society survey revealed that 28 percent of Israeli Jews are "very much bothered" by Christian missionaries, 20 percent "bothered," 20 percent "not so bothered," and 32 percent "not at all bothered."

Many Christians wear Jewish symbols to show their support for the Jews and Israel. But it is not always perceived in this fashion. Soon after I arrived in Israel, I bought a piece of Jewish jewelry for my wife to wear. A Jewish member of my staff asked her, "Why are you wearing that? It's a Jewish symbol. You're Christian." From that time on, we never wore Jewish symbols. I sometimes wear a cross on a gold chain; I did so proudly in Israel.

The Congregations

Two of the best-known men in Jerusalem are Christian preachers. One is Robert Lindsey, who wears two hats as pastor of the Baptist House in Jerusalem and scholar at the Jerusalem School for the Study of the Synoptic Gospels. Lindsey lost a foot in 1960 when he stepped on a land mine while escorting an Arab boy across the border. "I try very hard in preaching to help people understand the Jewishness of Jesus," Lindsey says.

The other is William Gardner-Scott, for years the rector of the Scottish Church of St. Andrews. Both arrived in Jerusalem

---

1. As reported in *The New York Times*, January 15, 1984.

in the 1930s. Now past eighty, Gardner-Scott has slowed hardly a step; most any day he can be seen, beret jauntily in place, scooting around town with his wife Darinka, an American, as devout as she is brilliant.

Lindsey, an Oklahoman, retired in 1986 as pastor. Baptist House, the energized "flagship" evangelical congregation in Israel, once was a struggling mission church. It now attracts 300 to 350 people every Saturday morning, overflowing the tent that has served as the congregation's house of worship since arsonists torched its chapel in 1982. While I was in Israel, the Baptist House featured music by Liz Kopp, who learned her bouncy, black-gospel piano playing as a white girl growing up in the black neighborhoods of Chicago. She and her husband Chuck are typical of a small colony of evangelical Protestants who have moved to Israel.

Lindsey attributes the growth in professions of faith at Baptist House to charismatic conferences in Israel in 1974 and 1976. The charismatic movement, which has burgeoned worldwide in recent years, emphasizes the Holy Spirit and the gifts of healing and speaking in tongues.

"It (growth) never happened until that (the charismatic movement) happened," Lindsey said in 1985. "The last five years have seen the change."

Lindsey's congregation has met on property the Baptists have owned for sixty years in the quiet, upper-class neighborhood of Rehavia, close to the center of the city. Orthodox Jews have fought Baptist efforts to rebuild on the same location and, despite Mayor Kollek's promise of assistance, the issue has yet to be resolved. Lindsey also is a researcher who believes the Gospels were derived indirectly from a Hebrew source, not a Greek text as is widely assumed.

David Elliott, dean of the beautiful St. George's Cathedral in East Jerusalem, led the very worshipful services in that congregation while we lived in Israel. A former jazz pianist and businessman, he was a superlative preacher and liturgist. An acolyte once described Elliott as "a good sacramentalist, a good preacher, and a good disciplinarian." I would say "great" in each case. John Peterson, an American, is the able dean of St. George's College.

The Lutheran Church of the Redeemer meets in one of the most impressive buildings in the Old City, in my opinion. This congregation sponsors the earliest of the multitude of Easter sunrise services, meeting at dawn on the Mount of Olives before the sun can be seen in the rest of Jerusalem to the west.

The Evangelicals

There are a host of evangelical educational institutions in Israel. The late Douglas Young, dean of Trinity Evangelical Divinity School in suburban Chicago, founded the Institute of Holy Land Studies in 1959. In cooperation with one hundred American colleges, some five thousand students have studied there for short periods since then. His wife, known to all as Snook, is one of Jerusalem's most gracious hostesses.

James Fleming, a historical geographer at Hebrew University, directs the Jerusalem Center for Biblical Studies with a curriculum specially tailored for students or preachers who can only spend a few weeks in Israel. St. George's College and the Ecumenical Institute at Tantur, founded after the Vatican conferences in the 1960s, also attract students.

One of the most significant evangelical Christian institutions is the aforementioned Jerusalem School for the Study of the Synoptic Gospels, headed by David Bivin, 48. Fellow Oklahoman Robert Lindsey and Jewish scholar David Flusser of Hebrew University also have contributed as scholars. Their theory is that the New Testament originally was written in Hebrew, not Greek. In their view, this theory explains why some of Jesus' sayings are confusing. When the translation was made into Greek, and then into English and other languages, difficult and hard-to-understand passages emerged. They say these difficulties often vanish when the Greek text is translated back into Hebrew, and then directly from Hebrew into the individual's modern language.

Matthew 6:22, 23, for instance, as translated from Greek to English, refers to the "good eye" and the "bad eye." Actually, Bivin says, the Hebrew word for "good eye" also means generosity, and "bad eye," miserly or stingy; if the gospels were written first in Hebrew, those were probably the intended meanings. In

Luke 10:9, explains Bivin, Jesus says the kingdom of God has "come near." But he points out that the Hebrew word "to come near" also means "already arrived," which in this case gives quite a different interpretation altogether.[2]

I knew other Christians: Rick Hurst, who opened the coffee shop inside Jaffa Gate; Merv and Meridel Watson, gospel singers; Jay and Marabelle Rawlings, who have produced film documentaries on Israel and Soviet Jewry; Charles Bennett, who broadcast for a station in Springfield, Missouri; Andrew Burrows, the Yale linguist and friend to all. Hurst, Burrows, and I got together weekly; it was a godsend.

The biggest foreign news staff in Israel is operated by Middle East Television, owned by Pat Robertson, founder of the Christian Broadcasting Network and former host of its "700 Club." Robertson, like many—but not all—evangelicals, is strongly pro-Israel, a position with origins in the belief that the Jews are God's chosen people and modern Israel is the fulfillment of biblical prophecy. MET's anchor, Peter Darg, is the match of any American anchor.

The evangelicals often are so strongly pro-Israel that they tend to overlook anything that the Jewish state does that is wrong, no matter how grievous. Theirs is a valid position, but they carry it far beyond the God of the Bible, who frequently scolded and punished the Israelites for not following his law (see Appendix D). And surely his law includes an obligation to be just and righteous. One American evangelical living in Jerusalem told me he would be proud to have his son serve in the Israeli army. Another said that the covenant of the Promised Land did not depend on the obedience of the Jewish people.

The most outspoken evangelical institution in Israel is the International Christian Embassy in Jerusalem, established in 1982 when Israel declared Jerusalem its eternal capital (and when many nations moved their embassies to Tel Aviv in protest). The

---

2. See further information in *Understanding the Difficult Words of Jesus: New Insights from a Hebraic Perspective*, by David Bivin and Roy Blizzard, Jr., with a foreword by Robert Lindsey (Austin, Tex.: Center for Judaic-Christian Studies, 1983).

Christian Embassy was established to declare that though others may leave, the Christians have *their* embassy in Jerusalem.

The embassy sponsors an annual Feast of the Tabernacles celebration in Israel, concomitant with the Jewish festival of the same name (Leviticus 23:34–36) commemorating harvest as well as the Israelites' wandering in the wilderness. People come to the Christian festival from many countries. But in recent years, attendance has dropped from six thousand to three thousand. The Christian Embassy attributes this drop to economic reasons and the fear of hijackings; but others say it is due to internal dissension.

Jan Willem Van Der Hoeven, 47, a Dutchman and an embassy spokesman, is best known for statements offered in aggressive support of Israel. The Christian Embassy, for instance, says Israel must continue to hold the West Bank because of "the indivisibility of the Land of Israel."

"Israel treats the Palestinian population . . . far better than Jordan, Syria or Egypt have treated the Palestinians," says Van Der Hoeven, who frequently points out that he is married to an Arab.

Much of the local Christian community boycotts the embassy. Yet Van Der Hoeven estimates that 80 percent of the 50 million evangelicals in the United States hold similar views concerning Israel. He says the Christian embassy has a constituency in approximately twenty countries, including some twenty thousand persons in the United States.

I once asked Van Der Hoeven if there was *anything* Israel could do to which he would object. He paused only a moment and said, yes, there was—to ease the availability of abortion in Israel.

Near Haifa, in the land of the tribe of Asher, other Christian fundamentalists have spent $13 million drilling for oil because Moses told the Israelites, "Blessed above sons be Asher . . . let him dip his foot in oil" (Deut. 33:24). So far they have had nothing but dry holes.

The American Colony

Horatio Spafford was a prominent Chicago lawyer in the late 1800s. He also was a committed Christian and a close friend of the evangelist Dwight L. Moody and Frances Willard, founder of the Women's Christian Temperance Union. In 1873, Spafford, his wife Valentine, and their four daughters were planning to take a ship to London for a holiday; when a business deal delayed him at the last moment, he sent them on ahead. At sea, on November 21, the ship collided with another ship and sank; the four Spafford children drowned. Mrs. Spafford went on to London and cabled her husband, "Saved alone." In his grief he wrote the touching hymn, "It Is Well with My Soul":

> When peace, like a river, attendeth my way,
> When sorrows like sea billows roll;
> Whatever my lot, thou hast taught me to say,
> It is well, it is well with my soul.

When the Spaffords had a fifth child who died of tuberculosis, their church in Chicago decided they must be terrible sinners for so much tragedy to hit them. Soon thereafter Spafford, his wife, and their new children moved to Palestine and there formed the American Colony to help the people of Palestine. The American Colony is now known the world over, especially by foreign correspondents, as the favorite hotel in Jerusalem. Once owned by an Arab pasha, it was bought by the Spaffords and converted into a hotel in 1902. T. E. Lawrence, the famed Lawrence of Arabia, British Field Marshal Lord Allenby, who conquered the holy land for the British in 1917, and a host of others have stayed there over the years.

One of the belles of the city today—as she always has been—is Anna Spafford Lind, now in her eighties. The silvery-haired Anna Grace, as she is known to her friends, drives with abandon all over Jerusalem and never fails to be in the pew at St. George's Cathedral on Sundays. She lives in the Spafford home that literally is part of the north wall of the Old City. From its rooftop, in the late nineteenth century, while having his devotions one day, the English general Charles Gordon looked out and noticed that the rocky hillside bore a resemblance to a skull. He surmised that this was Golgotha, "the place of a skull," referred to in the Gospels (Matthew 27:33, Mark 15:22, and

Luke 23:33), where Jesus was crucified. On this basis, the Garden Tomb was identified nearby and still is pointed out as the site most like in appearance where Jesus was buried. The "skull" now overlooks the teeming central Arab bus station. General Gordon made known his theory, and in time this rocky crag came to be known as "Gordon's Calvary"; tourists continue to be led to this spot today.

Anna Grace, after service as an officer in the U.S. Waves during World War II, helped run the hotel with her brother, Horatio Vester. She still operates the Spafford Children's Center, a clinic in the Old City for Arab mothers, treating thousands of patients every year.

The family is unusual in its mix of loyalties. Horatio Spafford and his wife Valentine were great supporters of the Palestinian cause. Anna Grace supports Israel with as much verve. In fact, during the 1967 War, when Jerusalem was unified, she brushed aside the Arab soldiers' order that they use her clinic. Then located in the family home, its door was locked and Anna Grace dropped the key in her apron pocket. Then she went to the roof and waved a welcome to Israeli soldiers advancing from the Notre Dame on the hilltop to the west. She even offered them lemonade.

Her brother Horatio died on Thanksgiving Day 1985 and is buried in the family plot on Mount Scopus.

But the family cheer lived on. A short time later, we had a dinner party and invited Val, still in her grief. She asked if she could bring her sister, Biddy. Of course, we said. Two of our other guests that night were Paul Reynolds and Keith Graves, both of BBC, the British Broadcasting Company. When the guests arrived and were introduced, Biddy remarked that she worked for BBC.

Over dinner, Reynolds and Graves, as reporters do, talked back and forth knocking BBC for one thing or another. As the meal wore on, one of them, wanting to draw Biddy into the conversation, politely asked what she had done at BBC, thinking she probably was a secretary or file clerk.

"I am vice chairman," she said, smiling. Reynolds and Graves choked in their embarrassment.

Guardians of the Holy Sites

Brown-robed Franciscan priests chant mass in the Christian holy sites in Israel every morning; to the tourist, they are the most visible of all the Christians in the holy land. These priests, along with the Greek Orthodox, Ethiopian Christians, Coptics (Egyptians), and Syrian Orthodox—numbering about two thousand in all—tend the holy sites and minister through hospitals and schools.

The various groups compete bitterly for turf at the Church of the Holy Sepulchre in Jerusalem and the Church of the Nativity in Bethlehem. They rigidly follow an unbelievably precise "status quo" agreement worked out in 1852 during Ottoman rule. One group dusts the floors, for instance, and another group dusts the steps. "The floor of the basilica is cleaned and the pillars up to the cornice are dusted daily by the Orthodox," the agreement says. But it gets complicated. What happens when the base of a column is removed, creating a few square centimeters of floor? Is the new floor area the jurisdiction of the group assigned to the floor? Or that responsible for the columns?

The Greek Orthodox repaired the leaky roof at the Church of the Nativity in the stealth of the night three years ago. Police had to break up a fight between the holy men of the Armenians and the Greek Orthodox at Christmastime 1984; they were arguing over who should do the ritualistic dusting of six inches of tile along the wall above the grotto!

The representative of Israel's Religious Affairs Ministry emphasized this conflict during an annual tour of Bethlehem for foreign correspondents. Naturally, the correspondents focused on that issue for their traditional Bethlehem stories that year. I suspect that the representative knew the journalists would do so, and focused on Christian discord for that very reason.

Three Christians bear the awesome title of "patriarch" in Jerusalem—Diodoros I of the Greek Orthodox, Giacome Giuseppe Beltritti of the Latin Church, and Yeghishe Derderian of the Armenian Church. Each is referred to as "His Beatitude." Their Moslem counterpart is Sheikh Sa'ad Eddin Alami, chairman of the Supreme Moslem Council. Two bishops of Jerusalem are Palestinians—Samir Kafity of the Anglicans and Daoud Haddad of the Lutherans.

The Roman Catholic Church's relationship with Israel is complicated by the Vatican's refusal to recognize Israel because of the Palestinian problem. The church emphasizes the problem is political, not theological. Pope John Paul II visited the great synagogue in Rome in 1986, but he has not budged on recognition of Israel. John Paul, however, did agree in 1987 to study the Holocaust and anti-Semitisim and issue a report. Pope John XXIII and Pope Paul VI visited the holy land. President Carter once privately asked John Paul to visit Israel, but he replied, "That would embarrass the pope." "What's wrong with that?" Carter asked, to which the pope replied, "Nothing, I guess." But so far he has not done so.

Father Jerome Murphy-O'Connor, a Dominican monk assigned to Ecole Biblique in Jerusalem, a graduate school in biblical and archaeological studies, points out that the monks in the monasteries also help hold title to their buildings, according to Middle Eastern practice. "They lead lives of desolation, but they perform an essential task in the Middle East," he says.

The Armenians

Hagop Antreassian, 43, is one of the best-known artists in Jerusalem. For his ceramics he takes the design—often flowers or a bird symbolizing paradise—from ancient Armenian manuscripts. Antreassian was born and raised in the Armenian Quarter, a walled city within Jerusalem's Old City. Antreassian was the son of a priest, but now he goes to the nearby third-century Cathedral of St. James only for weddings and funerals. When he got married a few years ago, he took for his bride a young woman, Armine, from Jordan.

The first Armenians arrived in Jerusalem at the time of the Crusades, and a second group went there in 1915, to escape the massacres of the Turks in their native land. Their numbers in Israel are declining. When Antreassian was a boy, fifteen thousand Armenians lived in Israel. Today only three thousand remain. And, as their numbers are declining, so the church-going habits of the people are diminishing as well. Armenians observe their Christian holidays by themselves; their Christmas, which marks both the birth and spiritual baptism of Jesus, falls on January 18.

9

The Bond to the Past

My strength is dried up like a potsherd, and my tongue cleaves to my jaws; thou dost lay me in the dust of death.

—Psalm 22:15

Israelis are a people living existentially for the moment. Theirs is a hedonistic approach to life that people long exposed to war often pursue. For whatever reason, they are surely not that much different than other Western peoples. Yet, Israelis also feel bonded to their roots in a land they claimed for themselves but had not been able to occupy for nearly two thousand years. Now archeological excavations dot the map of Israel, and are busy uncovering some of those roots. The excavations are not merely for the professional archeologist or student; many ordinary citizens sign on "digs" as a way to spend a short holiday. More significantly, the findings from archeological exploration have had profound meaning for the faithful around the world.

In this chapter, I want to review three of the most interesting discoveries.

The Jesus Boat

For Christians, perhaps the most fascinating recent discovery was a boat dating to Jesus' time. The boat was found on the Sea of Galilee's northwestern shore near the place Jesus often visited during his ministry. The 27-foot by 7.5-foot boat could conveniently have carried all twelve of the disciples, although the mathematical chance that this is actually a craft the Master used is small. Josephus, a leading historian of the era, wrote that hundreds of ships sailed the bustling Galilee in Jesus' time.

In 1986, when this ancient vessel was found, the level of the lake was several feet lower than normal because of a prolonged drought. The tractor of two brothers, Moshe and Yuval Lufan from Kibbutz Nof Ginosar, became stuck in the mud near the water, and in trying to free it, the men discovered a small, curved piece of wood in the earth. In digging, they quickly discovered a boat. Excited, they called Mendel Nun, an expert on the Galilee, who in turn contacted Shelley Wachsmann, Israel's inspector of underwater antiquities. After working night and day, only the lower part of the boat could be found, preserved in the soft, cheddar cheese-like mud. A cooking pot and a lamp found near the boat dated it to the first century A.D.. The boat was carefully lifted from the mud and sailed around the bend to Nof Ginosar where it was placed in a large tub-like structure to soak in special chemicals. The experts say that by soaking for several years they believe that strength will be restored to the wood.

The discovery of this boat also may shed light on the "nautical Masada" Josephus describes in his *Wars* (Book III). He wrote that 6,500 Jews sailed off Migdal into the center of the sea to escape the invading Romans. In an ensuing battle, most were killed. "The lake [was] all bloody . . . and the shore full of shipwrecks," he wrote. To fill out the picture, across the highway at Migdal, on the lake's western shore only a few hundred yards away, Franciscan fathers have found a mosaic from the floor of a Roman villa also dating to the first century. The mosaic shows the mast, bow, and sail of a boat. Thus, between it and the boat, there is a complete and accurate picture of the boats common during Jesus' day. From now on, the boats used to illustrate Sunday school lessons and discussed in scholarly works concerning Jesus' ministry along the Sea of Galilee can draw from this utmost example for accuracy of detail.

Computers and the Verbal Inspiration of the Bible

A team of Israeli researchers has used hi-tech methods to add evidence in support of the doctrine of verbal inspiration of the

Bible, the view that every word of the Bible is inspired of God. Dr. Moshe Katz, a Technion University biomechanic with a degree in Bible studies, and Dr. Fred Weiner, a computer specialist on Technion's medical faculty, fed the Hebrew Scriptures into a computer. Under programming by Dr. Eliyahu Rips, a Hebrew University mathematician, the computer scanned the Scriptures.

Something rather amazing was revealed. Words and messages leaped out when the computer used only every twenty-sixth or every fiftieth letter. Katz points out that these numbers are significant in the Bible. When its Hebrew letters are given their numerical equivalent, the Hebrew name *Yahweh* (usually translated Jehovah or LORD) becomes No. 26. Fifty, or seven times seven plus one, is also significant. There were seven days in the week of Creation. It is fifty days between Passover and Shavuot, the Jewish equivalent of the Christian Pentecost; farmers were told to work the land forty-nine years and rest it in the fiftieth, the jubilee year.

By counting every twenty-sixth letter, the computer found *Elohim*, Hebrew for God, hidden 147 times among the letters of the book of Genesis. Katz calculated that the probability of this happening by chance is 1:2 million to 1:3 million. In Genesis 12, which tells of the Lord promising Abraham the land of Canaan, the computer found the names *Jerusalem* and *Moriah* (the mount on which the temple was built hundreds of years later). In Genesis 28, when Jacob awakened after his dream about the ladder, he said, "Surely the Lord is in this place." By counting every twenty-sixth letter, the computer found the words *temple* and *Torah*, the Hebrew word for the Pentateuch, the first five books of the Bible. At the start and the end of four of these first five books, the computer counted every fiftieth letter and found the word *Torah*. Further, they found that if just one letter was removed from the Hebrew Bible, all the findings collapsed.

Since the nineteenth century, many biblical scholars have believed the Bible was pieced together centuries after the dates of the actual events described. Skilled editors, it is said, basically used four ancient sources—the J, E, D and P documents. Katz is reluctant to say the computers have proved literal inspiration. But when a reporter asked if Katz believed the Bible was dictated by God, he said: "It seems you came to the right conclusion." Jesus said that "not an iota, not a dot" would pass from the Law (Matthew 5:18).

My story on this research attracted more attention than almost any other news story or feature I wrote during my three years in Israel. It suggested to me that, as often is true in the history of faith, ordinary people are more prepared to believe the unusual or miracles than the intellectuals and scholars.

The Dead Sea Scrolls

Until a generation ago, the oldest manuscripts of the Bible dated back to about A.D. 1000. In 1947, an Arab shepherd boy named Mohammed Dehib, now dead, found scrolls in a Qumran cave near the Dead Sea. The scrolls were well-preserved in the desert conditions. Bedouins and archeologists scoured the Dead Sea cliffs and canyons, finding documents in eleven caves. They also found scores of documents reflecting the religious life and beliefs of the time. The documents dated to a three-hundred-year span of time, from the mid-third century before Christ until A.D. 68. This meant that the Old Testament texts found at Qumran were about one thousand years closer to the original texts than previously available manuscripts and, therefore, they were that much more likely to be accurate.

The manuscripts did reveal two additions to Jeremiah. But on the whole, they revealed few important changes in the Bible as it has been known for hundreds of years. This was important because people could continue to maintain that the Bible is error-free.

The first volume of the Dead Sea Scrolls was published in 1955 when Jordan controlled Qumran and East Jerusalem. French, American, British, and German schools of archeology each appointed a member to a committee of scholars under the sponsorship of the then-private Rockefeller Museum to take custody of the fragments and to control research and publication. So far, seven volumes have been published, and the late Pierre Benoit estimated that the remaining fragments will fill another six or seven volumes. Benoit, who was director-emeritus of Ecole Biblique, said that many of the documents are tiny, fingernail-sized fragments—

difficult to translate and even more difficult to place in a correct context.

More than forty years after discovery of the Dead Sea Scrolls revolutionized biblical study, more than half of them still have not been published.

Thousands of fragments from more than six hundred documents and almost every book of the Bible remain locked away at the Rockefeller Museum in East Jerusalem. For years they have been in the custody of six scholars, who had not finished their research and were barring others' access to the documents. So tight was their custody that when one of them died, he willed his rights to the fragments to the scholar of his choice.

Since 1985, however, the circle of scholars involved has broadened because the ones with custody realized that the work could not be completed in their lifetimes. Hershel Shanks, editor of the *Biblical Archaeological Review* in the U.S., also had proposed that the scholars should either let some of the scrolls be assigned to some of the host of eager, able young scholars, or allow the scrolls to be photographed for access to them in that fashion. Now nine scholars are at work on the biblical fragments. Israelis, previously barred because the scrolls were stored in what was then Jordan, have been added to the team.

Maggen Broshi, curator of Israel's Shrine of the Book, where the first published Dead Sea Scrolls are housed and are on display, says the unpublished documents include about two hundred fragments from every book in the Hebrew Bible except Esther.

"The surprising fact is they are, by and large, identical to the present texts. It is very significant," Broshi said. "It's substantially the same text," Benoit said.

Frank Moore Cross, a member of the international committee for editing the Dead Sea Scrolls, and a professor of Oriental languages at Harvard University, points out one example of the contribution the Scrolls have made to biblical interpretation. Recently he has set forth his view that the scroll of 1 Samuel found at Qumran near the Dead Sea, when the treasured scrolls were discovered in 1947, contains a few lines that are missing from the "received text"—the Hebrew text from which all translations were subsequently made. He says this recovered scroll takes us closer to the original and complete text of 1 Samuel, chapter 11.[1]

Scholars J. M. Allegro of Manchester, England, and M. Baillet of Bordeaux, France, have finished their work and published their findings. The scholars who have not finished are Cross; John Strugnell, also of Harvard; Jean Starkey of Paris; Polish scholar J. T. Milik, now of Paris; Eugene Ulrich of Notre Dame; and Benoit. Patrick Skehan died in 1980 and assigned his rights to Ulrich. Benoit died in 1987 and Strugnell succeeded him as general editor. Starkey was the first to share his documents with new scholars; Strugnell and Cross followed.

Honeycombing the Land

Dothan (Free)

I have previously mentioned my first trip to the Middle East in 1964, to participate in an archeological excavation at Dothan, on the West Bank. Dothan is a *tell*, or hill, that looms over the Plain of Dothan. It was the place where Joseph was dropped in a pit by his brothers (Genesis 37), and it has had continuous occupation ever since. The excavation was the ninth and final one conducted by Joseph P. Free.

During my season, we dug at three locations. One was a previously uncovered Late Bronze or Iron I tomb on the west side of the *tell* dating to the time of the Judges. It yielded 3,100 objects, making it one of the richest tombs ever found in the holy land. Another was on top of the *tell* where relatively recent (400-500-year-old) Arabic objects were found. I dug in the third location, in the network of walls that ringed the city. The walls were twenty-five feet high and eleven feet thick at the base.

During earlier excavations, Free had found the mammoth gateway by the simple but ingenious method of pinpointing the part of the hill closest to the water well several hundred yards

---

1. Frank Moore Cross, "Original Biblical Text Reconstructed from Newly Found Fragments," Part II, *Bible Review I* (Fall 1985): 26–35.

away. We concluded the room where we were digging was a fortress because it had no doorway and was built as part of the wall—similar to the citadels at Hazor and Megiddo. Whoever wanted into the fortress lowered himself through a window. The walls apparently had been crumbled in one violent action; my hunch was that this might have occurred when Joshua conquered the northern cities, although Dothan is not named in Joshua's account.

In the Late Bronze and Early Iron stratifications, there were at least twenty-one floor levels. We found more than eight thousand potsherds of Mycean and Cypriot ware, mostly *taboons* (Arab for "oven") and jugs.

In each group there were three or four students, ten to twenty Arabs, and a supervisor. We used picks and hoes, baskets and wheelbarrows. Tawfiq, the Arab pick man, was the aristocrat; the wheelbarrow boys who hauled away the dirt were at the bottom. Some of the boys who pushed those wheelbarrows of dirt were so light I could put my fingers around their biceps. Life "on the mound" was great. We used gasoline lights, ate rice, showered in cold water and had crude toilets. I conquered the cold water by putting a big panful in the sun each morning on the way to the dig; by mid-afternoon when we quit it was warm.

Joshua's Altar on Mount Ebal (Zertal)

Shechem already was a thriving place when Abraham stopped over four thousand years ago on his trip to the Promised Land. Several hundred years later, Moses told the Israelites that after they fled from Egypt and entered the Promised Land, they should build an altar of stones on Mount Ebal and offer burnt sacrifices there (Deuteronomy 27:4, 5). Joshua did just that (Joshua 8:30–35). During four excavations in 1982–84, archeologist Adam Zertal unearthed a compound, and in the middle was a nearly square, nine-foot-high heap of stones, filled with ashes and sheep bones, perhaps from sacrifices. Zertal said he could not be sure but it may well have been the altar that Joshua built.

The City of David (Shiloh)

The City of David, on the southeast side of the Old City and within view from our balcony, was the earliest Jerusalem dating back to the time of the Jebusites whom the Israelites were unable to conquer for several hundred years.

In his eighth and final season, Yigal Shiloh, head of archeology at Hebrew University, unearthed what he said was the oldest house ever found in Jerusalem, dating back two thousand years before David. It was the remains of a rectangular house sitting on the side of a fifteen-acre hill that made up the City of David.

Now the City of David is a state-of-the-art archeological garden of ruins, stone walkways, and steel railing. Shiloh also cleared the debris from Warren's water shaft and now one can crawl up it the same way that David's aide-de-camp, Joab, did in surprising the Jebusites (2 Samuel 5:6–10, 1 Chronicles 11:4–9).

Shiloh acknowledged that David could well have been resting on the flat roof of his palace when he saw Bathsheba taking a bath on another roof (2 Samuel 11). "It was very hot. They took baths outside," he said.

The Philistine Town Timnah (Kelm-Mazar)

Judge Samson courted his Philistine girlfriend, walking the five miles from his hometown at Sorek to her village of Timnah (Judges 14) in the lush coastal plain southeast of modern Tel Aviv.

More than three thousand years later, G. L. Kelm of Southwestern Baptist Theological Seminary in Fort Worth, Texas, and Amihai Mazar of Hebrew University excavated Timnah over eight seasons. They found seals, indicating the Philistines could write, and artistic Philistine pottery decorated with geometric designs. As in Dothan, they found a gateway. This one was L-shaped in a twelve-foot-thick city wall protected by a magnificent seventy-five-by-twenty-five-foot tower.

Jesus' Crucifixion and Resurrection

Scholars and the faithful still disagree on the sites of Jesus Christ's crucifixion and resurrection. The Garden Tomb, just north of the Damascus Gate, is a sylvan plot of aleppo pine, cyprus, fig, orange, lemon, and almond trees. A limestone hill in the likeness of a skull looms nearby. It *looks* like the place where Jesus should have been buried.

A half-mile south, among the narrow alleys and Arab shops inside the Old City, is the labyrinthine Church of the Holy Sepulchre. People in every cut of religious attire scurry about.

There is an archeological rule-of-thumb that a tradition dating back close to the time of the event is more likely to be authentic than a newly identified site. A 250-million gallon cistern and a winepress in the Garden Tomb area clearly date to the time of Christ; but this place was not mentioned as a possible site of his burial until 1883, when General Charles Gordon put forth his hypothesis.

Dan Bahat, Israel's chief Jerusalem district archeologist, like many other scholars, is convinced that the Church of the Holy Sepulchre is the actual site. The origins of the church date back to A.D. 327 when Constantine converted to the Christian faith, and his mother Helena went to the holy land and identified the sites of the crucifixion and the resurrection.

Bahat believes the church was built on the remains of first-century Jewish tombs. About 1972, thirty feet below the church's Armenian section, archeologists rediscovered a charcoal graffiti-type drawing of a boat dating to about A.D. 200. It bore the Latin inscription, "O Lord, we came." Bahat believes Western Christian pilgrims sketched the boat, an object figuring prominently in Christ's life, in a canyon behind Golgotha where Christians met secretly to worship. He believes they worshiped there because it was the site of Christ's resurrection.

Biblical Garden (Hareuveni)

Of the two hundred plants named in the Bible, Nogah Hareuveni has identified and planted 90 percent of them in a 550-acre plot of jagged Judean hills and valleys known as Neot Kedumim—the Biblical Landscape Reserve of Israel.

Hareuveni did more than stick plants between the rocks on the tons of soil he trucked in. He arranged them according to biblical theme. So the Bible student finds as much interest as the botanist in the Dale of the Song of Songs, the Forest of Milk and Honey, the Jordan River Thickets, or the Vineyard of Isaiah. Olive and fig trees are in profusion, of course. So are the rose of sharon and the lily of the valley, probably the most popular plants in the Bible. Of course, he points out that the rose of sharon is not a rose, and the lily of the valley is not a lily. "It's a tulip," he says, pointing out that a rose grows on a bush while a tulip grows from a bulb. The lily probably is a narcissus.

PART III
SHALOM

10

Common Guilt, Common Task

Behold, I will bring [Jerusalem] health and cure, and I will cure them, and will reveal unto them the abundance of peace and truth.
—Jeremiah 33:6 as translated by Frieda Lewis

"What should be the main objectives of our national policy for the next fifteen years to the time when we shall mark three thousand years since King David proclaimed Jerusalem the capital of his kingdom?" asked Yitzhak Shamir, then the foreign minister, on the eve of modern Israel's fortieth birthday.

I frequently asked the question—of Israeli officials, of Arab officials, of Western diplomats, and ordinary people—"What will the map of the Middle East look like in one hundred years?" "Or even twenty-five years?" Hardly anyone would venture a confident guess. One surgeon friend feels Israel will remain in a state of war and must maintain its defensive capability for the foreseeable future. Perhaps the most pragmatic reply came from an American official: "Israel exists at the will and ability of the United States," he said. "Both the will and the ability are *sine qua non* for Israel. If one is lost, Israel will go down the tubes."

Israel is in a formal state of war with all of its Arab neighbors save Egypt. And all those wars have never been formally concluded. Yet, one can also argue persuasively that a de facto peace prevails in Israel. The treaty with Egypt has proved durable; a de facto peace exists with Jordan, for the Jordan River Valley has been quiet for several years. The Saudis are passive. A tacit understanding probably exists with Syria not to go to war any time soon. Ironically, only the boundary with Lebanon is bloody, the one Arab country in years past that Israel thought it could deal with amicably.

227

Shalom, along with its Arabic equivalent, *salaam,* is not only the word for "peace," but also is the greeting and the farewell in Israel. Certainly the constant use of the word *shalom* represents the yearning of people and governments in the Middle East. But peace is more than the absence of war; it is the fullness of life. But in the stricken Middle East, even the absence of war is a significant achievement.

Common Guilt

The story we have presented on these pages, I hope, taken in all its dimensions, is a loving one. I say once again that I left the Middle East feeling deep affection and regard for both Jew and Palestinian, for Israeli and Arab. Yet I say once again in candor that I also came away convinced that neither side works very hard for justice and peace.

The Israelis must understand that nothing is more important than administering justice and mercy. This is the universal truth of their own Scriptures. We can accept the validity of the Promise of the Land for modern Israel and still insist that Israel treat the Palestinians justly and mercifully. In fact, Jew and Christian alike can subscribe to the validity of the prophecies concerning the regathering in the Promised Land and the end times—and face the chilling possibility that the prophecies don't refer to *this* regathering, that there must be yet another dispersion and persecution of the Jews before the regathering spoken of in biblical prophecies comes true.

The Arabs must understand that terrorism is inhumane. The bloodshed among the brothers, the use of religion to justify violence, is a violation of everything they hope to achieve.

It always seems to me that in times of conflict it is important to bring together the major antagonists, a role not easily delegated. I have never understood why Israel refuses to talk to the PLO and demands the same abstention by the United States. From the standpoint of *either* Israel or the PLO, it would seem the best chance for peace would be to get Prime Minister Yitzhak Shamir and PLO Chairman Yasser Arafat across the table from each other—just as Menachem Begin and Anwar Sadat were at Camp

David. It makes no sense for the Israelis to say they are willing to speak with Hanna Siniora or Abu Rahmeh. For these two Palestinians, no matter how able, speak for few but themselves. I frequently asked at Foreign Ministry briefings why Israel refuses to talk to the PLO—and got no answer. "There's Wes checking in with his monthly question again," laughed one American reporter, who has lived in Israel twenty years.

Why don't the PLO, as the legitimate representative of the Palestinian people, and Israel talk together? Why doesn't Israel, as a modest first step, stop referring to the PLO as a terrorist organization in each and every reference to it? Why doesn't the PLO recognize Israel's right to exist? How many wars will it take to convince the PLO that Israel is here to stay? These wars have taken thousands of Israeli lives—and thousands of Arab lives. Does the PLO care?

Indeed, why doesn't Israel allow the Palestinians to form a separate, autonomous state? This would satisfy the Palestinians' legitimate right to a homeland; even from *Israel's* point of view, the West Bank, existing separately and independently, would be much less a threat to the Jewish state than if it were tied to Jordan or another Arab country.

It is worth repeating that we in the West, Christians included, must accept a huge share of the guilt.

What if Britain and France had honored their commitments in 1921 and granted Arab sovereignty and independence in Syria, Lebanon, Transjordan, and Iraq, excepting only Palestine or a part of Palestine for a Jewish state? We do not know for sure. But I believe that at least some of the tension between the Arabs and the Jews might have been defused. Think of the wars that might have been avoided and the thousands and thousands of lives that might have been saved, but for British and French perfidy.

What if the superpowers, including the United States and the Soviet Union, stopped being the suppliers of guns and bullets to the Israelis and the Arabs? When one thinks of Western insensitivity, one need only recall the patronizing plea of U.N. Ambassador Warren Austin during a heated debate between Israel and the Arab countries. "Please," he said, "let's be Christian about this."

A Common Task

An Orthodox Jewish young man named Eleazer cleaned for my wife every other week. And Fayez, a Palestinian, did occasional carpentry or electrical work. One day, both happened to be in our apartment at the same time. "Hello," they said to each other rather tentatively, then they avoided each other. Becky was here and there around the apartment. Eleazer tried to draw out Fayez to little avail. Finally Fayez spoke.

"My son has just been falsely arrested for throwing stones in Hebron. But he did not do it," Fayez said. He added that he needed a large sum of money to get his son out of jail.

"Are you sure your son didn't throw rocks?" Eleazer asked. "I'm sure. He's my son," Fayez said. "Are you absolutely sure?" Eleazer pressed. "Yes, I'm sure. I didn't raise my son to throw stones." Three times this exchange took place.

Finally Eleazer said, "I'm genuinely sorry. You've got to trust God." Fayez turned full face and looked at him. "I'd like to trust God but I'm so tired. I'm sixty and an old man. I've lived here all my life and I haven't known anything but frustration and pain." It was a beaten-down response.

"I think your side wants peace," Fayez said. "We want peace. If only we could talk with each other."

They kept talking for a few minutes. Fayez left. Eleazer told my wife it was one of the few conversations he had ever had with an Arab. "I don't blame them for not wanting us here," Eleazer said. "The Palestinians say they want peace, but then I hear them saying they don't want us here. How do we distinguish between those who want peace and those who are willing to die with a suicide bomb in their car?"

Fayez was left with his pain.

In Sam Nissan's backyard on the western slopes of Jerusalem are an apparent biological contradiction—a palm tree, natural to the desert, and a cedar of Lebanon, which normally grows in the mountains to the north. Yet, there the palm and the cedar stand, side by side, carefully nurtured by Nissan's hands, as skilled with plants as with his surgeon's scalpel. In Scripture there is a precedent for two dissimilar living organisms sharing the same ground, for a palm tree and a cedar of Lebanon grew in Solomon's court-yard (Psalm 92:12, 13).

There is also plenty of precedent for Jews and Arabs living and working together in peace. True, Arab Moslems have often perse-cuted the Jews—in the ninth century in Sicily when Jews had to wear "a badge of shame," or in the eleventh century when Moslem Arabs massacred five thousand Jews in Spain, or when the Jews started returning in 1882. Yet, this persecution pales by compari-son to the Russian pogroms of the late 1800s and the Nazi Holo-caust of World War II. It is the West—and people who called themselves Christians, regrettably—who have visited the most persecution upon the Jews, not the Arabs.

Genesis 21, the same chapter that tells how Hagar and Ishmael were expelled into the Negev at Sarah's insistence, also tells how Abimelech, a local king, and Abraham swore to live in peaceful coexistence by dealing with each other honestly and loyally. There are modern precedents for such cooperation and coexistence.

Marvin Wilson, a Christian Zionist and Old Testament scholar, has offered a proper solution:

No solution to the problem of the land may be imposed on any people on the grounds that "it is willed by God." As a secular state, Israel is not the kingdom of God. . . . Therefore today's Christian should not blindly condone all her acts. Nevertheless, we strongly object to the practice of holding Israel to a different standard of morality from that applied to all other nation-states, especially those committed to Israel's destruction. Israel's own prophets call her to practice justice and com-passion to those they consider "strangers" in the land.[1]

There are remarkable parallels between Jews and Arabs in their nationalistic striving against Western imperialists. The 1897 Zion-ist congress in Basel, asserting the Jews' right to a national home, was paralleled by a 1913 Arab congress in Paris claiming full political rights for the Arabs. The 1894 trial of Dreyfus, the Jew-ish French soldier in Paris, was paralleled by the 1914 trial of

---

1. "'Real Estate' Theology: Zionism and Biblical Claims," The Evangelical Round Table: Christianity and the Arab/Israeli Conflict, Vol. 1, 1986 (St. Davids, Penn.: Eastern), 95–97.

ARMAGEDDON:
Will the last battle be at Megiddo?

By WESLEY G. PIPPERT
United Press International

FROM THE WINDSWEPT mound of Megiddo, looking out across the peaceful green valley of Jezreel, the visitor can almost hear the ancient cries of the dead and dying.

It is here, from the dawn of man, that the armies of the world have clashed. And it is here, some say, that the battle of Armageddon will be fought.

The mound of Megiddo, looming nearly 200 feet above surrounding terrain, overlooks the broad valley of Jezreel that stretches between Haifa and the Jordan Valley. Its place in the history books is marked by countless battles over thousands of years. More recently, however, it is a scenic wonder for Israel's tourist trade, attracting thousands of visitors per year.

Tel Megiddo is a strategically placed mound that overlooks the valley—a fertile region where wheat, cotton and vegetables grow in abundance.

It is just such a region that John describes in the Bible's Book of Revelation, saying that "the kings of the whole world" will war at Armageddon "on the great day of God the almighty."

Some Bible scholars maintain Armageddon refers to Megiddo, which is a Hebrew biblical proper noun, a place name with no known meaning.

Megiddo guards the narrow opening of the Eron Pass through the Mount Carmel range to the Mediterranean. It is the historic main route between Egypt and Mesopotamia, now Iraq.

TWENTY TIMES in the past 3,500 years, Megiddo has been overrun and conquered.

The Egyptian Pharaoh Tutmose III daringly went through the Eron Pass to conquer Megiddo in 1468 B.C. a short time later. Joshua took Megiddo during the Israelite conquest of the Promised Land.

Megiddo, spread over 15 acres, reached its greatest glory during the reign of King Solomon and the evil Ahab as one of Israel's main administrative centers, twice the size of Jerusalem.

But the mound was abandoned by its residents in the fifth century B.C. and has been uninhabited since. The site played a part both in the English push against the Turks in World War I and in the Israeli War of Independence in 1948.

In the 20th century, Megiddo has been excavated several times, most recently by Yigael Yadin in 1971.

Today, tourists can see the wall that surrounded Megiddo and the stone remains of stables for up to 450 horses dating from the time of Solomon and Ahab.

The immense L-shaped water system, which provided the model for James Michener's book *The Source,* allowed residents to go deep into the vertical shaft and then along the horizontal section to a hidden spring outside the city—safe from enemy detection.

But the main draw of the site may stem from the biblical tale of Armageddon. Many conservative Christians believe the battle of Armageddon will be an apocalyptic event in which, after the Second Coming, Jesus Christ will defeat the forces of evil and usher in a millenium of peace.

"My mother used to say the blood will flow ankle deep during the Armageddon," one visitor at Megiddo said.

Some Christians see a conflagration between the Soviet Union—"the anti-Christ"—and the United States occurring at Armageddon. Since the two superpowers are patrons of the hostile Middle Eastern states of Israel and Syria, it does not seem impossible "the kings of the whole world" could be drawn into the conflict.

"The excavations (at Megiddo) peel away the layers of history and despite the peace of the fertile valley, one can almost hear the advance of soldiers, be it Joshua or the war of independence," said Thena Ayres of Vancouver, British Columbia, one of thousands of tourists who visit each year.

"What stays with me are the questions: Will there really be a last battle? Will it be here?"

The Stars and Stripes, June 6, 1985

Major Aziz Ali al-Masri in Constantinople on charges of embezzlement, although his real "crime" had been organizing an association of army officers like the Arab secret societies. "His trial had shaken the Arab world more profoundly, perhaps, than any single act of Turkish tyranny, and greatly hardened the Arab will to freedom, for it had moved the masses as well as the thinkers," Antonius says.[2] And the 1917 Balfour Declaration, promising the Jews a national home, was paralleled by the 1914 promise of Lord Kitchener, the British agent in Cairo, to Hussein, the Sharif of Mecca, that if the Arabs would join the war against the Ottoman Empire, the British would support "the Arab nation" and "the emancipation of the Arabs."[3]

Faisal, the son of the Arab leader Hussein, and Chaim Weizmann, the Zionist who became first president of Israel, signed an agreement in 1919 recognizing "the racial kinship and ancient bonds existing between the Arabs and the Jewish people," and calling for "the closest possible collaboration" in developing Palestine. The agreement called for encouraging immigration of Jews "on a large scale" although it did not take up the question of a Jewish state. This germ of hope was snuffed out by the duplicity of the British and French at the end of World War I.

The cooperation can come in ways big and small. Israel sells irrigation equipment to Saudi Arabia through European dealers. Israelis have advised China on irrigation, even though the two nations do not have diplomatic relations. Israel and Egypt have cooperated for several years on a project on how to raise cotton in the desert.

Dr. Joseph Schenker, chairman of obstetrics at Hadassah Hospital in Jerusalem, once cancelled an appointment with my wife. The reason he gave later was that he had "to go to a country with whom Israel does not have formal relations to treat the wife of the leader." He did not elaborate, but the possibilities of whom he might have treated are awesome, indeed.

Many of Schenker's patients are Arabs. Many of Nissan's

2. Antonius, 121.
3. Ibid., 133.

patients are Arabs. What they are doing day-to-day—far removed from the political dealings—brings reality to the words of Frieda S. Lewis, national president of Hadassah. While in Jerusalem she pointed out that Isaiah and Jeremiah used the term "health" to mean not only physical health but righteousness, a love of peace and truth, possession of what these prophets call "the glory of the Lord."[4]

She quoted Isaiah: "Then shall thy light break forth as the morning and thine health shall spring forth speedily: And thy righteousness shall go before thee; the glory of the Lord shall be thy reward" (58:8, her translation). She also quoted Jeremiah in speaking of Jerusalem: "Behold, I will bring it health and cure, and I will cure them, and will reveal unto them the abundance of peace and truth" (33:6).

One afternoon in the spacious UPI bureau in the *Yedioth Ahrenot* newspaper in Tel Aviv, several of us reporters sat talking. I looked around the group. There were: Ohad Gozani, a sabra Israeli; Anan Safadi, a Palestinian Israeli; Gerald Nadler, an American Jew; and me, a Gentile—all of UPI; also there Georg Spieker, of the German Press Agency (DPA); and Vittorio Franleucci, of the Italian news agency ANSA.

Then I realized the significance of the make-up of the group—how many backgrounds and points of view were represented, and how much blood had been shed by our various countrymen fighting each other. Our conversation was easy and relaxed as we talked about the news of the day. Whatever our pasts, we were bound together by a common task: covering the news. I have never forgotten that scene. How I wish it could be imposed on the entire Middle East.

Every year, for several years, the mixed village of Neve Shalom ("Oasis of Peace") at the foot of the mountains west of Jerusalem has given free Christmas trees to whomever wanted them. Neve Shalom is a remarkable place, founded in 1970 by a Dominican monk, Bruno Hussar. Jews and Arabs live there now. When it sponsored an arts and music festival, UPI's Patricia Behre paid a

---

4. From remarks at the dedication of the Tannenbaum Tourist Center at Hadassah Hospital in Jerusalem.

visit. "On a day splashed with desert sunshine in this tiny village, the dimensions of the Arab-Jewish struggle shrink to jousting over a grassy patch from which to listen to music," she wrote. About five thousand Arab and Jewish youths have attended such workshops at Neve Shalom, and, as Behre put it, "they represent a small voice for peace amid a loud din of Arab-Jewish discord."

Professor Daniel Bar-Tal of Tel Aviv University, who found that 50 percent of the literature in Israeli grade schools put Arabs in a bad light (see chapter 3), began directing a program to help Jewish and Arab highschool teachers and principals learn to cope with each other's differences. He said that learning about each other's personal lives and problems is as important as lectures on Jewish and Arab history, society, culture, and religion.

One of the most courageous attempts to bridge the gap between Jews and Arabs was the film, *Beyond the Walls,* the story of life inside an Israeli prison. Produced by Israelis Uri Barbash and Rudy Cohen, the film is the story of the gradual development of a friendship between two prisoners—an Israeli criminal and an Arab charged with a political offense—who shared the same cell block. It was one of five films nominated for an Oscar as the best foreign film of 1985. Members of the Knesset condemned it, but thousands of Israelis lined up to see it.

Examples of individual cooperation could be noted. Sometimes it is the cooperation between Jew and Arab through the bond of the Christian faith. Sometimes Jews and Arabs have reached out to Christians. Sometimes the cooperation is between Jew and Christian. It always pleased me when Israeli musicians played Christian music, as they often did. For instance, I heard the Cameran Singers and the Kibbutz Chamber Orchestra perform Handel's "Messiah," and the Israel Philharmonic Orchestra perform Verdi's "Requiem" and Haydn's "Mass."

Obviously, when the Western Christian extends the hand of peace and reconciliation to the Jew or Arab, it must be done sensitively and cautiously. I attended a service on Mount Zion in which a group of Christians prostrated themselves in repenting and asking forgiveness for two thousand years of persecuting the Jews. Jewish friends who accompanied us to the service were embarrassed.

In a house appropriately close to the line that divided Arab Jerusalem from Israeli Jerusalem between 1948 and 1967, a group of fifteen Arab Christians and fifteen Israeli Christians have met for fellowship and prayer for some time. Their host, John Anthony, of Hope, Arkansas, who has been in Israel for twelve years, says they are "mature" Christians. One of the participants, an Arab Christian, said: "I grew up as a Christian knowing I was supposed to love Jews. But I had never met one. Then I met one. Then I met some Jews who are Christians."

One unusual form of peacemaking is so unusual as to warrant a fuller discussion.

Non-violence

"What Gandhi did in India can we do in Palestine?" asks Mubarak Awad, an American-trained psychologist and leader of the Palestine Center for Non-Violent Resistance. His brother, Bishara Awad, is president of Bethlehem Bible College. The movement's legal counsel is Jonathan Kuttab, son of a Nazarene minister in Jerusalem's Old City and a graduate of Messiah College. All are Arabs, and all are evangelical in conviction. Almost all of the other participants in the center, however, are Moslem Arabs.

Their method of non-violent resistance is patterned after that of Mahatma Gandhi and Martin Luther King, Jr.

In January 1986, some twenty Jewish settlers moved their fence outward to encroach on an additional five acres of Arab land at their settlement of Tekoa, the hometown of the Old Testament prophet Amos, who was, ironically, a biting proponent of social justice.

More than two hundred of Awad's Palestinian followers— joined by leftist Israelis and foreign volunteers—appeared in a show of non-violent resistance. A few Israeli soldiers came to the scene, looking bewildered, as if stonethrowing they could handle, but non-violent resistance they could not. The settlers buckled. The fence came down and was withdrawn to its original position.

The same month, a group of Arab farmers complained to Awad that the Israeli authorities had been uprooting hundreds of olive and almond trees near the village of Qattana, north of Jerusalem, and were selling them. What distressed the Arabs most was that sixteen of the trees had been sold to the municipality of Jerusalem to be planted along Martin Luther King, Jr. Street. Daoud Kuttab, managing editor of the *Al Fajr* newspaper in Jerusalem, noted it was ironic that olive trees seized from Palestinians should be used to honor a freedom fighter for American blacks.

Awad organized more than one hundred people to plant seedlings in an area where the trees had been torn up. Again, he said, Israeli soldiers on the scene appeared confused at what to do. When they jerked the seedlings out of the ground, the demonstrators merely replanted them, and offered the soldiers snacks of fruit and juice.

In the spring of 1986, Israeli authorities erected a high, mesh-iron fence on the sidewalk along Arab shops near the Jewish settlement in the center of oft-bloodied Hebron, and posted soldiers at each end. The purpose was clear: to discourage shoppers from patronizing the shops. Awad assembled about forty people in Jerusalem who drove to Hebron and, despite the presence of the military governor and twice as many soldiers, spent an hour shopping and buying more than $300 worth of goods.

In preparation for the demonstration, the shoppers went through training sessions that included role-playing as an Arab shopkeeper, an Israeli soldier, a Jewish settler, and a solidarity shopper. The shopping trips continued.

Awad and his followers printed fifteen hundred posters and put reminders in local newspapers urging people to eat and drink productions from the West Bank on the first Monday of each month. He said this was an attempt to help struggling Arab farmers who often must cope with restrictive marketing orders set forth by Israeli authorities.

After months of negotiation, the six thousand persons living in the village of Al Obideh finally got permission from the military governor to hook up to the Bethlehem municipal water system. The villagers previously depended on rain water, but a drought had forced them to buy tanks of water. The military governor had proposed the selection of one person to control the spigot, and thus the price, but the villagers insisted their democratically chosen village committee would control the water. In autumn 1986 the military governor yielded.

Almost six months after planting olive trees around the settlement of Susi near the Arab village of Yatta, Awad was arrested. Two Israeli plainclothesmen went to his office, charged him with trespassing and failure to present proper identification, and incitement; and after questioning him, released him on bond.

Awad believes he was arrested because he cooperated in the production of the British television program, "Courage Along the Divide," which discussed the morality of the Israeli occupation.

Awad's wife, Nancy Nye, an American from Ohio who taught in an Arab school in Ramallah, credits her husband's mother, a dedicated Christian, for the foundation of his ideas. Awad's father was killed in the 1948 War of Independence.

"She [Mother] told us never to seek revenge. We have to forgive and work so that other mothers don't suffer," Awad says.

Awad acknowledges also that he was influenced by his education at Bluffton College, a Mennonite institution in Ohio, and by spending four weeks in India becoming immersed in Gandhi's thought. Gandhi, a Hindu, led India to independence from British rule in 1947. The ninety-nine volumes of Gandhi's writings line Awad's cluttered third-floor office walls in Arab East Jerusalem.

Awad says twenty to twenty-five Arabs come every other Monday night for a lecture or discussion on non-violence. He reports that the biggest problem is their feeling that to be non-violent puts them in conflict with the Palestine Liberation Organization's (PLO) "armed struggle."

Conflict Resolution

Social psychologist Herbert C. Kelman of Harvard University[5] believes that neither the Israelis nor the Palestinians will enter negotiations that leave their right to national existence in doubt.

---

5. The following is based on personal conversations with Kelman as well as his "The Political Psychology of the Israeli-Palestinian Conflict: How Can We Overcome the Barriers to a Negotiated Solution?" his presidential address to the International Society of Political Psychology in Amsterdam, July 1, 1986, and printed in *Political Psychology,* Vol. 8, No. 3, 1987, pp. 347–363 and "An Interactional Approach to Conflict Resolution and Its Application to Israeli-Palestinian Relations," *International Interactions,* Vol. 6, No.2, 1979, pp. 99–122.

"Each party's need for assurance about its continued national existence is probably *the* central issue in the conflict and in efforts to resolve it. . . . Each party perceives the very existence of the other—the other's status as a nation—to be a threat to its own existence and status as a nation. Each holds the view that only one can be a nation: Either we are a nation or they are."

Kelman and his colleagues began holding "problem-solving workshops in conflict resolution" in 1971. Others were held in 1972, 1979, 1982, 1984, 1985, and 1986. They invite Israeli and Palestinian scholars and others to meet at Harvard for a weekend in a congenial, non-threatening atmosphere with confidentiality. The participants are not identified publicly. Kelman simply acts as a facilitator.

Kelman says his approach views international conflict as not only a conflict between nation-states but also a conflict of societies in which psychological, cultural, social-structural, and economic dimensions are central. The approach also tends to be suspicious about imposed agreements sponsored by the great powers.

Normally, Kelman says, representatives of conflicting parties express their grievances and proclaim their rights as firmly and as militantly as possible. "If the adversary describes atrocities in which hundreds were killed, they must counter with atrocities in which thousands were killed. If the adversary cites historical claims that go back a hundred years, they must counter with claims that go back a thousand years."

"The purpose of the workshops is to create a situation in which genuine social interaction between conflicting parties becomes possible and in which there is an opportunity for new learning. Participants are encouraged to attend to the other party, to try to grasp the other's perspective, and to examine their own impact on the other," Kelman says.

Over the years, Kelman has made these six assumptions:

- Nationhood. Both Jews and Palestinians perceive themselves as nations.
- Sharing the land. For both peoples, the search for political expression of their national identity centers on the same small territory. There can be no resolution of the conflict

unless each of the peoples ends up with at least some share of the land.

- Role of the Diaspora. Both Israeli Jews and Palestinians living in Palestine see themselves as members of a larger people.

- Legitimate Leadership. Despite its divisions and weaknesses, the PLO under Arafat's leadership continues to be the only agency accepted as legitimate by most Palestinians.

- Interest in Negotiations. Both sides consider continuation of the status quo to be extremely dangerous. Many Israelis see the incorporation of Gaza and the West Bank as a threat to the democratic and Jewish character of the state and to the integrity of their ideals. Palestinians see continuation of the status quo as leading to the loss of any territorial base at all for exercising self-determination.

- The Right to National Existence as the *sine qua non* of Negotiation. No Israeli or Palestinian leader will enter into negotiations that leave their right to national existence in doubt.

"In sum, as long as the only meaning of the other's national quest is perceived to be the destruction of one's own national aspirations, there is no basis for negotiation," Kelman says (*Political Psychology*, p. 362). "Once each side learns however . . . to recognize that the other side has needs, purposes, and visions apart from its desire to destroy one's own camp—there is a basis for accepting the other as a negotiating party."

Armageddon

I stood on Megiddo one day and looked out over the lush Valley of Jezreel. Megiddo is set at the pass of the historic highway between Egypt and Mesopotamia; over the centuries, many battles have been fought there. Revelation says the "kings of the whole world" (16:14) will gather there in the last days for the Battle of Armageddon. The fact that the two arch enemies, Israel and Syria, have as their patrons the superpowers, the United States and the Soviet Union, makes me realize that what my mother told me as

240

a boy—that blood would flow ankle-deep during the Battle of Armageddon—could well come true.

The blood has already flowed. Is this what the Middle East and its people, Jews and Arabs, are coming to? Or, do we put our trust in what the prophet Jeremiah said?

> At that time Jerusalem shall be called the throne of the Lord, and all nations shall gather to it, to the presence of the Lord in Jerusalem, and they shall no more stubbornly follow their own evil heart.
>
> —*Jeremiah 3:17*

Appendix A
Leaders of Israel

Patriarchs	Served	Chief Aides	Evaluation
Abraham			
Isaac			
Jacob			
Conquerors			
Moses		Aaron	
Joshua			
Judges			
Othniel	40 years		Israel Rested
Ehud	80 years		Israel Rested
Shamgar			
Deborah	40 years	Barak	Israel Rested
Gideon	40 years		Israel Rested
Abimelech			
Tola			
Jair			
Jephthah	6 years		
Ibzan	7 years		
Elon	10 years		
Abdon			Israel Oppressed
Samson	20 years		
Samuel			
Kings			
Saul	40 years	Abner	
David	40 years	Joab	Just
Solomon	40 years	Azariah	Wise

Leaders of Israel (*continued*)

Israel			Judah		
Kings	**Served**	**Evaluation**	**Kings**	**Served**	**Evaluation**
Jeroboam	22 years	Sinned	Rehoboam	17 years	Evil
			Abijah	3 years	Not wholly true
Nadab	2 years	Evil	Asa	41 years	Right
Baasha	24 years	Evil			
Elah	2 years	A drunk			
Zimri	7 days	Evil			
Omri	12 years	Most evil			
Ahab	22 years	Most evil	Jehoshaphat	25 years	Right
Ahaziah	2 years	Evil			
Jehoram	12 years	Evil	Jehoram	8 years	Evil
Jehu	28 years	Well	Ahaziah	1 year	Evil
			Athaliah	7 years	A killer
Jehoahaz	17 years	Evil	Joash	40 years	Right
Johoash	16 years	Evil	Amaziah	29 years	Right
Jeroboam	41 years	Evil	Uzziah	52 years	Right
Zechariah	6 months	Evil			
Shallum	1 month	Conspirator			
Menahem	10 years	Evil			
Pekahiah	2 years	Evil			
Pekah	20 years	Evil	Jotham	16 years	Right
Hoshea	9 years	Evil	Ahaz	16 years	Evil
(Conquered by Assyria, 721 B.C.)			Hezekiah	29 years	Right
			Manasseh	55 years	Evil
			Amon	2 years	Evil
			Josiah	31 years	Right
			Johoahaz	3 months	Evil
			Jehoiakim	11 years	Evil
			Jehoiachin	3 months	Evil
			Zedekiah	11 years	Evil
			(Babylonian Captivity, 586 B.C.)		

Modern Israel

Presidents	Served	Prime Ministers	Served	Party
Chaim Weizman	1948–52	David Ben-Gurion	1948–53, 55–63	Labor
Itzhak Ben-Zvi	1952–63	Moshe Sharett	1954–55	Labor
Zalman Shazar	1963–73	Levi Eshkol	1963–69	Labor
Ephraim Katzir	1973–78	Golda Meir	1969–74	Labor
Yitzhak Navon	1978–83	Yitzhak Rabin	1974–77	Labor
Chaim Herzog	1983–	Menachem Begin	1977–83	Likud
		Yitzhak Shamir	1983–84, 86–	Likud
		Shimon Peres	1984–86	Labor

Appendix B
Chronology

To get a fix on Middle East chronology, it is convenient to recall that sweeps of history often are 400 years in length. The Israelites were in slavery in Egypt 430 years (Exodus 12:40); from the Exodus to the monarchy was approximately 400 years (1 Kings 6:1); and the monarchy lasted about 400 years. From just prior to the time of Christ until A.D. 330, the Romans ruled Palestine. From 395 to 636, the Byzantine Empire ruled Palestine from Constantinople. With the birth of Islam and the bursting forth of the Arabs, they ruled the Middle East from 632 to 1096—first from Damascus and later from Baghdad. The Crusaders had an abbreviated rule, from 1096 until shortly after Saladin conquered them in 1187; then the Mamelukes ruled until the Ottoman conquest in 1517, and the Turks ruled until 1917. The British mandate lasted until 1948.

Ancient Israel

ca. 1900–2100 B.C.—Abraham
About 1440 B.C.—The Exodus and the Conquest*
1400–1000 B.C.—The Judges
1000 B.C.—King David
960 B.C.—Solomon builds temple
721 B.C.—Conquest of Israel by Assyrians
586 B.C.—Conquest of Judah by Babylonians, Jerusalem sacked
538 B.C.—Return from Babylon, rebuilding of temple
A.D. 70—Destruction of temple

Modern Israel

A.D. 1882—First *Aliyah*
1897—First Zionist Congress in Basel
1917—Balfour Declaration

---

*See John J. Bimson and David Livingston, "Redating the Exodus," *Biblical Archaeological Review*, 13-5 (Sept.-Oct. 1987), 40.

1922–1948—British mandate

1939—British white paper seeks to limit Jewish immigration

Nov. 29, 1947—U.N. General Assembly approves partition of Palestine, including a Jewish state

May 14, 1948—Israel proclaimed a nation

1950—Law of Return affirms right of every Jew to live in Israel

1956—Sinai Campaign

1962—Israel executes Nazi Adolf Eichmann

1964—Palestine Liberation Organization is founded

1967—Six-Day War, Israel captures the West Bank, Golan, and Gaza; unifies Jerusalem

Nov. 22, 1967—U.N. Security Council passes Res. 242

1967–70—War of Attrition

1969—Yasser Arafat becomes chairman of PLO

1970—Jordan expells PLO

1973—Yom Kippur War

1974—Arab League designates PLO as sole legitimate representative of the Palestinian people; U.N. General Assembly passes Resolutions 3266 and 3267 endorsing the designation

1977—Menachem Begin becomes prime minister, ending string of Labor prime ministers

1981—Israel bombs Iraqi nuclear reactor; annexes Golan Heights

1982—Israel returns Sinai to Egypt; later invades southern Lebanon to rout the PLO in June; hundreds of Palestinians are slain in Sacra and Shatilla refugee camps in September as Israelis stand by

Author's Assignment in Israel

1983

Oct. 10—Knesset approves Yitzhak Shamir to succeed Menachem Begin as prime minister.

Nov. 4—Suicide bombers kill 61 at Israeli military headquarters in Tyre; Israel resumes air raids for first time since 1982.

Nov. 24—Israel trades 4,500 prisoners at Ansar, southern Lebanon, for 100 Israeli soldiers.

Dec. 6—Bomb explodes in Israeli bus in West Jerusalem, killing 6.

Dec. 23—Yasser Arafat leaves Tripoli, Lebanon.

1984

Jan. 15—Inflation rose to 190.9 percent in 1983.

Jan. 27—Jews attempt to attack Temple Mount.

Feb. 9—First rockets fired from Lebanon on Metullah in nine months.

March 5—Lebanon abrogates May 17 agreement with Israel.

April 12—Four Arabs hijack an Israeli civilian bus on Ashdod-Ashkelon coastal highway; all 4 guerrillas and a passenger are killed.

April 26—Tel Aviv celebrates 75th birthday anniversary.

April 28—Police find bombs on five Arab buses; leads to breaking of ring of Jewish settlers who conducted reign of terror against Arabs.

May 1—Syrians capture three Israeli diplomatic personnel north of Beirut.

May 28—Commission finds 2 of the April 12 hijackers were beaten to death.

June 5—First Israeli-Syrian clash in Golan in decade.

June 27—Israel swaps 291 Syrians and 20 other Arabs for 6 Israelis.

June 27—Israel bombs Rabbit Island off Lebanon, killing 19.

July 23—National elections, with Labor winning 44 seats in the Knesset and the Likud 41. Rabbi Meir Kahane wins a seat.

Aug. 24—Mild earthquake in northern Israel.

Sept. 6—Shimon Peres of Labor and Yitzhak Shamir of Likud agree to form "national unity" government.

Sept. 14—Central Bureau says Jews are no longer in majority in Galilee.

Oct. 23—Israel's toll hits 600 in Lebanon War.

Nov. 8—Israel and Lebanon start military withdrawal talks in Lebanon.

Dec. 24—Prime Minister Peres visits Bethlehem Mayor Elias Freij's Christmas party on the Occupied West Bank.

1985

Jan. 1—Inflation in Israel was 451 percent in 1984; population was 4,235,000, an increase of 1.9 percent in 1984.

Jan. 3—Airlift of 3,000 Ethiopian Jews to Israel in the last month is revealed.

Jan. 14—Israeli Cabinet votes three-stage withdrawal from southern Lebanon.

Jan. 16—Knesset defeats Orthodox "Who is a Jew?" bill, 62-51.

Jan. 16-24—Federal jury in New York finds that *Time* magazine defamed Ariel Sharon on the Sabra and Shatilla story, that the story was false, and that *Time* acted without malice, thus meaning Sharon lost the suit.

Jan. 24—Israeli-Lebanese peace talks break down at Naqoura, Lebanon.

Jan. 27—Israel and Eqypt resume talks on future of Taba on the Gulf of Aqaba.

Feb. 3-5—Hearings on the twins who were subjects of experiments by Josef Mengele during World War II.

Feb. 11—King Hussein and PLO Chairman Arafat agree to work toward a joint Jordanian-Palestinian delegation to negotiate with Israel.

March 10—Suicide bombing kills twelve Israeli soldiers in Lebanon.

March 16—About 20,000 Peace Now demonstrators converge in Tel Aviv.

April 2—Israel releases 752 Shiite Moslems from Ansar prison and transfers 1,200 to Atlit, Israel, in what the Red Cross charges is a violation of the Geneva convention.

May 7—Prime Minister Peres tells Knesset that President Reagan's visit to Bitburg concentration camp was a "terrible error."

May 20—Israel swaps 1,150 Arabs terrorists, perpetrators of worst guerrilla attacks against Israel, for three Israeli prisoners of war.

June 6—Israel completes withdrawal from southern Lebanon except for 3-9 mile "security" belt along the border.

June 6—Mengele's body discovered in Brazil.

June 11—Train hits schoolbus near Haifa, killing 22.

June 14—Shiite Moslems hijack TWA jet, demand release of 766 prisoners at Atlit.

June 30—American TWA hostages freed in Damascus.

July 1—Israeli Cabinet adopts economic austerity program.

July 17—Prime Minister Peres rejects list of Palestinians submitted by Jordan for joint Jordanian-Palestinian delegation.

July 27—Jewish settlers say they are "almost" ready to start buying land in Nablus on the West Bank.

Aug. 4—After rash of Jewish slayings by Arabs, Cabinet votes to expel terrorists, impose "administrative detention," and study possible use of death penalty.

Aug. 15—Inflation in July was 27.5 percent, highest ever.

Sept. 10—Israel releases last 119 Shiite prisoners from Atlit, presumably as part of deal that led to release of TWA hostages.

Sept. 25—Three Israelis killed by terrorists on a yacht in Cyprus.

Oct. 1—In retaliation, Israel bombs PLO headquarters in Tunis, leaving 73 dead.

Oct. 5—Egyptian soldier kills 7 Israeli tourists at Ras Burka on Sinai.

Oct. 7—Hijackers seize Italian cruise ship *Achille Lauro* and demand release of 50 Palestinian prisoners.

Oct. 10—Israel cracks Fatah network that planted 8 bombs in Jerusalem since April.

Oct. 16—U.N. General Assembly rejects Arab move to expel Israel, 80-41.

Oct. 21—Prime Minister Peres, in U.N. General Assembly speech, proposes direct negotiations with Jordan and an "international initiative" for peace.

Nov. 19—Israeli jets down 2 Syrian jets in first air clash in 3 years.

Nov. 21—Jonathan Pollard arrested in Washington on charges of spying for Israeli embassy.

Dec. 1—Israel apologizes for Pollard spy affair.

Dec. 13—U.S. customs agents search 3 businesses in the northeast for illegal export of weapons technology to Israel.

Dec. 27—Guerrillas attack El Al counters in Rome and Vienna, killing 18.

1986

Jan. 7—Egyptian Sgt. Suleiman Khater, convicted in October slaying of Israelis, commits suicide in Cairo jail.

Jan. 8—Knesset members and Moslems get in fist fight on Temple Mount.

Jan. 18—Spain and Israel establish diplomatic relations.

Feb. 4—Israel intercepts and forces down a Libyan plane near Haifa in erroneous belief high-ranking PLO officials are aboard.

Feb. 11—Soviet Jew Anatoly Scharansky is released from Soviet prison and arrives in Israel.

Feb. 19—King Hussein breaks off attempts with Yasser Arafat, chairman of the PLO, to initiate a joint peace process with Israel.

Feb. 26–28—Conscript policemen riot in Egypt.

April 15—U.S. bombs Libya.

April 23—Five Israelis are among seventeen men arrested by U.S. customs agents in Bermuda in connection with planned arms sale to Iran.

June—Rash of burning of Jerusalem bus shelters by ultra-Orthodox Jews protesting "lewd" advertising.

June 8—Former U.N. Secretary-General Kurt Waldheim, accused by Israel of World War II crimes against the Jews, is elected president of Austria.

Appendix C
Population in Palestine

	Jews	Palestinians
6th century (at time of Islamic immigration)	approx. 30,000	0
1882 (at start of Zionism)	50,000	500,000
1948 (before Israeli War of Independence)	650,000	1.2 million
1988		
Israel	3.5 million	750,000
West Bank	65,000	813,000
Gaza	2,700	525,000
Total	3,567,700	2,088,000
Worldwide	13 million	4 million

Based on estimates from the state of Israel, demographers Dov Friedlander and Calvin Goldscheider of Hebrew University, the West Bank Data Project, and Palestinian sources. Meron Benvenisti of the West Bank Data Project points out that population figures for the West Bank and Gaza were based on official 1985 figures. He projects that, on the basis of 1984–85 growth rates, the Palestinian population in the West Bank at the end of 1986 was 835,000; the total for Gaza was projected at 542,000.

Appendix D
Ancient Israel

Secure Borders and National Security

The Conquest

Israel has had problems of national security and terrorism from its most ancient of days. Joshua moved his people up the east side of the Dead Sea (Joshua 1, 2), crossed the Jordan River, and took Jericho (chapters 3–6); and then he thrust quickly southward to take Hebron and the Negev (10), and northward to capture the Galilee (11). But many pockets of Canaanites and other resisters remained. There was frequent highway piracy, when caravans ceased and travelers kept to side roads (Judges 5:6, 7), and when guerrillas destroyed Israelite crops and herds (6:3, 4).

The Judges

Men and women rose up to attack the guerrillas and, on the strength of their victories, became leaders of the new Israelite nation, much in the pattern of modern-day Israel's David Ben-Gurion, Menachem Begin, Yitzhak Rabin, and others—using their terrorist or military prowess to propel them to political leadership. Deborah, the Golda Meir of her time, defeated the Canaanites and their tanks in the north (chapters 4, 5). Jephthah tried negotiations but eventually went to war to defeat the Ammonites, who hailed from the area of what is now Amman, Jordan (11, 12). Samson used brute force to defeat the Philistines in the south (14–16). But the resistance, especially by Israel's neighbors, was not totally eradicated.

251

Justice and Mercy

From Judges to the Monarchy

In the transition from the Judges to the monarchy, Hannah, the mother of Samuel, prayed:

> He raises up the poor from the dust;
> He lifts the needy from the ash heap,
> To make them sit with princes and inherit a seat of honor.
> —1 Sam. 2:8

Despite their grandmother's prayer, Samuel's sons as judges over Israel "did not walk in his ways, but turned aside after gain; they took bribes and perverted justice" (1 Sam. 8:3). During Samuel's farewell appearance to the people at Gilgal prior to the monarchy, he asked them to evaluate him in terms of whether he had defrauded or oppressed them. (Time and again in a study of the leaders of Israel and Judah, we are confronted with the problem of godly leaders whose children were not godly, or vice versa. In all probability the good leader's family life suffered, or, the bad leader's children looked elsewhere for models.)

David

Upon assuming the throne, David and his chief of staff, Joab, captured Jerusalem by going up the still-existent water shaft at the Gihon spring. David whipped the Philistines, the Syrians, the Moabites, and the Edomites, driving all the way to the Euphrates River. His warring was so bloody that God denied his last wish of building the temple. This surely is a commentary on God's view of warmaking. But David had secured Israel's borders—temporarily.

David, handsome, courageous, cunning, a good speaker, a gifted musician, was a complex man guilty of more than his share of indiscretion, even felonies. His affair with Bathsheba and his arranged slaying of her husband Uriah were notorious.

His treatment of his chief of staff, Joab, was particularly ungrateful and despicable. After Joab killed Abner, Saul's chief of staff, David denied responsibility for the slaying, but apparently refused to prosecute him. Joab was a coconspirator with David in arranging the slaying of Uriah. David sent Joab to defeat the Ammonites and to besiege Rabbah. Joab conducted the census, which angered the Lord. In short, Joab was David's enforcer, his hit man. But after Joab scolded David for mourning for his son, Absalom, who had rebelled against the throne, David turned on him. "Do not let his gray head go down to Sheol in peace" (1 Kings 2:6), David darkly told Solomon from his deathbed. Solomon dispatched his own chief of staff, Benaiah, to kill Joab.

Given this kind of a record, why was David so loved of God? Why was he praised for doing right in the eyes of the Lord "except in the matter of Uriah"? Why was he more reknowned than any king of Israel, before or since? Much of the answer, of course, is that David repented and was contrite. But part of the answer also must lie in that he executed justice over all the people (2 Samuel 8:15 and 1 Chronicles 18:14). David's own words reveal, despite his lapses, a fundamental commitment to justice:

> For the needy shall not always be forgotten,
> And the hope of the poor shall not perish forever.
> —*Psalm 9:18*

> For the word of the Lord is upright;
> And all his work is done in faithfulness.
> He loves righteousness and justice;
> The earth is full of the steadfast love of the Lord.
> —*Psalm 33:4, 5*

When he crowned son Solomon his successor as king, David admonished him, in the familiar phrase, to walk in the ways of the Lord and to keep his laws and commandments. Again, we infer that David was instructing Solomon, among other things, to be a just ruler.

Solomon

As in the case of his father, Solomon presents difficulties. In his initial acts as king, he put his adversaries to death. When his brother Adonijah, who had tried to seize the throne, merely asked for Abishag to be his wife, Solomon had him assassinated. Solomon ordered the execution of Joab, David's chief of staff. Despite David's pardon of Shimei, Solomon ordered his death. Finally, Solomon took a foreign wife, the daughter of the Egyptian pharaoh, one of seven hundred wives and three hundred girl friends. Then, his bloody deeds behind him, Solomon asked the Lord for discernment between good and evil and for an understanding heart. The Lord replied that if Solomon would walk in his ways, keep his laws, and execute his judgments, the Lord would dwell among the Israelite people. Certainly, Solomon, like David, aspired to justice. His writings in Proverbs are sprinkled with statements indicating a sensitivity to justice.

> The king's heart is a stream of water in the hand of the Lord;
> He turns it wherever he will.
> Every way of a man is right in his own eyes. . . .
> To do righteousness and justice is more acceptable to the Lord than sacrifice.
>
> —*Proverbs 21:1–3*

Solomon prayed for guidance in various situations—when two neighbors were at odds, when Israel was defeated, during drought, during famine and pestilence, during war and captivity; and of special significance, for mercy on behalf of strangers. Again the Lord's reply was familiar—if Solomon would walk in his ways and keep his laws, the Lord would establish the throne of Israel forever. Solomon enjoyed relative peace. He established diplomatic relations with King Hiram of the Mediterranean coastal city of Tyre over the construction of the temple. Their negotiations suggested, however, that Israel trailed its neighbors in technology during the Iron Age. Solomon needed Hiram's skill in working with brass. The building of the temple pushed Solomon to worldwide glory as a monarch.

But Solomon, despite his wisdom that exceeded "sand on the seashore" (1 Kings 4:29), depleted the treasury in building the temple and the royal mansion. Despite his prayer for strangers, he made slaves of foreigners. The Queen of Sheba complimented Solomon for administering justice, but the seeds of decay had set in. He loved many foreign women and they turned his heart. The Lord got angry; the harm was done.

Rehoboam and Jeroboam

His son Rehoboam ignored the wise counsel of elders to be a servant—perhaps the true purpose of power—and listened to young advisers. It split the kingdom, which was the beginning of the end. Rehoboam, as king of the southern kingdom of Judah, married cousins and forsook the law of the Lord, implying he was unjust. But Jeroboam, his brother, who became king of the northern kingdom of Israel, was equally if not more evil. In fact, Jeroboam was held up as the measure of evil for future kings of Israel. Jeroboam always was identified in the Hebrew Bible, not as Solomon's son but as the son of Nebat, Solomon's slave woman.

Kings of Israel and Judah

Most of Israel's kings were evil, far more in number than those of Judah (the southern kingdom). Yet, despite all this, even in them there was an element of justice. "We have heard that the kings of the house of Israel are merciful kings," King Ben-hadad of Syria said (1 Kings 20:31).

King Asa of Judah, the great-grandson of Solomon, presents an almost classic study. Initially he kept the law of the Lord: He broke down foreign altars, and did "that which was right"; his heart "was perfect" (2 Chron. 14:2). Ten years of peace followed. But when the prophet Hanani told Asa that he had done foolishly by seeking a treaty with Syria rather than relying on the Lord, Asa resorted to oppressive policies. Disobedience dulled his conscience and led to oppression and injustice.

Ahab was the worst king of Israel to that point—and he had

followed a series of evil kings. The unscrupulous, spineless Ahab even submitted to the demands of King Ben-hadad to turn over his wives and children. He called the prophet Elijah "you troubler of Israel" (1 Kings 18:17), but Elijah quickly retorted that hundreds of false prophets ate at his wife Jezebel's table. In one of the most blatant cases of greed and injustice, Ahab demanded the vineyard of Naboth and when Naboth refused, Jezebel had him stoned to death on a phony charge. When Ahab finally humbled himself, the Lord consented to delay the evil on his house until the next generation. But the Lord was furious at him.

Judah's King Jehoshaphat, who followed in his father Asa's footsteps, did right in the eyes of the Lord and kept his commandments. He recognized that power and might come from God. The greatest builder on record since Solomon, Jehoshaphat erected garrisons as well as castles and cities of store. He appointed judges for every city in the land and instructed them:

> Consider what you do, for you judge not for man but for the Lord; He is with you in giving judgment. Now then, let the fear of the Lord be upon you; take heed what you do, for there is no perversion of justice with the Lord our God, or partiality, or taking bribes.
>
> —2 Chron. 19:6, 7

But his successor, King Jehoram of Judah, did evil in the sight of the Lord. The prophet Elijah told Jehoram that he had not walked in the ways of his father, Jehoshaphat, or his grandfather, Asa. Instead, he married the daughter of Ahab of Israel. Edom and Libnah revolted against him. In one of the most ignominious epitaphs ever, the biblical historian wrote: "His people made no fire in his honor . . . and he departed with no one's regret" (2 Chron. 21:19, 20a).

Ahaziah of Judah did evil in the eyes of the Lord. It was no wonder because his mother, Ahab's daughter, was his counselor. King after king had done evil. Evil led to bloodshed. In one of history's bloodiest scenes, Jehu killed King Jehoram of Israel, ordered King Ahaziah of Judah killed, and "slew all that remained of the house of Ahab in Jezreel, his great men, and his familiar friends, and his priests, until he left him none remaining" (2 Kings

10:11). The Lord was so angry at the house of Ahab that he praised Jehu for doing this! This may suggest graphically how angry the Lord gets at injustice. Even more astounding, after all this bloodshed, Jehu, now the king of Israel, walked in the sins of Jeroboam and not in the law of the Lord.

Ahaziah's mother, Athaliah, tried to usurp the throne and destroy all of the royal seed, but her treachery came to an end at the point of a sword. Ahaziah's child Joash had been hidden away and Joash took the throne at age seven. Even though Ahaziah followed the sinful advice of his mother, Joash chose a different path than his father and grandfather. He did right in the eyes of the Lord. We may infer that such a statement referred to his being a just king, for the biblical historian points out that Joash did not remove the high places of false worship, the people still sacrificed and burned incense, and Joash had two wives.

Joash began to repair the temple and worship was restored while the priest Jehoiada was alive. But after Jehoiada died, at age 130, Joash and the people promptly forsook God and served idols. Jehoiada's son Zechariah, suggesting they had turned to injustice, told the people they had transgressed the law of the Lord. "Because you have forsaken the Lord, he hath also forsaken you," (2 Chron. 24:20), Zechariah told them. Josiah, not remembering Jehoiada's kindness to him, joined the people's conspiracy and commanded them to kill Zechariah. By the end of the year, Judah was sacked by the Syrians and Josiah fell victim to a conspiracy of his own servants.

Meanwhile, Jehoahaz succeeded Jehu on the throne of Israel and, like his father, he did evil in the eyes of the Lord. The biblical historian suggests that the Lord's anger was responsible for Israel being oppressed by Syria all during Jehoahaz's reign.

Another Joash, the son of Jehoahaz, took the throne of Israel and he, too, did evil in the sight of the Lord and departed from his ancient grandfather Jeroboam's sin.

In Judah, meanwhile, Amaziah followed his father Joash to the throne. Initially, he did right in the eyes of the Lord "but not with a perfect heart" (2 Chron. 25:2b). He did not remove the high places and the people still sacrificed and burned incense. But Amaziah's treatment of the conspirator-killers of his father suggested an acute sense of justice, and that is perhaps why he was credited with doing right in the eyes of the Lord. On the basis of Mosaic law, he executed the killers but not their children: "The fathers shall not be put to death for the children, or the children be put to death for the fathers; but every man shall die for his own sin" (2 Kings 14:6; see Deuteronomy 24:16).

Amaziah, however, fell into bloody war. He hired 100,000 Israeli mercenaries to battle Edom—but dismissed them following the advice of an unidentified man of God on grounds the Lord was not with Israel. On his own, Amaziah slaughtered the Edomites, and then for some bizarre reason, he started worshiping the gods of the defeated Edomites. The Lord was angry and determined to destroy Amaziah. When diplomacy between Amaziah of Judah and Joash of Israel failed, the two went to war. It would not be the last time the Lord's people have battled each other.

The Words of the Prophets

From here on, in the waning days of Israel and Judah, the written prophets appeared on the scene.

Jeroboam II, the son of Joash, reigned over Israel, doing evil and making the nation sin as well. But the Lord used Jeroboam II to restore the boundaries of Israel. Ironically, Jonah, the prophet and an intense nationalist, got very angry when the Lord reached out and saved the people of enemy Ninevah. The prophets Amos and Hosea condemned the injustice of Israel during the reign of Jeroboam II in the harshest terms:

> This is what the Lord says:
>
> Because of outrage after outrage committed by Israel I will not relent!
> For they have sold the innocent for a handful of silver,
> And needy men for a pair of shoes.
> They grind the faces of the poor into dust,
> And force the humble out of his rightful path.
> Father and son use the same temple-girl,
> And so defile my holy name,
> Beside every altar they lounge on garments which they took in pledge,

And in the houses of their gods they drink away the money they imposed in fines.

—*Amos 2:6–8* PHILLIPS

Now hear what the Lord says, you people of Israel,
For the Lord has a quarrel with the inhabitants of the land!
There is no honesty nor compassion nor knowledge of God,
But an outbreak of cursing, murder, stealing, and adultery,
And bloodshed follows bloodshed.
This is why the land is withered,
And everyone who lives in it has lost heart.

—*Hosea 4:1–3* PHILLIPS

Isaiah, Hosea, and Amos were the prophetic voices when Uzziah and Hezekiah were kings of Judah, and Jeroboam II reigned over Israel. Uzziah did right in the eyes of the Lord, although he did not remove the high places and the people still sacrificed and burned incense. He built Eilat, which was the port city for the copper refineries at Ezion-Geber. He rebuilt cisterns for the cattle throughout the land. He was a skilled husbandman and engine-maker. He rebuilt the army—"he became very strong" (2 Chron. 26:8b).

Despite all this, the prophet Amos condemned Judah for "outrage after outrage" and for having "spurned the Word of the Lord and failed to keep his commandments" (2:4, PHILLIPS). The prophet Isaiah saw that having defeated the Philistines, Judah became infiltrated with soothsayers and fortune-tellers.

Their land has become full of idols.
And they bow down to the work of their hands,
To things which their fingers have fashioned,
And I will not forgive them.

—*Isaiah 2:8* PHILLIPS

It truly was prophetic. It is said that power corrupts. Uzziah's power corrupted him. The biblical historian wrote, "But when he was strong . . . he grew proud" (2 Chron. 26:16). He trespassed against the Lord and became furious at priests who warned him about burning incense on the altar. He died a leper.

The End of Israel

Not surprisingly, a series of mediocre kings followed Jeroboam II on the throne of Israel as it speeded toward dispersion. Zechariah did evil. Shallum was a conspirator. Menahem ripped up women with child. Pekahiah and Pekah were evil. All went the way of the slave woman Nebat's son Jeroboam.

Finally, the Assyrians carried the Israelites away into exile.

The End of Judah

Judah lingered on. There was a roller coaster of good kings and bad. Jotham, the son of good-then-bad Uzziah, did right in the eyes of the Lord. But the people still sacrificed and burned incense and were corrupt. Jotham also engaged in much construction; he built cities in the hill country and towers and castles in the forests. He subjugated the Ammonites and took booty of silver, wheat, and barley. The biblical historian declared a direct relationship between his right doing and his strength, saying "so Jotham became mighty, because he ordered his ways before the Lord his God" (2 Chron. 27:6).

Ahaz did not do right as his father Jotham had done, raising again the question of why children of godly parents sometimes do wrong. Ahaz made his son walk in fire. The people sacrificed and burned incense in high places as well as on hills and "under every green tree" (2 Chron. 28:4). The allied forces of Syria and Pekah of Israel besieged Ahaz but failed to conquer Judah. Vulnerable, Judah was sacked by the Edomites and the Philistines. The prophet Obadiah condemned the Edomites:

> But you should not have gloated over the day of your brother in
> the day of his misfortune;
> You should not have rejoiced over the people of Judah in the day of
> their ruin;
> You should not have boasted in the day of distress.
>
> — *Obadiah 12*

Ahaz turned to Assyria for help, offering silver and gold from the temple as a tribute—and his sins increased. He made burnt offerings, looted the instruments of the temple, and then sealed its doors. The biblical historian concluded: "For the Lord bought Judah low because of Ahaz the king of Israel, for he had dealt wantonly in Judah and had been faithless to the Lord" (2 Chron. 28:19).

It was during Ahaz's reign that the Lord promised a virgin would conceive and bear a son named Immanuel. This son would contrast sharply with Ahaz in the way he was a leader.

The prophet Micah condemned the injustice in Judah. His comments obviously were aimed at Ahaz in view of the stature of Hezekiah subsequently:

> Woe to those who imagine wicked schemes,
> Who work out evil plots while still in bed;
> When daylight dawns they act
> For the power lies in their hands.
> They covet fields and seize them.
> They covet houses and take them for themselves.
> They break a man and his household;
> Yes, they crush him and all his rightful inheritance.
> —*Micah* 2:1, 2 PHILLIPS

Hezekiah succeeded his father, the evil Ahaz, on the throne of Judah, and did right in the eyes of the Lord. Rather than looking at his father, Hezekiah probably benefited from the prophetic messages of Isaiah, Amos, Hosea, and Micah. He was nonpareil. "He trusted in the Lord the God of Israel; so that there was none like him among all the kings of Judah after him, nor among those who were before him" (2 Kings 18:5).

Hezekiah sent a decree to the people: "For if you return to the Lord, your brethren and your children will find compassion with their captors, and return to this land. For the Lord your God is gracious and merciful, and will not turn away his face from you, if you return to him" (2 Chron. 30:9). He cleansed and reconsecrated the temple, observed Passover, appointed priests, and commanded the people to tithe. "And every work that he undertook in the service of the house of God and in accordance with the law and the commandments, seeking his God, he did with all his heart, and prospered" (2 Chron. 31:21).

Hezekiah threw off the Assyrian yoke and defeated the Philistines, but was forced to pay tribute to Sennacherib of Assyria. With the prophet Isaiah advising him and the Lord intervening, Hezekiah defeated the insolent Sennacherib on what is now the Russian Compound in Jerusalem and won worldwide acclaim.

Let the biblical historian tell it: "He was exalted in the sight of all nations from that time onward. . . . And Hezekiah had very great riches and honor; and he made for himself treasuries for silver, for gold, for precious stones, for spices, for shields, and for all kinds of costly vessels; storehouses also for the yield of grain, wine, and oil; and stalls for all kinds of cattle and sheepfolds. He likewise provided cities for himself, and flocks and herds in abundance; for God had given him very great possessions" (2 Chron. 32:23, 27–29).

But it was Indian summer. His son Manasseh retreated from Hezekiah's glory, rebuilt the high places, raised up altars for Baal, and did evil. He, too, made his son pass through fire and practiced augury and sorcery and shed much innocent blood. The biblical historian says Manasseh made Judah more evil than other nations. The children were sacrificed in the Valley of Hinnom; this valley separated our apartment from Mount Zion. We were reminded of Manasseh's sin daily. But after the Assyrians bound him and took him to Babylon, perhaps remembering his father, Manasseh humbled himself, prayed, and was restored to the kingdom. He put away the strange gods and idols and rebuilt the altar of the Lord. But the people still sacrificed in high places.

Amon, as king of Judah, did evil but he did not humble himself as his father Manasseh had done. His own servants conspired against him.

Josiah, taking the throne of Judah at age eight, followed in the path of his great-grandfather Hezekiah, not his father Amon. He returned to the Lord with all his might, according to Mosaic Law. But it was not enough to atone for his grandfather Manasseh's wrongs. Josiah purged Judah of high places, broke down the altars of the false gods, and smashed the idols to dust. He repaired the Temple, and in a remarkable discovery, he found the Torah, ordered it read to all the people, and made a covenant to walk with the Lord and keep his laws with all his heart. Surely justice and

mercy are implied in the description of Josiah's reign, for he broke
the houses of the sodomites and he put away people who had
wizards, teraphim, idols, and abominations.

Despite all this, the prophet Zephaniah still found injustice in
Judah:

> Woe to her that is rebellious and defiled, the oppressing city!
> She listens to no voice, she accepts no correction.
> She does not trust in the Lord, she does not draw near to her God.
> Her officials within her are roaring lions;
> Her judges are evening wolves that leave nothing till the morning.
> Her prophets are wanton, faithless men;
> Her priests profane what is sacred, they do violence to the law.
> The Lord within her is righteous, he does no wrong;
> Every morning he shows forth his justice, each dawn he does
> not fail;
> But the unjust knows no shame.
>
> —*Zeph. 3:1–5*

The prophet Jeremiah was even more harsh:

> For wicked men are found among my people. . . .
> They have grown fat and sleek.
> They know no bounds in deeds of wickedness;
> They judge not with justice the cause of the fatherless, to make it
> prosper,
> And they do not defend the rights of the needy,
> "Shall I not punish them for these things?" says the Lord.
>
> —*Jer. 5:26–29*

As always, however, the prophet held out hope: "For if you truly
amend your ways and your doings, if you truly execute justice one
with another, if you do not oppress the alien, the fatherless or the
widow, or shed innocent blood in this place, and if you do not go
after other gods to your own hurt, then I will let you dwell in this
place, in the land that I gave of old to your fathers forever" (Jer. 7:5).

After Josiah died, his sons Jehoahaz and Jehoiakim followed
him to the throne of Judah and they, too, did evil. They did not
heed Jeremiah's words. Jehoiakim, who had been put on the
throne by Egypt, taxed the people for silver and gold to give to

the pharaoh. Jehoiachin, who was Jehoiakim's son, became king of Judah and did evil in the sight of the Lord. He fell victim to the siege by Babylon. The biblical historian notes that he paid no attention to Jeremiah, and he was the last king of Judah.

Spirit of Wisdom

What had happened to the promise of David and Solomon? The biblical historian summarizes in 2 Kings 17: The people of Israel and Judah walked in the customs of other people and did not keep the laws of the Lord. The Lord sent prophets, "but they would not listen, but were stubborn. . . . They despised his statutes . . . and the warnings he gave them" (vv. 14, 15). Surely an insidious part of the malignancy was the injustice so prevalent among the leaders and the people.

During the reign of one of the worst kings, Ahaz, the Lord sent the promise of a new leader who would be merciful and just:

> There shall come forth a shoot from the stump of Jesse,
> And a branch shall grow out of his roots.
> And the Spirit of the Lord shall rest upon him,
> The spirit of wisdom and understanding,
> The spirit of knowledge and the fear of the Lord.
> He shall not judge by what his eyes see,
> Or decide by what his ears hear;
> But with righteousness he shall judge the poor.
> And decide with equity for the meek of the earth.
>
> —Isa. 11:1–4

Index to Scripture

Index to Persons and Subjects

Jerusalem School for Synoptic Gospels, 206-07
Jesus boat, 215-16
Jesus Christ, 19, 20, 24, 67-68, 79, 120, 198-214, 222-23, 264
Jews: *aliyah*, 166-67; American, 135, 141; anti-Semitism, 75-76; Ashkenazi, 150, 154-57, 174; Black Hebrews, 169-70; Conservative, 149; dispersion, 159-60; Egyptian, 171-72; Ethiopian, or Falasha, 169-71, 247; Holocaust, 30, 88-89, 93, 127, 165, 167, 190, 214, 231; in Arab countries, 171-74; Iranian, 140; Law of Return (1950), 167; Messianic Jews, 203-05; other persecution, 30, 162, 231; Reform, 149; secular, 152-54; Sephardic, 150, 154-57, 174; ultra-Orthodox, 27, 145-51, 249; Who is a Jew? legislation, 149
Jewish religion: and missionaries, 206; Chief rabbinate, 157, 170, 206 (see also Eliyahu, Shapira); Hanukkah, 92; observance, 150, 152, 158, 170, 206; Passover, 29, 92; Purim, 92; Rosh Hashanah, 92; Shavuot, 92; Succoth, 92; Yom Kippur, 92
Johnson, Lyndon B., president, 32, 59, 138
Jordan, 69-71, 107, 111, 172, 229
Joseph, 96, 120
Josephus, historian, 216
Joshua, 43, 158
Jradi, Khalil, Shiite guerrilla, 196
Judea and Samaria, see also West Bank, 98

Kach, see Kahane
Kafity, Samir, bishop, 213
Kahane, Rabbi Meir, Knesset, 83-84, 93, 119, 156
Kalandia, see Palestinian refugees
Kalb, Marvin, professor, 15
Karp, Judith, Israeli official, 122
Katsover, Zvi, Jewish settler, 116
Katz, Moshe, computer specialist, 217
Kedumim, see settlements
Kelman, Herbert C., psychologist, see also conflict resolution, 238-40
Kelm, G. L., archeologist, 222
Kennedy administration, 137-38
Kfar Darom, see settlements
Khalif, Karim, Arab mayor, 104
Khartoum Conference (1967), 60
Khomeini, Ayatollah Ruhollah, Iranian leader, 140, 192, 195
Khoury, Elias, bishop, 203
Khrushchev, Nikita, Soviet leader, 137
Kibbutzim, 37-39; Deganiah, 166; Ein Gev,

44; Huldah, 43; Lavi, 37; Merhavia, 167; Nof Ginosar, 37, 216
King David Hotel, 50, 126, 133, 165
Kiryat Arba, see also Hebron, settlements
Kiryat Shomna, 46
Kissinger, Henry A., secretary of state, 136, 138-39
Knesset, 31, 33
Kollek, Teddy, mayor of Jerusalem, 24, 27, 45, 147, 198, 207
Kopp, Chuck and Liz, 207
Kuttab, Daoud, Arab editor, 201-02, 237
Kuttab, Jonathan, Arab lawyer, 13, 110, 202, 236

Labor party, 33-34, 149, 156
Lahad, Antoine, South Lebanese militiaman, 179
Land, 24, 34, 121, 158-59, 189, 239-40
Lavie, Mark, journalist, 82
Law of Return, see Jews
Lawrence, T. E. (Lawrence of Arabia), 129
League of Nations, see also Balfour, British, French, 131
Levinger, Miriam, Jewish settler, 117-19
Levinger, Rabbi Moshe, Jewish settler, 112, 117
Levy, David, Israeli politician, 33, 156
Levy, Moshe, Israeli chief of staff, 101
Lebanon, 61-63, 71-75, 227, 246-47; Christians, 187; Gemayel assassinated, 62; Jews in, 172-73; 1978 Litani Operation, 61; refugee camps, 111; Shiites, 194-97; World War I and French mandate, 129-33
Lewis, Frieda, Hadassah president, 234
Libya, 172-73, 249
Likud bloc, 33-34, 149, 155
Lilienbaum, Moses, Zionist, 163
Lind, Anna Grace Spafford, see also American Colony, Spafford, 211-12
Lindsey, Robert, minister-scholar, 205-07

Maagen Michael, terrorist attack, 46
Ma'ariv newspaper, 194
Malachi, prophet, 199
Mandates, see British and French
Maoz, Baruch, minister, 204-05
Maoz, Moshe, political scientist, 66, 104, 108, 187
Marriages, mixed, 83
Masri, Zafer, mayor, 104-05, 109
Mattar, Ibrahim, Palestinian economist, 99
McMahon, Sir Henry, British official (see also British, Arab, Hussein), 128
Mecca, birthplace of Mohammed, see also Islam, 128, 191

THE MIDDLE EAST